BRING OSCAR

LANCE FRIEDMAN

Copyright © 2021 Lance Friedman.

ALL RIGHTS RESERVED. This book contains material protected under International and Federal Copyright Laws and Treaties. Any unauthorized reprint or use of this material is prohibited. No part of this book may be reproduced or transmitted in any form or by any means, electronic or mechanical, including photocopying, recording, or by any information storage and retrieval system without express written permission from the author/publisher.

ISBN: 978-1-64184-590-8 (Paperback)
ISBN: 978-1-64184-591-5 (Ebook)

Dedicated to the dogs who can't read this,
yet provide the companionship, courage, composure,
and comedy described in these pages.

Contents

Introduction 1

Part I: West 3

Part II: South 95

Part III: East 137

Part IV: Alaska 267

Epilogue 389

Credits 391

Introduction

I've flown around the world and throughout the United States. During each trip, I had to leave my dog, Oscar, at home. It might be for three or four days or as long as two and a half weeks during international travel. Oscar had run of the house with access to the backyard via a doggie door, allowing him the freedom to go in and out. While gone, I left him in the best care. When I returned, he'd wag his tail, and we'd wrestle in the living room.

One summer, I decided to take an extended vacation. I imagined a road trip that would require at least a month—I'd have to bring Oscar with me. At the time, traveling with a dog seemed a hassle. Or, was it? And, there were limitations. Or, were there? We would find out.

Oscar and I ended up traveling over thirty-five thousand miles in the car and walking at least twenty thousand miles together. Friends, family, and people we met along the way suggested, "Do you have a blog? You have some great stories," or "You should write a book." Well, here is the book!

These pages are my thoughts, experiences, and impressions as we glided across the country. Everything in this story is true, with the exception of a few name changes (so that I don't get in trouble).

PART I
WEST

EVANSTON, ILLINOIS to MINNEAPOLIS, MINNESOTA

I WALKED OUTSIDE, carrying a bag of dog food. Oscar watched with anticipation as I put it in the trunk of the car. He knew something was going on. He'd seen me countless times carrying groceries from the trunk, which meant rotisserie chicken for him. And, he'd seen me lugging large bags of dirt and mulch to the backyard. But, this time, I was *loading up* a car.

I went inside the house and returned a minute later holding Froggie and Sylvester, Oscar's two favorite stuffed animals (both muddy and shredded, but recognizable). I tossed them on the back seat.

As I walked past Oscar, I reminded him, "going road trip!"

His sideways ears perked straight up.

I went inside, and Oscar followed me. I grabbed the cooler off the kitchen counter and any remaining perishables from the refrigerator. We went back outside. As I packed the final items in the car, Oscar watched with his tongue hanging out. "Yeah, you're coming with," I assured him. "Big road trip!" He wagged his tail.

There wasn't much preparation. I prepaid my bills for two months, arranged for my neighbor's kid to collect my mail, and tried to finish eating all the perishable food in the refrigerator. I hate wasting food.

For the trip, I threw the following into the car:

- Two dog bowls (water and food)
- One old 64 oz. plastic juice bottle to hold water
- United States map
- Laptop
- Camera
- Credit card and cash; roll of quarters for tolls or parking meters
- Flip phone cellphone
- One duffel bag with clothes
- A cooler with energy bars and snacks
- Oscar's favorite pals, Froggie (missing an eye) and Sylvester (caked in dirt)
- Oscar's blanket and pillow

In the trunk of the car, I stored the following in cardboard boxes:

- Dog food (bag of dry and a couple of cans of wet)
- Paper towels and regular towels
- A few small plastic bags and a few garbage bags
- Simple Solution (a cleaner for pets)
- Car first aid (jumper cables, oil, and basic tools)

That's it. To be honest, I was winging it. If I forgot something, I could always buy whatever it was at a store along the way. I figured if I had a credit card and some food and water (in case the car broke down), what could go wrong? If the trip was a disaster, we could just turn around and go home.

I chose the destination of Emmett, Idaho, where my mom lived. Once we got there, Oscar and I could spend a week (or so) visiting family, relaxing, and taking a break from driving. Plus, free housing would cut costs. Along the way, we'd get a chance to pass through South Dakota to Mount Rushmore. A bit of Wyoming. And, eventually back through Montana. A friend had mentioned that the Badlands and Devils Tower are cool places. Otherwise, looking at the map, I had absolutely no idea what we would find in between. But, at some point in time, we'd get to Idaho. After packing up the car, we did a final walk through the house. Lights out. Empty fridge. Computer off. Oven and appliances off. As I was locking the front door, Oscar skipped over to my old Acura. Perhaps he was anticipating a trip to the park or the lake.

At the time, I had two cars. The "dog car" was a nineteen-year-old Acura Integra. It used to be my car, but eventually rust, mud, dog hairs, and wear and tear turned it into a very, very used car. When I finally bought a new car, I kept the old Acura. It was a stick shift, which I loved, and I also appreciated the fact that I could use it to hit the gym, transport a muddy dog, or fill it with junk from Home Depot. It didn't matter about clean-up. The other car was a Nissan Altima, and it remained spotless. It still had new car smell and a clean interior because it was seldom used.

"Oscar, come this way." I guided him away from the rusted '94 Acura with its bumper held by duct tape. (It wasn't going to make it across the country.) "We're taking the Nissan."

I opened the back door. Oscar paused and looked up at the seats. They were a bit higher than the Acura. Plus, there were extra blankets and pillows covering the leather seats. As I prepared to assist him into the backseat, Oscar climbed up and in, dragging his back paws, but he managed to generate enough lift! Even at over thirteen years old, Oscar could still make it into the car. I shut the back door, and then I went around and got into the driver's seat. Oscar poked his head between the seats and licked my face. "Nice job, buddy. Thank you."

I turned and could already see some dirt and hairs on the wrinkled blanket and exposed backseat. I just shrugged. After four dog-free years, I thought, *It's OK. Just let it go.* I had no illusions. I knew the car interior would get trashed. "Let's get rollin'!"

We pulled out of the driveway and started toward the freeway. Mile 1—2000 to go. Oscar placed his two front paws on the armrest, completely disregarding the blankets and comfort that I had carefully prepared in the backseat. Then he rotated into the front passenger seat.

"OK, so you're going to break in the freshly cleaned leather seats on day one."

Oscar sat comfortably—tongue hanging out, a slight smile, looking content—as we headed into our adventure. I rolled down the passenger window, and he stuck his head outside to enjoy the wind blowing in his face.

We drove north on I-94, passing neighborhoods, restaurants, and places I'd seen countless times. Then, an hour later, we crossed the border into Wisconsin. The interstate road beyond Kenosha and toward Milwaukee took me into territory that was less familiar. Then we encountered construction and traffic. *Really? Friday at 11:00 a.m.?*

Patience, I reminded myself. *This trip is a marathon, not a sprint.* We had plenty of time to cover ground each day, and we had weeks to complete the journey. There was no hurry.

After grinding through Milwaukee traffic, then passing Miller Park where the Brewers play baseball, I looked for a suitable stop beyond the city limits. It seemed reasonable to take a break every two hours or less, allowing Oscar to relieve himself and stretch his legs. When I didn't see any interstate rest areas, I just pulled off at a random exit.

We ended up in Waukesha in the parking lot of an abandoned shopping center and a lone Kentucky Fried Chicken. I wasn't hungry, but it was a chance to use their facilities. Since I observe an animal-friendly diet, I ordered a Coke and fried potatoes—I felt obligated to buy something. After using the restroom and refilling Oscar's water jug, I went back outside, sat down on the curb next to my pal, and handed him a dog treat. He paused, looked around, and meandered to a little parking lot island with rocks and a bush. He pawed at the rocks, creating a little hole, and placed the treat in the rocks. Then he used his snout to push the rocks on top of the treat, partially burying it.

"What are you doing? Saving that snack for later?" Satisfied with his cover-up work, he trotted to me. "Dude, we ain't comin' back here." I was hoping he realized that unlike the snacks buried in the backyard, he couldn't retrieve this one later.

We continued our journey, bypassing Madison, the state capital, and neared Wisconsin Dells, which is known for its resorts and water parks. I exited the I-90/94 and started looking for an intriguing lunch place. Indoor dining was out, and I could eat at a chain restaurant any time—I wanted to try local places. Fine dining was also out. I'm not cheap, but I just don't appreciate fine meals like some others do. I like quality food but at a better price.

I spotted a large, colorful beer mug sign—Brat House Grill. As we approached, I noticed outdoor tables under umbrellas. Perfect! A casual place with outdoor seating and shade to keep Oscar cool. I tied him to a picnic table and ran inside. It was a typical tavern decorated with Brewers and Packers memorabilia and televisions showing various sports channels. I took a quick look at the menu. Every minute inside was a minute Oscar was on his own and out of my sight. I easily defaulted to a veggie burger, waffle fries, and a Coke and asked the bartender to bring the meal outside. I refilled Oscar's water jug and trotted outside where he was sitting in the same position I had left him. He seemed amused by the new environment, watching diners at the other tables.

I struck up a brief conversation with a family who had two terriers with them. They were from a suburb of Chicago and were spending the week at the Dells. I mentioned our month-long trip, and they took an interest in Oscar.

"What kind of dog is that?"

"He's a Shepherd Lab mix with a bit of Schipperke; maybe some terrier."

"A bit of everything," the mother added.

"Yeah, his mama got around," I joked. She laughed.

"What's his name?" one of the daughters wanted to know.

"Oscar."

"Cute name!" she said

"Named after Oscar Madison."

"Who?" asked the mother.

"Ever watch *The Odd Couple*?" I asked her.

"Oh, yeah! Oscar," she remembered. "Then, are you Felix?"

"Oh, no. Oscar is definitely my sloppy, likable roommate. But, I'm no Felix."

The waitress came outside with a tray holding my lunch. I started to dig in and Oscar joined me. When I gave him some of my veggie burger, he started lickin' his chops. A few minutes later, the family stood up to leave.

"Nice meeting you," they said.

"Bye, Oscar," one of the daughters said as she gave him a pat on the head.

"Take care," I told them. This was the first of countless brief encounters Oscar and I would have. Our first lunch stop was a success.

We returned to the I-90/94 west toward Minnesota. As cars raced by us, we continued cruising around sixty-five mph. I usually drive fast, shooting down the Chicago expressways, but today, I took my time winding through the green valleys. I enjoyed the company of my canine pal. Why rush? Driving long distances may seem boring or something you want to hurry through. But, it's a mindset. I viewed it as a new and interesting journey. Plus, it gave me lots of time to think and daydream.

"What the hell?!" Suddenly, a bunch of flashing lights appeared in the distance. I wondered if there was an accident, but it turned out to be an ordinary speed trap. Many of the people who had sped past me in a racing cluster had been rounded up. As we drove past the flashing lights, Oscar watched the scene through the window. *Getting a speeding ticket on day one would suck*, I thought. *Especially an out-of-state ticket.*

I looked at Oscar. "Good thing you're here. Otherwise, I might've been speeding with them. You may have saved me a big hassle—and a bunch of money. It's like a doggie dividend."

Oscar stared at me with his tongue hanging out. "Or, maybe a bow wow bonus. What do you think?" He tilted his head trying to understand. "Nothing? I'll work on it."

As we left northern Wisconsin, I noted the lush green landscape and valleys formed by lakes and rivers. I also couldn't help but notice a lot of fireworks shops, a couple of casinos, a few adult stores, and a slew of fast food. What does that say about American interests?

In the late afternoon, we passed over the St. Croix River on a substantial, crowded bridge that connected Wisconsin and Minnesota. Just beyond the "Welcome to Minnesota" sign, I spotted a rest stop. This was a good time to take a break and double-check the directions to our hotel. As we pulled in, I noticed a walking path and doggie bags for waste. Nice. I gave Oscar a treat and let him sniff around. "Oskie, this is all you." He led me along a dirt path to explore some of the wooded areas.

"Holy cow!" The "Land of 10,000 Lakes" is the land of ten billion mosquitoes! Oscar flicked his head as the insects surrounded his ears and went relentlessly at my legs. After five minutes, I couldn't take it. We raced back to the car and made an escape for the hotel. Following the map, I maneuvered through downtown Minneapolis traffic and turned south to the Richfield suburb.

The night before, I had picked the Candlewood Suites. The photos and reviews seemed fine, and they accepted pets. Besides, "Suites" sounded better than "Motel." This would likely be our longest driving stretch—four hundred miles—so why not treat ourselves?

As we approached the front doors, we paused and looked at each other. *Do we just walk in?* I wondered. *Or, should I leave him in the car? Tie him up outside the doorway? Maybe there is a side entrance for pets?* I had never stayed at a hotel with a dog before, but since this place had pet-friendly rooms, I concluded that we could both enter the lobby. So, that's what we did.

We were greeted by a young man behind the reception desk who handed me two key cards (Was one for Oscar?), and we proceeded down the hallway to our air-conditioned room. It was definitely a suite. It was spacious with a nice kitchen area, business workspace, and living room. I popped on the TV and plugged in my laptop, flip phone, and camera to recharge.

I was pleased that the first place was a terrific hotel! Or, maybe it was the novelty of staying at a hotel with a dog.

I connected to the Wi-Fi and started looking at destinations for the next day. I wanted to stick to my original plan of going through South Dakota first. On the way home, we'd pass through North Dakota. After thirty minutes of Internet research, I booked a room near Sioux Falls, South Dakota. The photos, description, and reviews of the hotel seemed fine. In the end, I just wanted a clean, safe, fair market-priced place in a decent area that took a dog. With my reservations complete, I climbed into bed and turned on the television. This was a late-night treat. I didn't have a TV in the bedroom. (Before you know it, you're sleeping less and watching TV more.) After thirty minutes of channel surfing, I cut myself off and went to sleep.

MINNEAPOLIS, MINNESOTA to SIOUX FALLS, SOUTH DAKOTA

I WOKE UP to the sound of the air conditioner cranking, which I had set low for Oscar's sake. He was a cold temp pup. In the winter, I'd look out the window and often spot him sitting in the snow, contently basking in the arctic air.

There were two possible routes to our next destination: either straight through Minnesota along minor highways or via the interstates. Because I'm a curious person, I usually default to the route I haven't seen, but in this case I hadn't been either way, so I chose the faster and smoother path. As we cruised on I-35 through new territory beyond Minneapolis, Oscar sat in the backseat snacking on a treat.

It was then that I began appreciating this "traveling with a dog" concept more and more. There were lots of pros, like no awkward silences in the car and you get to pick the radio station. But let's acknowledge the cons. There's no one to split costs or driving with, no planning input (although an occasional tail wag was informative), and you must skip places that don't allow pets. Plus, I had to schlep all of his stuff. I liked to joke that Oscar needed to pull his weight!

Just past the I-35/I-90 junction, we stopped at a rest area southeast of Mankato. I remembered Mankato from *Little House on the Prairie*. I had considered including the Laura Ingalls Wilder Museum in Walnut Grove, Minnesota, in our itinerary because I had fond memories of watching her stories on tv as a child, but it was far off the main interstate, and it didn't seem to offer anything for Oscar.

After a bit of people watching at the rest area, Oscar buried another treat in the high grass. Soon after, an older gentleman approached us. "So, it's just the two of you?" He seemed harmless.

"Yep, just me and the dog," I replied. "Long road trip."

"And he can stay in hotels?"

"Actually, there are lots of hotels that permit pets. More than I thought."

"Well, that's great. We had to leave our dogs at home. The road gets to be too much for them."

"He seems to like it," I said looking down at Oscar. "Lucky for me. It's tough to find people to travel with. They either have work, or most of my friends are married with kids."

Oscar started tugging on the leash. He was signaling that he wanted to move along.

"I think your friend wants to go," our new friend said.

"I think so," I said as Oscar tugged harder on the leash. "Gotta go!"

We resumed our journey, heading west on I-90. I remembered seeing something online about a Jolly Green Giant statue around this area, so we took the exit leading into Blue Earth, Minnesota. It was lunchtime though, so I pulled over at the Pizza Hut. After sharing a mini pizza, I took out a ball from the trunk, and we went into the neighboring open field to play catch. I threw the ball, and Oscar chased it down. He picked it up and took three steps back toward me. Then he dropped the ball and started sniffing around.

"That's not the way it's played," I called out to him. I walked over to the ball and picked it up. He looked at me and wagged his tail. I threw the ball in the other direction. He took a quick step toward the ball, then he abruptly stopped and started sniffing and exploring in the other direction. "OK. This game is over. The only one fetching is me." I watched Oscar wander around the open field with dark clouds behind him. When it started to sprinkle rain, we went back to the car and began our hunt for the Jolly Green Giant. As it came into view, I learned it was evidence that all sorts of random things are in the US.

I took a few photos of the enormous attraction, and that's when the dark clouds really started coming in. Then it began to rain, but I still wanted to get some photos of Oscar and me with the Giant before it really started pouring. I saw an older couple taking pictures, so I approached them for assistance. They looked like veteran tourists, and the gentleman graciously agreed to shoot a few pictures of Oscar and me. I showed him the buttons on my digital camera while his wife introduced herself to Oscar.

After handing him the small camera, I rushed Oscar over to the massive statue. We walked up the steps and stood between the two enormous green feet. Ignoring the inconvenient rain coming down, our photographer patiently took several nice pictures: a few close-up shots of us between the huge feet and then a couple of shots from a distance, extending from head to Green Giant toe.

Standing with the Jolly Green Giant

We darted back to the car as the rain picked up. However, just before climbing in, Oscar walked right through a small puddle of mud. I imagined Tony Randall playing Felix Unger and moaning, "Oh, Oscar, Oscar, Oscar," as Jack Klugman playing Oscar Madison made a mess in their apartment.

"You couldn't just walk around that?" I suggested. With complete indifference, Oscar left a trail of paw prints on the front seats. I grabbed a towel from the trunk and wiped some of the paw prints off the driver's seat. Then, I lightly wrapped Oscar to get the excess rainwater off of him. After going through the convenient Dairy Queen drive-through, we exited Green Giant Lane and hit the road again.

While driving in the on-and-off rain, I counted down the miles on the signs to Sioux Falls. They passed quickly, unlike when I was a kid and driving took forever. I can remember my mom driving fifty-five mph as countless cars passed us. Her slow driving was not as bad as her choice in music. A twelve-year-old is not going to sing along to "I Am Woman." Occasionally, she'd choose the Bee Gees or The Grease Soundtrack, which was more appealing. But we didn't have a choice—she drove, she chose.

I also remembered that our seat positions were decided by rock paper scissors or by which kid hollered "call front seat!" first. Car bingo got old. Counting license plate states got old. Looking at the landscape through the window got very old. Oscar should be grateful he was on a road trip with me - first-class ride!

In the afternoon, we cruised past the "Welcome to South Dakota" sign. It's always exciting to reach a new state. A quarter mile farther was a sign—Speed Limit 70. Nice. Being able to pick up the pace and the spacious scenery offered a good first impression.

It's interesting to observe the contrasts between states. It seems the US is composed of several "regional countries." The Southwest, South, Pacific Northwest, Northeast, Southeast, and Midwest are all unique places. As we crossed the border into South Dakota, the change was noticeable. Suddenly, instead of Minnesota potholes and crowded roads, the South Dakota highway was wide open with smooth, freshly paved roads. We passed the next speed limit sign—75. Awesome. Within thirty minutes, we were at the hotel.

The nice gentleman at the front desk of the Sioux Falls Econo Lodge handed me two room cards. Again? One for you, Oscar! We walked down the hallway to our room and found two queen beds. I threw the bags on one bed and sat on the other. "Oskie, here's your blanket with Froggie." I laid his blanket on the ground with his stuffed animal, then I flipped on the TV.

Oscar looked up at me. They don't call them puppy-dog eyes for nothing. "Alright." I lifted him onto the bed beside me, and we watched TV. "Just don't leave any paw prints on the bed."

There's a beige couch in my living room that was practically new and perfect—until two hours after I got Oscar. He ran into the house and sat right on the cushions. I tried to wash out the mud, but it was never the same. He kept climbing onto his comfortable couch spot until he was trained to stay off. But by then, the couch was history. So I gave up and let him sleep on it. "No paw prints in the hotel, Oscar."

It was June, and the sun didn't set until around ten o'clock. We had time to do some evening exploring, so we headed out to Sioux Falls. It looked cool, and it was dog friendly—the perfect activity. Once we arrived, we were greeted by extensive sidewalks and grass areas among rocks and waterfalls. It was a nice place to hang out. Plus there was a festival going on with food, music, arts, and crafts. We grabbed a snack and found a spot with a good view. *There's something intriguing about stepping into a place where nobody knows you.* I had a front-row seat to watch how the people of Sioux Falls spent a summer evening. They seemed like friendly folks.

We also took some time to explore the nearby statues and art pieces, picking up some history about the falls themselves. That's when I noticed Oscar had stopped and his head was gyrating back and forth. His stomach started heaving. Uh-oh. Yes, Oscar puked his snack on the ground. I looked around, and fortunately, nobody was looking at us. Between doggie bags and handfuls of napkins I managed to clean it up without anybody noticing. *If a dog pukes in a park, and nobody sees it, did it happen?*

At this point, the sun was lower in the horizon, and most of the festival vendors and artists were packing up their booths. We were also ready to leave and pick up dinner, but most of the food places had already closed their tents.

On our walk back to the car, Oscar stopped to greet a family sitting at some covered picnic benches.

"Like your dog."

"Thanks! He's a good one," I said. "Are you from around here?" I was curious, plus I intended to ask for a restaurant recommendation.

"No, we are here for the festival and to visit the falls. We live in Iowa, about an hour and a half away." We made small talk about the merits of South Dakota and our common experiences in and around Chicago.

"How old is your dog?" the husband asked.

"I think about thirteen. I got him at a shelter. They said he was one at the time."

"You've had him a long time."

"Yep. Adopting him was the best forty bucks I ever spent."

"You're right. We have two rescues at home."

"I found a good one. Picked him out at the shelter—or, he picked me. When I got to his cage, he stood up from the back, walked right up to the front, and looked right at me."

"Sounds like it was meant to be," the wife said.

"Where are you headed?" the husband asked.

"We're going west all the way to Idaho and back. Looking forward to Mount Rushmore and Montana."

"You'll love them both!" she said.

"Do you know much about North Dakota? Is there anything to see?"

"Not much," he said. "It's all oil tankers on the roads. South Dakota is much prettier."

It didn't matter. I was going there regardless to see it for myself.

Oscar leaned over toward their little kid. The boy reached out his tiny hands, and Oscar started to lick his fingers like a kid licking frosting from the mixer.

"I kinda want to see what's in North Dakota. I hear the Badlands are cool."

"Yes, they are interesting, but it's only part of the state. The rest is just open road and oil fields." This seemed too simplistic to me. I couldn't believe there wasn't more to see. In a few weeks, I would find out.

After leaving Falls Park with no restaurant recommendation, we stopped at a convenient Subway. Inside the sandwich shop, there were two high school kids working. It was around 9:15, and there were no customers. Billy Idol's "Flesh For Fantasy" was playing over the radio.

Eighties hard rock, I thought. *My kind of town.* I ordered a turkey sandwich and cookies. The turkey was for Oscar, and the rest of the fixings would be for me. The two teens seemed to be enjoying their summer jobs. One was singing along to the music, then he stopped and enthusiastically asked me what I wanted on my sandwich.

As he prepared it, he bobbed his head to the guitar of Steve Stevens. Then he handed my sandwich to the other worker, and she asked if I wanted chips and a drink. They both had a sincere smile and energy, like this was the best sandwich, the best job, the best time ever. It inspired thoughts in me about attitude, gratitude, and perspective toward work. "I like the spirit," I said to them and happily left money in their tip cup.

When I got back in the car, Oscar sniffed at the bag. "Not yet. Ten more minutes." Once we arrived back at the hotel, Oscar eagerly followed me—or rather eagerly followed the bag of dinner! I unlocked the door to our room, turned on the TV, and we both started chowing down. "Glamorous life on the road, huh?" Oscar was enjoying his dinner of "turkey on dry."

SIOUX FALLS, SOUTH DAKOTA to RAPID CITY, SOUTH DAKOTA

THE NEXT MORNING we checked out of the Econo Lodge, and I pulled out the map and a yellow highlighter. I continued to trace the path of our journey, pleased with the distance we had covered so far: almost seven hundred miles. I shoved the map back into the glove compartment and started racing west on I-90.

Mile after mile, we passed towns, rest areas, and attractions. The decision to stop usually depended on timing. Did Oscar need to walk? Was I hungry? Did we need gas? Also, I was not above being influenced by a billboard promoting a tourist site. The farther the attraction was off the highway, the less likely I was to stop. But, in the end, I usually defaulted to having a look, because it would kill me to learn later that I had missed a cool sight simply because of fatigue, laziness, or impatience. Sometimes, weeks after a trip, I discover a spot I had completely missed. I usually write it down because someday I plan to get back there.

The billboard that caught my eye this time was for "The World's Only Corn Palace." Corn Palace? I was intrigued. The drawing was curious, but what would it really look like? Since it was advertised as a palace, it must be quite regal and ornate! We decided to take a "tour detour" and pulled off at Mitchell, South Dakota. For fifteen minutes I followed arrows through town. I started to have reservations, but we were committed. After following a maze of directions leading to the middle of town, we finally found it!

On our way in, we passed a few buildings with a carnival/county fair/Vegas feel. Upon arriving at the front of the Palace, I thought, *Yes, it is unique.* As I peeked in the window, a lady waved us inside. "Hi! I saw the Corn Palace sign on the road. Just wanted to see what this place is all about."

"Well, come on in," she invited us with a smile.

"Him, too?"

"Of course, he can come inside."

Oscar and I walked through the turnstile and entered the Corn Palace. I stopped to thank her for letting us inside, and she went on to tell me about the over one hundred years of history of the Palace and the Mitchell community. She clearly loved talking to us, and I enjoyed hearing her personal tidbits about life in South Dakota. After the nice chat, Oscar and I walked through the lobby area. As Oscar mingled through the crowd of visitors, some kids and parents stared at the only dog walking around, but most ignored us. Instead, they were admiring the corn themed attractions and interior decorations.

We came to the arena with seating and a nice scoreboard in the middle. It was used for basketball games, concerts, or in today's case, a market with souvenirs. It definitely had a nifty motif of agricultural murals and corn decor. At this point it had been twenty minutes, and Oscar had yet to mark his territory, so I decided not to push our luck. We headed back outside to take a few photos of the Corn Palace front and admire the architectural style. Then, I noticed a giant smiling corn across the street. We had to get a picture! I asked a stranger to take the souvenir shot, and he happily agreed. As I hoisted up my fifty-three-pound pal, passersby turned to watch us pose for a humorous photo. Oscar can really draw a crowd. Plus, he always takes a good picture.

A "corny" picture of Oscar and me

After spreading some Oscar love to the people who had gathered and answering some questions about our road trip, we were back on the road, flying down I-90 west through South Dakota. The roads seemed freshly paved and smooth, and there was little traffic. The speed limit was seventy-five, so going eighty miles per hour with the truckers made it easy to cover a lot of ground. It was mostly open scenery with towns every twenty or twenty-five miles. And, of course, there were consistently spaced billboards doing all they could to lure me off the highway.

Two hours later, we passed a few billboards promoting an "1880 Town" near Midland, South Dakota. This got me reminiscing about the Old Tucson theme park I had visited as a kid in Arizona. It was a western town replica where you could do things like pan for gold and watch a gunfight reenactment.

Harkening back to my good memories as a child, I couldn't help but pull off the highway and steer us in the direction of the Original 1880 Town. Before heading to the entrance, I offered Oscar some water. As we approached, I looked at the ticket prices—around twelve bucks just to walk inside and see the town, with the highlight being some original props from the Kevin Costner movie, *Dances with Wolves*. Well, we're here. I forked over the entrance fee, and Oscar and I went inside to see what was behind door number one.

We were welcomed by gravel and dirt separating wood buildings. It was barren, and some of the buildings were a bit run-down. I half-expected tumbleweeds to roll down the main walkway. We did see the *Dances with Wolves* items, but they were anticlimactic. There was also some ancient farming and Old West equipment that looked as if they hadn't been touched or maintained since 1880. Inside one of the old wooden buildings were exhibits filled with aged photos and items someone in the nineteenth century would've had. With the exception of a few covered wagons and some pioneer relics, it seemed more of a garage sale than an antique exhibit.

Nevertheless, I had to look on the bright side. Oscar found places to sniff, we met a few nice people, and we stretched our legs. Also, there was a nifty pet area with three red fire hydrants, a ceramic life-sized dog, and a little doghouse. There was a sign that read "South Dakota's Original 1880 Town Pet Rest Area" with a cartoon dog sketch. It was a thoughtful, cute setup. This tour detour wasn't a total loss. While it didn't live up to my childhood memories, we got some exercise and the weather was pleasant.

Once we were back on the road, we passed countless Wall Drug billboards along the interstate. This was one attraction I had no trouble passing by. Despite being a popular shopping destination, trinkets and tchotchkes don't interest me or Oscar. Neither do crowds, so we passed. Besides, we were on our way to something much more exciting: Mount Rushmore. And by skipping Wall Drug, we still had time to get there in the same day. I was eager to reach this monument, then it felt like the Black Hills would never end. *How much farther?*

We persisted through some winding roads, until suddenly around the corner was a face.

Amazing! I stared up in awe at the profile. There was an enormous face in the rocks! Incredible.

I wanted to get a picture, but unfortunately, the road didn't have a suitable shoulder for pulling over. We followed the scenic highway, eventually arriving at the main entrance and parking structure. That's where we learned dogs were not allowed beyond the park entrance. Many visitors left their pups in their vehicles—not me. It's either both of us, or none of us. Oscar and I walked past a motorhome, listening to a dog bark near the window. Then we passed a big truck with two dogs sitting inside, the windows cracked to let in some air. That wasn't for us.

We walked to the edge of the allowed designated area. We couldn't enter the park, but I still had a view where I could see the four carved faces of the presidents. As we walked along a paved path, I admired the massive monument in the distance while Oscar inspected the plants, the path, and a garbage can. His interest was ground level. At one point on the path, I was able to line Oscar up for a photo.

A National Treasure and Mount Rushmore in the background

It was a moment: standing near Mount Rushmore. It took a long time to get here, and I didn't know when I'd return. I wanted to take advantage of this time. *Be in the present.* I just sat and admired it. Wow. That took some serious artistic talent. I stared at the etchings in the mountain and wondered, *How the hell did they do that?* It would have required incredible ingenuity. The project was started in 1927 before computers, cell phones, and other technologies. I facetiously imagined some guy hanging from a rope chiseling away. Meanwhile, the others were at the bottom yelling, "A little to the left. Now take a little more off the nose." Or, I pictured another person running half a mile away to draw what he saw and then came running back with a hand-drawn sketch. I wondered what would have happened if they made a mistake. Could they put pieces back? Super Glue ain't gonna work. As I was deep in thought, Oscar tugged on the leash and pulled me away. That was my cue. He was done with Mount Rushmore.

Before getting back on the main highway, we took a pit stop in the nearby town of Keystone. We both needed a snack, and I wanted one last look at the view of the Black Hills.

Outside a souvenir shop, a kid approached and asked, "Can I pet your dog?" In the distance, his parent yelled out, "Make sure you ask permission!"

There's no doubt that traveling with a dog makes it much easier to meet people. If I were alone, there's no way a stranger would suddenly start talking to me. And, if they did, would I even bother to engage? But, when traveling with Oscar, lots of curious people wanted to chat.

"Of course," I answered. "He likes meeting people." We chatted about his name and breed.

"We used to have a Lab," the boy said. I sensed the boy had a dog because he was comfortable with Oscar. "How old is he?" By now, his parent and a girl joined us.

"Not sure, probably about thirteen," I told them. "See the gray on his chin. But, he's still got some pep. We were running 5K races when he was eleven."

"I like his ears," the girl said happily. "They go in different directions!" On cue, Oscar's left ear went straight up while his right ear lay down. They continued asking questions while petting and hugging Oscar. Then, a few others joined in to pet Oscar and talk about him. I didn't mind. I enjoyed talking about our adventure, and Oscar enjoyed the attention.

After everyone got their fill of loving on Oscar, we left Keystone and aimed for Rapid City to find our hotel. Unfortunately, somehow and somewhere, I made a wrong turn. I found myself driving through open area with fewer and fewer cars. I turned around and started retracing our path. There were no buildings, and I was disoriented. I stopped on the shoulder and looked at the maps on my laptop, but I couldn't figure out my location. I needed to get to civilization to ask someone for directions. Ideally, I wanted to find a gas station where the cashier or a person in line could reset me in the right direction. I was also fine with going online at a Starbucks, McDonald's, or Dunkin' Donuts with free Wi-Fi.

I hoped it wouldn't take long to find a person. As I drove aimlessly in western South Dakota, I finally noticed a landmark: an odd-shaped building I knew we had passed earlier. From there, I started to deduce which way to the town. Then, around the next turn, a gas station appeared! I ran inside to confirm my directions. The cashier assured me that I was headed the right way. After the thirty-minute detour, we were back on track.

At last, we reached the Americas Best Value Inn next to a Chili's restaurant by a shopping mall. There was a lot of concrete, leaving only small patches of grass for Oscar. There were better locations in Rapid City, but being near Mount Rushmore and the Black Hills, the hotels were quite expensive. In the end, we just needed a quick stop with a bed and a shower. I did, however, spend an extra fifteen dollars on an upgraded "executive room." I've found that when you pay just a little bit more, you usually get significantly more space, and perhaps a couch or a kitchen area. Also, I suspect someone paying extra would expect a cleaner room and likewise would treat the room better. Same goes for rental cars.

Our executive room was terrific. There was lots of room to spare—everywhere. I cranked on the air conditioner, and we popped on the bed to watch TV and figure out where to get dinner.

Regardless of what I was up to, Oscar seemed excited about the new room.

The thought occurred to me that we'd visited more fast-food joints in three days than I had in three months: KFC, Pizza Hut, Subway. Plus, I had snuck in a Dairy Queen and a bag of Doritos chips. With better nutritional balance in mind, I found an Italian restaurant where I picked up some pasta, a salad, and meatballs for Oscar. After dinner in our room, I followed the routine of looking for the next day's itinerary and hotel.

During an ordinary search for "hotels with dog," I discovered a website called BringFido.com that lists hotels and restaurants that are pet-friendly. While their database isn't necessarily complete, it became my default place for researching hotel options because it offered a ton of information, including pet fees and some user comments. After booking the room, I started searching the towns we'd pass along the way and read more about Mount Rushmore, Crazy Horse, and the history of this area. Meanwhile, Oscar wandered around the opposite side of the room. He picked out a comfortable spot beside the refrigerator, sat down, let out a deep sigh, and closed his eyes.

RAPID CITY, SOUTH DAKOTA to SHERIDAN, WYOMING

AFTER A BRIEF morning walk with Oscar and a quick bite to eat for breakfast, I printed screenshots of online maps, anticipating the cool sites we could see today. I also sent some photos and emails to friends and family. Then, I posted a few Oscar photos on Facebook. I'm not real big on Facebook. People telling strangers about their personal stuff. Same goes for texting about a great moment rather than actually watching it. Facebook feels like you're sharing with your friends about the fun you're having without inviting them to come along. And what's the point of having hundreds of "friends" that you rarely talk to? An old friend of mine described Facebook as a "time suck." In any event, maybe some friends or family of mine would like to see Oscar out on the road.

    I closed the laptop and packed it in the bag. Oscar followed me to the front desk to check out. He was getting the hang of the hotels. And, I was very happy with the trip so far. In fact, seeing Mount Rushmore alone made the drive worthwhile. Looking at Oscar that morning, I thought, *We should've done these road trips years ago.*

Upon entering the car, I glanced at the odometer and saw the miles we had piled on—nearly eleven hundred. I took out my yellow highlighter and traced more distance on the map. Yesterday, we had basically gone across the entire state of South Dakota. Time was moving faster and faster, and the trip was cruising along.

We resumed our travels on I-90 west along the Black Hills, passing by Sturgis, which is home to the huge annual motorcycle rally. Before we knew it, we were at the border, and there was the sign—"Welcome to Wyoming: Forever West" with a silhouette of a cowboy on a horse. A new state! I decided that the Welcome Center would be a good place to stop. As I took the off-ramp, Oscar sensed the car slowing down, woke up, and assumed his "Washington Crossing the Delaware" pose in the car. He liked standing on the arm rest, and I had a few theories about this. I assumed he was curious and liked watching through the window. Maybe he just likes licking my face. Or perhaps it's more comfortable to stand there than sit in the back. Or it could be that he likes the air conditioner blowing directly into his face.

Before exploring the area, I gave Oscar fresh water, then we trudged off to inspect a large bronze wildcat and a view of open land in the distance. No doubt, there is a lot of space in this part of the country. After speaking with a helpful woman at the information desk in the Welcome Center, we were back in the car with a plan to detour off the main interstate onto Highway 111 to Highway 24. I-90 was sparse, but this local highway was almost empty! We passed the sign for a town called Alva. "Population: 50." Yes, lots of space.

We were making our way to Devils Tower National Monument. A friend had mentioned it to me prior to our trip, and the Welcome Center confirmed it was a popular attraction. So I drove with anticipation. And drove. And drove. Suddenly, a plateau-like mountain in the middle of an open plain appeared in the distance. It was unique and eye-catching. I started to understand why Devils Tower was a must-see.

As we pulled in, I grabbed Oscar's leash. "Let's check this out!" He seemed up for it. We walked around the park in a long, grassy section where pets were allowed. We had a great view, so I persuaded Oscar to pose for a photo. It wasn't difficult. He was a bit tired and quite content to sit still. His tongue was hanging out of his mouth, so he presented a perfect smile! I marveled to Oscar about how they should include him on a Wyoming postcard! There are plenty of Devils Tower pictures out there, but I preferred a shot with a personal touch.

An angel in front of Devils Tower

After marveling at how few visitors there were, even during the summer vacation season, we got back on the road headed toward a little town called Hulett where we'd stop for lunch. I found a place with the curious name of R Deli. What really caught my attention was the countless white animal horns on the eave and roof in the front of the building! I decided not to ask where they came from and instead ordered a big chicken sandwich for the two of us to share. Oscar got the chicken; I took the veggies and cheese.

As we ate comfortably under a shaded awning around the corner from the deli, I noticed a Hulett Museum Art Gallery. What could possibly be inside that place? After lunch, we went across the street to find out. Sure enough, it was another pleasant surprise! There was a nicely displayed collection of Western items, and it was run by a historical collector from the area. It had shiny finished-wood floors and immaculate displays, so understandably, pets could not enter. Fortunately, the weather was pleasant, and there was a wooden bench with solid railing. So Oscar sat at the entrance under the bench. He seemed content, clearly having no interest in the exhibits inside.

The owner/curator, who was wearing a western shirt, jeans, and cowboy hat, introduced himself. He was from Tucson, among other Western spots, and had acquired tons of items for his own personal collection. After having accumulated enough stuff, he opened this museum, alongside items on loan from the Smithsonian's storage and pieces from collectors in the area. It was a substantial display of artifacts and antiques. He was quite welcoming and offered some cool historic tidbits. As I looked at the items, I could still see Oscar sitting at the museum entrance. He seemed to be OK, watching an occasional car or person go by.

Thirty minutes later, we left Hulett and took the scenic side road out of town headed toward Sheridan. I continued to admire how wonderful and remote this land was, but at the same time I thought, *What if the car breaks down? How long would it be before I could get some help?*

What a sight that would be: Oscar and I walking along the interstate for miles. Fortunately, the two-hour stretch to Sheridan went by quickly. Tonight's destination was Mill Inn. Its towering structure was visible from a distance. It's a former flour mill, which seemed interesting, and it was listed as the number one hotel in Sheridan on Tripadvisor. It was worth a try.

To get into the lobby, we passed under the hotel emblem: "Best Rest Out West" with a silhouette of a cowboy riding a bucking horse. Our room was small but nicely renovated. Overall, the Mill Inn was a score! Oscar and I explored the hotel grounds with a keen interest in the high silos. Although, I think Oscar sniffed the bushes with greater interest.

When it was time for dinner, I decided to try Taco John's. I had seen several of them along the way, and curiosity got the best of me. Plus, it was located two blocks away, so we could walk rather than drive. At the restaurant, I left Oscar in the outside patio. I went inside and ordered a taco salad for me, Santa Fe chicken on the side for Oscar, and a Coke. As they prepared my meal, I gave a quick wave to Oscar through the window. I think he saw me. He was waiting patiently.

After dinner and custard dessert, we returned to the comfortable, air-conditioned room. Oscar found his spot for the night.

SHERIDAN, WYOMING to DILLON, MONTANA

IN TAKING A cross-country road trip, there are inherently long stretches of driving. Today's leg would be four hundred and twenty miles, enabling us to get to Boise in two days. In total, we had nearly seven hundred miles left. At least, these long periods of time in the car were relatively comfortable. I can remember in the late 1980s when I was going to and from college, it took about six or seven hours by car from Phoenix to LA. I did the three hundred and sixty miles of driving through the desert in a 1970 Dodge Challenger—with no air conditioner. I called the system "4-40 air conditioning," which meant I rolled down all four windows and went forty. I'd also leave as early in the morning as possible, and sometimes, when the temperature gauge rose toward the red line, I would turn the heater on with the hope that it would add ventilation and help the engine heat escape through the opened vents, thus cooling the radiator. The ride was a furnace on wheels.

Today, as an adult, driving is a more comfortable journey. There can be long stretches of the same road, but it's exciting not knowing what town or site is around the corner. I found driving two hundred and fifty miles per day with Oscar to be enjoyable. Listening to XM radio, which included dozens of classic stations, was an improvement from old cassettes. And, of course, there was plenty of air conditioning.

On this day of driving, we got an early start and crossed into Montana. It truly was Big Sky Country. The scenery was beautiful: green pines, white-capped mountains, and the blue sky. It's hard to describe, but when you look in the distance, it really does look like a "big sky" that goes on forever. Occasionally, I just had to stop on the side of the road for a photo. Each time, I'd look up and down—*big sky*. The height from the horizon up to the sky seemed larger than normal, as if it were an optical illusion.

We remained on I-90 west, driving around Billings, until we hit an official rest area twenty miles west of town. There was a pretty view of mountains, along with Yellowstone in the distance. Oscar and I took a moment to walk around and enjoy the fresh air. It was at this rest stop that it hit me how much easier (and appealing) it was to learn facts, history, and geography during this trip compared to textbooks or a classroom.

I found yet another good photo op and asked a young man if he could take a photo. He agreed, not enthusiastically, but he was nice enough. I handed him my little digital camera, and he seemed a bit perplexed. Perhaps, in this day of smartphones, traditional cameras were becoming less familiar. I showed him which button to push and where to view the shot then picked up Oscar, walked twenty feet away, and posed. The guy took a few pictures, handed me the camera, and rushed off. I looked at the digital photos, and realized there were no pictures! He had pressed the wrong button.

I tried another guy, repeating the process. Photographer number two took the photos and walked off. I looked at my camera, and there were photos, but they weren't centered. At least I could crop them later. *Can't anyone take a picture with an ordinary digital camera anymore?*

Before returning to the car, I ran across a kid wearing a Boston Bruins t-shirt. "Aren't they playing the Blackhawks?" I asked. The Stanley Cup Finals was the extent of my hockey knowledge. Then I mentioned that I was from Chicago.

"Yeah," he answered. "We're up 2-1." The kid seemed to be boasting. I'm not sure why. After all, I wasn't playing. Nevertheless, he seemed nice enough.

"Hey, you mind taking a photo of me and my dog?" Third time's a charm. In the end, this Bruins hockey fan took a nice, well-centered shot of us.

During the next stretch, we passed ranches, cattle, and railcars carrying coal or minerals. Then, the spacious road went through a few passes along the Gallatin Range. It was a beautiful mountainous view of pine and green grass. Some homes in the mountains caught my eye, so I wrote down the nearby town's name, Livingston, so we could pass through on the way back. Twenty miles farther, we stopped at a rest area near Bozeman. Oscar scouted around while I read a few illustrated timelines related to the Lewis and Clark National Historic Trail; another lesson, courtesy of the Montana Department of Transportation.

Montana rest stop—Green grass and Big Sky

Shortly after passing the Continental Divide of the Americas, a significant position dividing the flow of water into either the Pacific Ocean or Atlantic Ocean, we reached the eighteen hundred miles of traveling mark via I-90 and switched onto the junction of Interstate 15 heading south toward lower Idaho. An hour later, we reached Dillon, Montana, where we were staying at a Motel 6 for the night. The room rate was only fifty-eight bucks, so I was prepared for anything. At the reception area, Oscar and I encountered a friendly student, originally from Mesa, Arizona, working the front desk.

"Really?" I said. "I grew up in Phoenix."

"Small world."

"And, you ended up in Montana?"

The student explained when and why she moved. Mostly, she liked the climate and lifestyle of Montana. "But maybe I'll go back some day," she added.

Oscar popped his paws onto the front desk countertop. She seemed to like dogs and gave him a friendly glance. "Sorry about that," I said. "He's excited about checking in."

I pulled the car around back, closer to our room. I lifted Oscar out and placed him on the ground. Then, I went to the backseat and pulled out my small bag with one night of clothes and toiletries. I grabbed a bottle of water and my laptop, then locked the car.

Where's Oscar? I looked around. The dog was gone.

"Oscar," I called out. *Where did he go?* "Oscar, where are you?" It was useless. I noticed his hearing had begun deteriorating a few months earlier. He may not be able to hear my voice, even if it was loud. I put the bags down and walked twenty feet in each direction. *What the hell? I know you can't go far.*

I called his name a few more times. Suddenly, I heard the rattling of his collar from above. I traced the sound to an outdoor stairwell around the corner. I walked over, looked up, and saw Oscar frozen near the top of the stairs! "How's it going up there?" I asked him. Oscar could work his way up a set of stairs, and if possible, he would patiently, methodically, slowly come back down. Unfortunately, sometimes his old legs found it too difficult to come back down steep or separated steps.

He looked down at me with the expression, *are you coming?*

"Oscar, we're not on the second floor." I went up the stairs and carried him back down. Then, I retrieved the bags and bowls, and we went to our room.

Motel 6 can get a bad rap, yet the room turned out to be a great deal—quite spacious, two beds, good Wi-Fi, and air conditioning. Plus there were no blood stains, crime scene chalk lines, or funny smells. It seemed like a good deal and safe place, and there was no pet fee. It was a bit noisy, but we could live with that.

The only downside to this remodeled place was lack of extras. I didn't see any shampoo or soap; so, I used leftovers I had collected from other hotels along the way. And, the bathroom had flimsy white towels, (the kind we had in seventh-grade gym class).

After unpacking, we did a bit of exploring. Two blocks away was a huge running area for people and dogs, and farther down the street, there were restaurants and a great walking path. Oscar and I started along the expansive path through the woods and along the ponds near the motel. Then, we continued to an open field where two dogs were wrestling with each other. Oscar gave it a try and joined in the wrestling, albeit a half step behind the young Labs. Eventually, he walked away and started sniffing and yawning. "Yeah, Oscar. Your best days are behind you."

After returning from the afternoon walk, we drove ten minutes into the downtown area, searching for a place to grab dinner. Starting at the Beaverhead County Courthouse, we drove around the area until finally settling on Papa T's Family Restaurant. "Family restaurant" usually implies decent prices and a menu full of choices. Plus, on the awning it said "Taste of Montana Hospitality"—sounded like an endorsement to me! I went inside and placed an order to go. While the food was prepared, Oscar and I walked around the block, looking at the shops, a tavern, and other Dillon businesses. It was a Tuesday evening after seven o'clock, and although it was bright and sunny outside, many of the places were closed.

During the ride back to the motel, Oscar sniffed the bags. As we walked to the room, Oscar led the way—he was anticipating dinner! Following dinner, I checked email and reported to my mom that we had made it to Dillon. Then I flipped on the TV and relaxed. As Oscar sat next to me on the bed, I scratched his back and massaged his ears. That's when I felt something on his back. I rubbed my finger over it again. When I pulled back the fur, it looked like a dark red pimple. *Maybe it's a tick?*

I checked online, searching "How to remove a tick from a dog." Apparently, I was supposed to use tweezers, but I didn't have tweezers. Fortunately, a few days ago, I had packed plastic utensils. So, using a plastic knife and fork—and some bad lighting in the motel room—I started to pick at the "pimple." After a few times of picking at it, the thing changed position. So, it was definitely not a pimple. *It's alive!*

I kept prodding with the fork and knife. Then, I could see it!! It was a tick, with the little legs still moving. I managed to pluck it out, like chopsticks. After squishing it, I tossed it in the garbage. I kept thinking, *Damn, that thing was alive.* Yuck.

DILLON, MONTANA to EMMETT, IDAHO

IN THE MORNING, Oscar eased his way out of the bed onto the carpeting, cleverly using the hotel comforter to help himself down. Each night at home, when I went to sleep, I'd hear Oscar's paws on the wood floor: clop...clop...clop...clop-clop-clop, and then a leap into the bed. Until one day, he couldn't do it. The bed became too high for him, so he would walk over and stand next to the bed, waiting for me to lift him up. Getting off the bed wasn't bad. He figured out how to drape his paws along the side and "slide" off the side. And that became our routine.

Oscar landed all four paws on the ground and wandered to the toilet for a drink of water, bypassing his bowls set on a towel. *Dogs do something funny, stupid, or gross every day.*

With no breakfast offered, we checked out sooner. I led Oscar to the car and opened both the passenger door and the back door. "Which seat do you want?" He chose the backseat and climbed up. It was a bit high, so his hind legs slipped back to the ground. I caught him and gave him a lift. "Backseat it is."

Bring Oscar

After closing the doors, Oscar retrieved a leftover dog treat lodged in the backseat. I sat in the driver's seat, placed the Motel 6 printout on the pile of receipts in the compartment under the armrest, and started the engine. After an hour on I-15, we approached Monida, Montana. Exit 0, the last stop before crossing into Idaho. I started looking for a rest spot. Then I saw a sign: "Spencer, Idaho—Opal Capital of the World." It was approximately fifteen minutes down the road.

Opal Capital of the World sounded alluring. *Of the world? Let's see if they live up to it.*

We pulled into this small town, which would be our last stop for gas. I drove into the lot with an old-school gasoline pump, the sort I hadn't seen since I was a kid. It was like stepping into a forty-year time warp. There was a café with a gift shop that sold opal-related souvenirs. Also, you could pay to go into the back and mine for opal. A few senior citizens were outside trying their luck. We might've joined in the opal search, but no dogs were allowed. It's too bad. Oscar would've been great at digging up the ground!

After fueling up the car, we walked down the road and passed a sign that read, "Since 1897, Spencer, Idaho, Elevation 5898." The elevation seemed a heckuva lot higher than the population. We also came upon what appeared to be an old mining stop. There were railroad tracks and what looked like an old depot stop. I snapped a picture, and that was the extent of our tour of Spencer.

We resumed our drive down I-15 through desert landscaping as well as lava formations that created porous rock surfaces and scenery. Just past Idaho Falls, there was a place called Hell's Half Acre. The name choice struck me as odd. Are they trying to attract visitors or discourage them?? It sounded like a miserable, ominous place. So, of course, it piqued my interest!

Hell's Half Acre turned out to be a lava field. There was a trail that did a full circle through the desert and island of cooled lava. Along the way were boards with information and history about the area. It would make a good field trip for a geology class. It also proved to be a good place to walk with Oscar. We just had to bring water because it was hot as hell in the desert!

Staying cool during a summer day in Hell

Back in the car, we continued along I-15. Oscar was sitting in the front seat, soaking up the view and a back massage from me. At the interstate split, we turned onto I-86 west. This merged into I-84 west/Route 30 west toward Boise. At four o'clock, I realized I'd made a rookie mistake as we cruised straight into Boise's four-lane highway packed with cars. It was the middle of rush hour traffic on a Wednesday. Over the past few years, Boise had exploded into a rather large city. This brought restaurants, entertainment, and real estate development. It also brought traffic and other downsides of sprawling growth. There was no way around it. We were going to grind our way through Boise toward Gem County.

Once we made it through the traffic, we enjoyed the ups and downs of some small mountain passes, and we stopped at the Pearl scenic overlook. In the parking area, signs explained its history as a bustling gold mine town around 1900. Eventually, the ore ran out, and it became a ghost town. Our last scenic stop for this leg of the drive was overlooking Emmett, Idaho. We looked at the beautiful view of the mountains and the valley below. At last!

EMMETT, IDAHO – At Mom's House

WE PLANNED AHEAD of time to spend about a week at my mom's house. This would be a chance to visit family, take a driving break, get some laundry done, clean the car, and relax. It would be a reset. We'd use each day to explore an area around Emmett and nearby Boise. Spending a day or two touring a place gives an impression, but spending a week living in a place helps immerse you and produces a better understanding of the people. You may cover less territory, but it'll be more thorough.

After picking up some groceries for the week, I decided to check out the neighborhood gym. It's important to me to stay active, especially after so much time in the car. My mom, Oscar, and I walked three blocks to get there, and I tied Oscar to a bench just outside the gym entrance.

"He'll be fine," my Mom assured me. "Nobody in town will bother him."

"I know. I just want to be sure he doesn't block the sidewalk." I gave Oscar a quick pat on the head. "Wait here. We'll be right back."

We went inside the building to check out the facility. It was a bit run down, with older equipment, but the people were super nice and the gym provided enough to get a workout. After all, dumbbells, pull-up bars, and stationary bikes are timeless. I explained that I was in town for a week, so signing up for a gym membership wouldn't work. However, they improvised and offered me a two-week pass—ten gym visits—for a whopping fifteen dollars. My local gym cost almost fifteen bucks for one guest pass. Small town wins again. The manager handed me a business card to use as a makeshift membership card. He told me they'd put a stamp after every visit. Perfect. "I'll be back later today."

We continued walking along the main streets of the small downtown. My mom pointed out places she frequented: a flower shop, a diner, an antique shop, the local bakery. A few blocks away, there was a large grocery store, restaurants, and an ice cream shop. And, there was a place to wash the dog. Lucky for you, Oscar. Across the way, there was the local car wash called the Car Tub, which was located next to the Gem County Fire Department. One mile away, there was a public sports complex with a track and open field. Plus, there was a concrete area for skateboarding. Along the way, the locals greeted us. Meanwhile, I kept noticing the surrounding mountains that rose into view behind the town.

The first few days, we slowed down and adjusted to small town living. Instead of miles of driving in the car, we were enjoying the extra free time. Each day, I'd walk Oscar. We'd pass by familiar shops, or we'd try different residential streets. People in trucks would say hi or wave as they passed by us. When I was younger, if you asked me to describe Idaho, I'd probably say "potatoes and militia." But now I was seeing rural Idaho firsthand, and so far, in Emmett, I'd begin by describing it as "nice people and mountains."

During most evenings, I'd check email, write, set my itinerary, or watch a movie on my mom's DVD player. One mile away, there was a Redbox, containing plenty of one-dollar films to rent. Meanwhile, Oscar made himself at home, resting in different spots around the house, unknowingly leaving his hair behind in each location. And, every few hours, I watched Mom straighten the house or sweep the floor.

Oscar enjoying his vacation (Nearby, my mom is sweeping up dog hairs!)

One evening, we left Oscar in my mom's place and walked down the street to the Emmett Community Movie Theater. This week's feature film was *The Fast and the Furious*. The ticket was about three bucks, the popcorn was a dollar, and the soda was a buck fifty. What a deal! We took our seats, where I enjoyed lots of legroom. While talking to Mom, I scanned the theater and looked at the scene. There were teenagers sitting up at the front, and two old ladies wearing tennis shoes in the row next to us, cheerfully gossiping about events in the town. A mix of townspeople of all ages filled the theater. Just before the show started, I trotted up the aisle and got another bag of popcorn. It was just one dollar, and I was happy to support the theater.

Before the start of the movie, the owner came out and introduced the show. He thanked everyone for attending and made a few announcements about upcoming movies and current events in town. After the film, which was thoroughly entertaining, everyone filed down the aisle and exited, each saying goodbye to the theater owner standing at the entrance. Small towns truly are a wonder.

My mom and I walked three blocks back to the house. Inside, Oscar was waiting for us. I was relieved that there seemed to be no accidents nor any damage—until I noticed the blinds over the door window. Apparently, Oscar was trying to see outside? Or, get out? Nevertheless, he did OK.

Oscar posing next to his handiwork

That night, we took Oscar around the neighborhood. At 10:00 p.m., the summer weather was pleasant and the town was quiet. We walked by a small bar and restaurant, one of the few places that was open. Then, we continued past a few empty streets before turning back and calling it a night.

EMMETT, IDAHO – Day 5

ON THE FOLLOWING Monday morning, I got up and took Oscar outside for a walk. When we returned, my mom was awake and offered to make breakfast for everyone. While we were eating, she got up to sweep the floor again. "He's just going to leave more hairs," I reminded her. In the hot summer, Oscar consistently shed his black coat.

"I know," she said, "but I like to keep it clean." I didn't bother to stop her.

"So, are we still going to your brother's today?"

"Yeah," I said. "I'm not sure if we should stay overnight or return tonight."

"Either is fine with me," she said. "I can pack a small bag."

"I'll throw our stuff in the car, too."

My mom, Oscar, and I took a beautiful drive to Baker City, Oregon, passing through mountains and high desert. We stopped along the way to get a glimpse of a part of the Oregon Trail. A couple of hours later, we reached Baker City where we passed lampposts with pictures of their 2013 high school graduates. *I like small*

Bring Oscar

town communities. There were a few cafes and a random general store, as well as several antique dealers.

We pulled in front of my brother's two-story house. Eric's two sons were playing in the front yard and happily led us inside. While Oscar browsed, my brother and nephews gave me the brief tour of the house. Thirty minutes later, Eric, Oscar, and I got into the car and drove to see his land, cattle, and bed-and-breakfast.

We began the forty-five-minute drive to Halfway, Oregon, stopping at a remote, scenic rest stop overlooking the valley with ranches and cattle and horses. After taking in the view, I lifted Oscar back into the car—and he tumbled into the backseat. "Are you OK, buddy?" Oscar leaned forward between Eric and me. *That was weird.*

We continued driving through the winding road, climbing in elevation, with the windows cracked open letting in the mountain air. Oscar pushed his snout against the window. He seemed to be sniffing the fresh air or enjoying the breeze. Or, maybe he was trying to get a better view of the scenery?

We turned off the paved road onto a dirt path that led to the bed-and-breakfast. After we parked in the gravel lot, I lifted Oscar out of the car and noticed he was limping a little bit. But then he started walking ahead of us. As my brother described the buildings and land on the ranch, I watched Oscar from the corner of my eye. He began making a wincing sound. "Maybe he twisted his leg," I thought out loud. "Sometimes, he gets a sore leg and eventually walks it off."

We continued walking behind him. Then he began acting oddly. He was sort of chasing his tail. Perhaps he was stung by a bee? Or, trying to sweep away an insect pestering him? He appeared to be desperately running in a circle.

We caught up to him. "Oscar?" Nothing. "Oscar!" He didn't respond to my voice.

I grabbed him, but he was stubbornly trying to go in circles. I held his body, and it was in a contorted circular form. I tried to straighten him, but his stiff body resisted. Then, I wrapped my hands around his neck and looked at his face. No expression. I waved my hand in front of his face. Like a blind person, there was no reaction.

I looked into his eyes and saw an eerie look of emptiness, fear, and stoicism. Then, his eyes started twitching!

"What the fuck is that?!"

My brother looked at the eyes. "I have no idea." He waved his hands, but Oscar did not respond. "Is it a seizure?"

"Shit, I don't know. I've never seen anything like that." Could it be a stroke? His body was stuck. How did it happen so suddenly? He was walking around, then suddenly, his eyes were twitching. And, he was crooked.

"If it is a stroke, we need to get him to a vet fast."

"Maybe it isn't? It suddenly happened. Maybe he'll snap out of it?"

"He doesn't look good."

I carried him around for a bit. Then, I let him walk. Suddenly, like a drunk, he veered to the right and stumbled. I helped him up. Then, I watched his thirteen-year-old body wobbling and walking crooked, and then falling. I looked at him, and he stared vacantly back at me. We started to walk again. Then he began walking in circles.

"You're right. We gotta find out what's wrong. Is there a vet in this town?"

We drove back to Baker City. I wondered if these winding roads had given him vertigo. Or, when he fell at the rest stop, did it hurt him like some sort of concussion? Meanwhile, Oscar sat in back, looking medicated and vacuous.

Forty-five minutes later, I carried Oscar into my brother's house and set him gently in the middle of the living room. Meanwhile, Eric went on the computer to get information. The others came into the room, curious about what happened.

Oscar staggered a bit, and then he suddenly puked—on the nice rug. This was a new low.

"Oh God," my brother groaned as he looked over his shoulder. "That was a new rug."

Murphy's Law: Oscar didn't throw up in the car, or in the yard, or on the kitchen floor. He let it out on the new carpet.

Eric turned back around and continued doing Internet searches about Oscar's symptoms.

"I'll pay for another," I mentioned.
"It's a handstitched Persian rug."
It sounded expensive. "I'll get you another."
"I bought it from an old guy in Pakistan when I was deployed."
"Oh," I sighed.
"Ah, whatever. I'll just move a piece of furniture on top of the stain." My brother's dry humor could come out in any situation.

My mom and nephews rushed to get paper towels and cleaning materials to minimize damage to the rug. Then, I noticed Oscar's eyes start twitching side to side again.

"It's like he's possessed," I called out. "Hey, Eric, do a search on 'dog twitching eyes.'"

My sister-in-law returned to the room with an address of the local vet. "He's there right now. I told him you're on the way."

My brother jumped off the computer, I grabbed the dog, and we rushed down the street to the vet's office.

After describing everything that had happened during the day, the young vet speculated it could be brain damage from a fall, stroke, or old age. Or, maybe not. "We could do an MRI, but it would be expensive. And, if it is a stroke, there isn't much we could do here. You're better off going to Boise where there is a surgical team and more advanced equipment."

"That's three hours," I said. "Is that too much time to help him?"

The vet couldn't provide a definitive diagnosis, so we had to drive back to Boise to see a specialist at the emergency animal hospital. If it were a stroke or seizure, we had a small window of opportunity to help him—if at all. I wondered if a dog stroke was different than a human stroke.

The vet offered the name of a specialist in Boise. "Here's her information and the address of the clinic. And, I'll send the records to her." We started racing back to Boise, consistently checking on Oscar in the backseat. He was just sitting in his spot, staring aimlessly in no direction.

"He seems calm," my mom said hopefully.

I was watching the clock and the speedometer. And, I was worried. "Well, his eyes are open. I suppose that's a good thing." When

I had a concussion, it was important not to pass out. If his eyes were open, then he wasn't dead.

Suddenly, my gas gauge alert light appeared. "What the hell is going on?!!" The gas level plummeted. "Come on!"

"What's the matter?" my mom asked.

"It says we're almost out of gas. I don't know why!" The gas gauge was fluctuating as we went over and through the mountains. Suddenly, the gas alert showed low fuel. "Now this is happening! There should be plenty of gas!"

Time was of the essence, but I couldn't risk running out of gas. After twenty miles, I gave in and pulled into a gas station. I quickly grabbed the pump and noticed you had to pay first.

"I'll go inside," my mom said.

While she walked inside, I looked at Oscar. He was still. "Don't die," I pleaded with him. "We'll be at the vet soon. Don't die." He was only thirteen years old. I always knew the day would come, but I didn't think it would be this abrupt. "You're my best friend."

It was twelve years earlier when the big day happened. I went with two friends, Carrie and Phil, to find a dog. We started at a nearby rescue where their policy did not permit visitors around the cages. Instead, volunteers brought out potential adoptees one at a time. The lady showed us a couple of dogs that weren't a fit. Then, she brought out another twenty-pound terrier.

"No, I'm looking for a Shepherd-like dog," I reminded her. "Don't you have any bigger dogs?"

"Let me go look," she said.

As she took the little dog inside, I said to my friends, "Are they even listening to me?"

"It doesn't look like it," my friend said. "What are they thinking? They haven't brought out one dog that you described."

"Maybe they don't have what I'm looking for," I suggested. "Or, they're trying to get rid of certain dogs."

The director seemed reluctant to let us see many dogs. "How many hours do you work?" she asked. "And, the dog would be alone?" she asked skeptically. "It's just you?"

When she went inside, my friend asked, "What's the deal with her? She's totally giving you the third degree." A shelter ought to be careful on behalf of the animals, but were they trying to find homes for these dogs or not?

"She probably thinks I'm some irresponsible, single guy." Then, I added cynically, "I had no idea it was so difficult to rescue a dog."

This lady didn't realize I was the biggest dog person out there. In fact, I had bought a house with a backyard, put up a fence and a gate, and installed a doggie door to prepare for this moment. "If I didn't want a dog, I'd still be in my apartment," I joked. "I basically bought a very expensive doghouse."

When the lady returned with an eight-year-old midsize dog, I turned to my friends. "We gotta go somewhere else," I said, giving up. "We're wasting our time here."

On the way out, another volunteer suggested a place where we could look at all the dogs. So, the three of us drove to Orphans of the Storm Animal Shelter in Deerfield.

At Orphans, we walked up and down the aisles, past the individual cages. I was excited with anticipation. Which dog would I rescue? I picked out two dogs and separately walked around with each. Then, I resumed looking up and down the rows, until I reached a seemingly empty cage. In the back, sitting in the shade was a little black dog. He looked at me, stood up, and walked to the cage fence between us. He looked me right in the eye. No excitement; just a definitive understanding.

He was a black shepherd mix, a breed that I was seeking. Plus, he was big enough to roughhouse, wrestle, and run with, but small enough to lift and handle. The volunteer opened the cage, and I took this black dog for a walk. We wandered along a small path, where he sniffed and explored the tree-lined section. Then, in a grass area, my friends and I sat down with him. We played a bit, and he seemed comfortable and responsive.

After returning him to his cage, we continued looking at other available pets. But, after ten minutes, I went back to him. I knew that was my dog. The name on his cage was "Pepper." The volunteer took him out again and handed me the leash.

"Do you know anything about him?" I asked.

"He was found on the streets three weeks ago," the volunteer answered. "We think he's about one year old."

"He seems well-behaved," my friend mentioned.

"Yes, he's a sweet dog. And, he's housebroken and healthy. He's a little underweight, but that's expected."

I led the black dog outside for a confirmation walk. He was comfortable walking along with us. Then, when he was looking the other way, I called out, "Hey, Pepper."

He didn't turn around or react.

"Pepper," I repeated. There was no response.

That was the end of that name!

"So, what are you going to name him?" my friends asked.

I had thought about it days earlier. "What do you think about Ripley? Also, I was thinking of the name Oscar."

"Oscar," Carrie immediately said. "I like that name."

I filled out the paperwork at the front desk. After paying the adoption fee, they handed me a few pet items and a leash. Oscar was mine.

As we walked—and Oscar strutted—along the cages, the other dogs yelped and barked. Suddenly, one dog leaped onto the fence as we walked by him.

"What the—!" Phil laughed with amazement.

The sleek dog barked while grasping the fence three feet above the ground. It was a cross between Spiderman and Cujo.

"I'd love to take all of you," I said as we continued toward the exit. "But, this is the one."

Ever since I took Oscar home that day, he's been a roommate and a friend. He had an uncanny understanding. If I was mad, he'd dart outside and wait in the backyard. If I was sad, he'd climb onto the couch and sit on my lap. Or, if I was excited, he'd run around and leap up to me. He didn't know what the reason was, but he was happy too. Through ups and downs, he was there.

When I saw my mom come out from paying for the gas, I gathered myself and started filling the tank. Then it was back to the race to Boise. During the drive, awful thoughts came to mind. It'll have been nearly four hours since the event. If he'd had a stroke, then he's done for. If he needed surgery, what would that involve? I'd pay whatever it cost. If he died, then I imagined having to drive two thousand miles back home without him. It would be a nightmare road trip. *Did I do this to him?*

After two and a half hours on the road, we were back in Boise. "I have the address," my mom told me. I followed her directions. Meanwhile, I watched Oscar in the rear view mirror. He had a haunting, glazed look with no response. I looked closely and noticed his eyes were twitching again. That helpless stare was saddening. "I know he is aware that something is wrong."

We pulled into the large parking lot of the veterinarian clinic. I lifted Oscar out of the backseat and carried him into the waiting room. We rushed up to the receptionist. They were expecting us, so we were immediately received. "The vet has the info from the Baker City clinic," the assistant told us. "She knows he has received a steroid and blood thinner."

In the hallway, Oscar was somewhat mellower, but he couldn't walk straight so I carried him into the examination room. A few moments later, Dr. Lefkowitz entered. I explained everything that had happened, describing the drive across the country with no issues. The drive up to Baker City and Halfway. The walking in circles, the twitching eyes, and the vomiting.

"Is it a stroke or a seizure?" I asked.

"I recognize this," the vet immediately answered. "It looks like vestibular disease. They call it 'old dog syndrome.' It is the most benign emergency case you can hope for," she assured me.

I asked if it was caused by the winding roads and loss of equilibrium when he was sitting in the backseat.

"We don't know what causes it," she explained. "Has he had any cases of this before?"

"Nope, first time," I said. "So, the winding roads and elevation were just a coincidence?"

"Anything might have caused it."

I was incredibly relieved.

Then, she added, "He should improve. But, he'll unlikely be one hundred percent."

"So, eighty percent? Ninety percent?" I asked hopefully. "What does that mean?"

"Well, he should recover, but he might have occasional dizziness. And, an episode may occur again. But, it's not fatal."

"So, it's not damage to the brain?" I checked. "He did throw up."

"No. It's unlikely. And vomiting and nausea does occur from the loss of equilibrium. You can give him some pills for motion sickness."

"I take Dramamine on my cruises," my mom added.

So, rest, Dramamine for motion sickness, and let him adjust to the "drunkenness." I could live with that.

"Usually, it takes about a week or so to recover."

"So, no driving?"

"It's best that you wait, if possible."

So, one week in Idaho would become two weeks.

"Mostly, Oscar needs to take it easy." Then the vet did a quick blood test and tasks that might occur at his regular check-up.

"We'll see if he improves before trying an MRI search for any brain lesions," she repeated. "Most importantly, don't let him hurt himself."

We left the vet incredibly relieved. He's not dying.

"It seems like an extreme case of vertigo," I guessed. "He just needs to recalibrate his head."

"Well, that's a relief," my mom said. "Are you OK?"

"Just hope he gets better." I looked in the backseat, and Oscar just sat in the seat staring. Just staring.

Before the trip, I told myself that we could turn around at any point for a few reasons: 1) Oscar wasn't doing well, 2) the car wasn't doing well, 3) Oscar didn't like the hotels, or 4) I ran out of money—although, I always had the credit card. However, in this case, we were sort of stuck. Oscar had to recover first.

We drove forty minutes from Boise to my mom's house in Emmett. I lifted Oscar out of the car and tried guiding him to the porch. Suddenly, like a stumbling drunk, he veered to the right and landed in the bushes. *Oh God, my bad,* I thought. *Shit.*

"Lance, hold on to him." My mom firmly repeated the vet's instructions. "Guide him, and prevent him from hurting himself." It was like holding up a toddler. I carefully lifted him inside the house.

We fixed a light dinner. What a long day. It was supposed to be an easy overnight trip to visit my brother. Oscar crept into the kitchen and slowly tried getting water from his bowl. I went down to his level and noticed his eyes were twitching less. He staggered, but he did seem more aware. I wondered if he was going to get better and how long it would take. Then Oscar slid down on the floor, closed his eyes, and rested.

A few hours later, Oscar came into the living room. I looked up from the computer. "How you feeling, buddy?" He stumbled closer to me. "Wanna treat?" I handed him a dog biscuit. He let it drop to the ground. "No?" He stared at me. "How 'bout a walk?" There was a slight perk in his expression. I grabbed his leash, and he stumbled toward me. "This will be a short one," I said. "Get you on the road to recovery."

Since the day I got Oscar from the shelter, I vowed to walk him twice a day, every day. Sunny, cloudy, cold (we had a fifteen-below-zero walk once), or snow. He especially loved the snow. The powder on his face reminded me of a cocaine fiend. The exception was rain. Snow, yes; but rain, no. That was the social contract: twice a day, every day.

We stepped outside the house. I picked him up and carried him down the three steps off the porch. Then, we resumed. Oscar veered, stumbled, and leaned. I crouched over to guide him along the sidewalk. Then, I figured out a remedy. I straddled him, and he stood between my legs. Then, he looked ahead and started walking. As he fell leftward, my left leg stopped his fall. He centered himself and continued. When he fell rightward, my right leg stopped his fall. I was a human guardrail. Thirty minutes later, we finished a single block, but he was happy.

EMMETT, IDAHO – Day 6

I HEARD A clopping sound on the living room floor. Oscar had awakened, so I jumped out of bed to take him outside. As he sniffed the bushes, he staggered like a wobbly drunk. I watched him brace himself on all four legs. Suddenly, he stumbled a few steps to the left, catching himself and avoiding a fall.

"Are you OK?" He tilted his head to the right, appearing to maintain equilibrium. It was heartbreaking to watch, but at least he recognized me. He did come to my voice and was trying to do the things he ordinarily would do.

My mom stood in the doorway. "How's he doing?" she asked.

"He's trying to walk around," I pointed out. "But look at his head."

"Oy, poor thing."

"Yeah, but the vet said it would take a week or so," I said. "He's better than yesterday." *And, he's not dead.*

"Does he want to eat?" my mom suggested.

"I'm gonna make his breakfast."

I went into the kitchen and microwaved some chicken. I added a Dramamine pill for dizziness plus the medicine for his joints. Ah, the modern world of doggie drugs! When I put the bowl on the floor, Oscar took a sniff, and then a bite full. After finishing most of the bowl, he took a quick drink of water. Then, he wobbled over to the air conditioning vent and plopped down.

"Oy, so *aoysgematert*," Mom said to the dog. It was Yiddish for exhausted.

The next morning, Oscar showed more energy and less twitching in his eyes. We walked a bit farther this time, and finally his bowels were functioning again. He appeared to have a smile on his face and a clearer look in his eyes. He still staggered, and he needed a bit of guidance, but it was progress.

I watched him compensating; when he swayed, he would catch himself instead of falling. It's as if he were slowly learning to walk differently. Part of me felt sad and worried. But, when he stood there like a heavyweight fighter, staggering in the fifteenth round, with his head tilted and tongue hanging, I started to find some humor in it.

"Damn, Oscar. You are fucked up," I said in a cheerful voice. "But, you are a warrior!" After the walk, I grabbed a treat from the kitchen counter and handed it to him. He took the snack and found a comfortable spot on the floor.

In the afternoon, I went for a jog. Upon my return, I found my mom watching TV. Oscar was lying beside her.

"How's he doing?"

"Fine," she said. "He's just been sitting with me. Resting."

At dinner, Oscar struggled to lower his head into his food bowl. It made him lose his equilibrium. So, we sat on the ground and handed pieces of chicken to him. Then we lifted his bowls of food and water to face level, so that he could easily eat and drink.

EMMETT, IDAHO – Day 10

DURING THE RECOVERY, we followed a routine. Oscar would rest. Maybe a short walk around the block. He'd stagger and tilt his head. Then, return for more rest. Meanwhile, I'd go down the street for a workout then watch a Redbox rental or two. Today, it was *Skyfall*, the latest Bond movie. In the evening, we'd have dinner at the house or a neighborhood place. I liked to walk later when it was cooler. I thought the nighttime is better for him. Maybe there were less conflicting images and visual stimuli; perhaps less disorientation.

Five days after the incident, there was a change: Oscar had his first burst of energy! It was overcast with a cooling breeze, and suddenly he did two sprints up and down the front lawn. Not bad for a thirteen-year-old! Then, he did a quick digging routine in the rocks by the plants. The wrecked flowers wouldn't please Mom. But, he's recovering!

"Were you digging up the flowers?!" I said to him. "Are you having fun?!" His ears perked up, and he wagged his tail as he stood next to me. His eyes were returning, the number of stumbles was decreasing, and his energy level seemed to be picking up.

EMMETT, IDAHO - Day 11

IT WAS TIME for a trial run. My mom and I decided to take an excursion to Black Canyon Diversion Dam outside Emmett. It was a good chance to see the scenery around Idaho, and we could see how Oscar would respond to being in the car for an extended period of time. We drove along State Highway 52 to Horseshoe Bend, which was a stopping point before recreational people ascend into the remote mountains. It was hot, so I grabbed some water for Oscar. I placed it in the shade behind the car. He took a few gulps. Then he put his front paws in the water bowl.

"Cooling the tootsies?!" Oscar started splashing and digging his paws into the water bowl. Water was flying everywhere.

"What's he doing?!?!" my mom asked.

"Oh, he does that a lot. I'm not sure if he's digging or splashing or whatever." At home, from time to time, I'd hear splashing sounds coming from the kitchen. I'd walk from the living room into the kitchen to find Oscar sitting next to his empty water bowl—with puddles of water all over the floor.

Once Oscar was satisfied, we continued on to the dam. We made our way down the dirt trail through the brush. As we got closer, Oscar got out front and started dragging us faster to the water. Then, around the corner, there was a shoreline into the reservoir. Oscar immediately stepped into the shallow area, delighted to cool off his paws. In the background, we could see the dam and water flow. The short road trip turned out to be a success. There were a few winding roads through the hills and mountains, which I tried to take slowly. Overall, Oscar took the drive quite well.

Cooling his tootsies at Black Canyon Reservoir, Emmett, Idaho

EMMETT, IDAHO – Day 13

OSCAR WAS SHOWING good progress, being able to walk farther each day. It also appeared his vision was improving. Occasionally, he would do a brief ten-foot trot through the grass. His head still tilted, but he seemed happier. His progress was not a surprise to me—Oscar is a warrior. When he passed ten years old, we still ran races together. I'd enter 5Ks, and he'd join me. The first mile, he'd race ahead, dragging me behind. Then, the second mile, we'd run in lockstep. At the end of the third mile, I'd be dragging Oscar to the finish line. Pacing himself was not his strength!

When we'd play, Oscar would go one hundred percent, running and swimming at the lake or chasing his ball in the park. Later, he'd limp around the house. At first, I worried he had torn a ligament. But, a day or two later, he was fine. It was just aches and pains, like a runner after a huge endurance race. "You should've paced yourself," I'd explain to him.

Back at my mom's house, I was on the computer checking a few things related to the drive home. That's when Oscar appeared in the doorway. He was holding steady on each of his legs, and his head was tilted to the right, and his tongue was hanging to left.

What a sight! But, he seemed pleased. "Yep, you're still doing it!" I encouraged him.

We'd been in Emmett almost two weeks. Oscar was recovering, and it was almost time to go. I was OK with the routine, but I didn't want to wear out our welcome. Unbeknownst to me, we were wearing out our welcome a bit. Months later, I was talking with my sister and explained how great Mom did with Oscar and how she didn't seem to mind him staying there. That's when my sister revealed that when I was out of the house, my mom was on the phone complaining to her about the dog hairs and her house getting disorganized.

"Really?" I couldn't believe it. "She never complained to us."

"Oh, yeah," my sister went on. "She'd tell me, 'that dog sheds so much; drives me crazy.'"

"Really?"

"Don't worry. I put her in her place. I told her that she promised to be OK with the dog. I said to her, 'you knew Oscar would shed! And, you promised not to worry about it. Then I reminded her that she invited you for at least a week, instead of a hotel. So she needed to keep her mouth shut."

"Well, she never said anything to us," I told her. "Kinda funny, though. She enjoyed having the dog around, making lunch and dinner for him. Also, she took him for walks to the donut shop. They were bonding."

My mom loved Oscar. She accepted the shedding, although she did sweep a lot! Mostly, I could see she liked when Oscar followed her around, and she enjoyed giving him snacks and extra attention. In fact, numerous times, Mom went out of her way to spice up Oscar's dinner bowl with homemade gravy or chicken broth.

EMMETT, IDAHO – Day 14

IN THE MORNING, I went down the street to the gym. Inside, the young man put another stamp on my card. Then, I did intervals on the bike, pull-ups, and used some of the weight machines. An hour later, I walked back to the house. When I returned, Mom and Oscar were out.

After a shower, I went onto the porch with the laptop and checked email. Suddenly, I saw my mom strolling up the street with Oscar beside her. Oscar would take a few steps then look up at the white bag. Then take a few more steps and peek up at the white bag. I grabbed my camera and took a few photos.

"Hi," she said. "We took a walk to the bakery."

"Of course, the bakery!" I knew Mom loved her walks. But I also knew it was a great excuse to grab some donuts or cinnamon rolls, especially if she brought Oscar along.

"It was Oscar's idea?"

My mom laughed. "Well, it's good for him to get some exercise."

I uploaded the photos of Mom, Oscar, and the white bakery bag, and emailed them to my sister. Then I grabbed one of those cinnamon rolls.

Today there were mild, scattered clouds and a clear mountain view. My mom suggested a ride around Emmett. The three of us took a tour, visiting cherry orchards, views that overlooked the Emmett valley, and Little Gem Cycle Park (an off-road spot used by ATV and motorcycle riders). Oscar enjoyed the variety and open air. When we returned, I checked messages on the laptop and found an email from my sister.

> *Those photos are fantastic! I am glad Mom has had Oscar around for a while. She used to love when I would have her watch Toby for a few days. She doesn't want the full-time responsibility of a dog, but loves them for a few days....Oh, I am sure there is an excuse in there someplace regarding you or Oscar for the cinnamon rolls. There is nobody better at justifying pastries than our mother!...Does Oscar have any interaction with Walter? I felt sorry for Walter last summer. Only Mom and I talked to him.*

I went outside to look for Walter. Oscar followed me into the closed-in backyard. My mom had put up a short fence for Oscar a month before we arrived. Next door, was a family with a sweet hound named Walter. Sadly, he got little attention. Sometimes, Walter was just tied to a chain outside in the backyard. Sometimes, he could freely wander around the yard by himself. My mom would go outside and say hi to Walter and toss him a biscuit when the family wasn't around.

He seemed so kind and lonely. Part of me wanted to go next door and offer to buy their dog. (And part of me wanted to take him!) It's just a sad reality that many people think their dog is an animal that they can just throw in the backyard. Or a toy they play with whenever they feel like it.

In the distance, I could see Walter sitting in the shade. My mom came outside. "Hi, Walter," she called out. He perked up a bit but remained in his spot. My mom tossed a few biscuits into their backyard. Walter walked over and picked them up.

"He's a nice dog," I said. "It's too bad he's by himself out here. Isn't it hot for him?" Walter wandered closer to us. Oscar and he looked at each other. I felt bad thinking this poor dog sat for hours and hours alone, sometimes tied to a chain. Also, I compared Walter to Oscar, a dog who's getting endless attention and a trip around the country.

EMMETT, IDAHO – Day 15

IT WAS A true "dog day of summer." Another hot one. This morning, I saw a guy getting out of a truck with his dog. The golden retriever came up to the fence and greeted Oscar. The dog was happily dripping wet. Had he been in the canal four blocks away? The man smiled and wished us a nice Fourth of July.

In the afternoon, there was a little break in the temperature. It was overcast, plus every so often, a breeze tried to get through. I decided to get in a quick run. Meanwhile, my mom offered to take Oscar for a walk, so we both left the house at the same time. As I stretched, my mom walked down the steps of the porch, but Oscar didn't want to go. He kept looking at me, waiting for me to follow. Finally, after I disappeared behind the house, Oscar went along with my mom. Glad to know I was still his number one guy.

I beat Mom and Oscar back to the house. When they returned, Oscar was a bit wet. "Where did you go?"

"I took him around the neighborhood. He walked through some sprinklers, and we went to the canal like yesterday." No doubt, Oscar looked happy.

He's recovering, and I like the spirit! I thought to myself as Oscar was excitedly pulling on the leash, dragging my mom toward me. I wanted him to come up by going around to the front steps, but instead, he adamantly tried to take the shortcut and jump onto the porch—and missed—his hind legs fell back as he struggled to get up to the porch platform. Finally, he fell back, and with my convincing, went around to the steps.

We attended an annual Fourth of July picnic outside Emmett. It was held at a friend's place, which was a large ranch. Where else could you be eating pasta salad and dessert, look past a hanging tire swing, and see cows grazing?! The area was filled with nice local people. I particularly enjoyed a conversation with an eighty-year-old named Doyle. He had been in Idaho for over forty years after stints in the seed business that took him around the world. Listening to his experiences and wisdom, I learned a bit about sledging/panning for gold and silver, growing crops and watering rights, the blossoming of different fruit trees, land, EPA/government, and more.

EMMETT, IDAHO – Day 17

ON OUR FINAL day before heading back home, I realized that we had developed a routine in Emmett. In the morning, Oscar and I walked around the town. Afterward, I headed to the gym for a workout. Then, I returned to my mom's house, had a snack, and used the Wi-Fi to check email and do a bit of work. In the afternoon, we found an activity. Yesterday, my mom, Oscar, and I took another short excursion around Idaho. Today, we stayed in and watched a movie. Then, when the temperatures cooled a little bit, Oscar and I went for another walk. I realized that much of my activities became similar to the routine I had back home: walk Oscar, workout, have a meal, do some work on the computer, walk Oscar, watch some TV, and go out at night.

On this particular day, we went to a few favorites: Idaho Pizza Company for lunch and Arctic Circle for ice cream. With one day left before our journey home, Oscar and I took it easy around the house. I rented two movies from Redbox: *Trouble with the Curve* and *The Perks of Being a Wallflower*. It was a solid double feature. In between, I made some preparations for the return drive. I gave the car a needed cleaning, both inside and out. Then I started repacking

Bring Oscar

the luggage into the trunk of the car and printed the first few local road maps. In the evening, my mom and I left Oscar at the house and went for a final dinner at a nice local restaurant.

EMMETT, IDAHO to IDAHO FALLS, IDAHO

AFTER NEARLY TWO weeks of recovery, Oscar seemed fit for our journey home. I anticipated that we'd pass through some familiar sites, scenery, roads, and towns from a few weeks ago. When possible, we would hopscotch our way back, stopping at certain places for the first time, while skipping others we had already passed through. We may decide to revisit a favorite location, but mostly, we would try different stops.

Once we were back on the road, we diverged off Interstate 84 and took Highway 30 for the scenic route through Thousand Springs. It started at a town called Bliss. "Entering Bliss Pop 318," read the sign. "So, we have found bliss in Idaho," I said to Oscar.

We drove south on Highway 30 around Buhl along the Snake River to the Twin Falls area. We made our first stop at Shoshone Falls, which was recommended by my mom.

Oscar and I walked around to various viewpoints of the canyon and falls. It was impressive, showing the contrast between the desert and rock background and the flowing waterfalls along Snake River Canyon. Better yet, it happened to be sunny with a bright rainbow!

We continued exploring Shoshone Falls Park, which included a vast grass area for walking, sitting, picnicking, and viewing the scenery in the distance. Off to the side, there was a snack bar. This seemed like a good spot to take some quality time as we started our return journey. After sitting in the shade for a while, sipping a snow cone, we got up and took one more look at the views. Picture perfect.

The afternoon drive was tougher. The weather was in the high eighties, and the road was more crowded. Then, thirty miles from our destination, there was a long accident delay on the interstate. But, overall, Oscar seemed to be OK. I had made sure to slow down during steep ascents and descents, and I kept the air conditioner cranking.

After three hundred miles, we reached Idaho Falls and our motel, the Super 8. I quickly learned that this one wasn't so super. The person at the front desk wasn't very friendly—and they were very reluctant to take Oscar because he was not staying in a crate. I explained that he was over thirteen years old, mellow, and harmless. Since adopting him, Oscar had never been in a kennel or crate. They weren't too thrilled, but conceded the room to us.

Before settling in, I wanted to see the nearby falls and pick up dinner. We got back in the car and drove to the main part of town to pick up some food at the Snow Eagle Brewing & Grill. I picked a parking spot in the shade, left Oscar in the running car with the air conditioner blasting, and raced in to place a quick order.

"Do you want to sit at the bar or wait for a table?"

"Can I get it to go?" I asked. "I got my dog outside."

"No problem," he said and handed me a menu.

"Chicken breast, fries, side pasta and salad, and a Coke to go."

"It's the dinner rush, so it'll be about thirty minutes. Is that OK?"

"Perfect." I wanted to walk up and down the riverfront anyway.

Oscar and I walked across the street toward the water. Idaho Falls had a nice walking path that winded along a grassy area with benches and view of the Snake River. On that walk I realized just how huge the Snake River is, about one thousand miles. We had seen part of it back in Wyoming a few weeks ago. There were lots of birds for Oscar to look at, and dream of chasing, and the temperature in the shade was pleasant. I was pleased with today's itinerary: we got in two quality excursions at Shoshone and Idaho Falls. And, Oscar seemed to like these long walks.

After thirty minutes we returned to the restaurant. Oscar waited near the entrance. I walked inside, and the bartender saw me. "I got your order right here. I threw in some utensils and napkins."

When I walked outside, Oscar saw me—and the bag of food—and his ears perked up.

"Yep, I got you some chicken," I assured him. "Let's get rollin'."

Back at the hotel, Oscar dove right into his food, and I was pleased that he was able to maintain his balance while enjoying his meal. After dinner, I opened up my laptop to check messages and plan for tomorrow only to find that I had no Wi-Fi connection. "OK. It's official. This Super 8 sucks." After watching TV until 11:00 p.m., I tried the Wi-Fi one more time. Fortunately, the evening connection improved from zero to two bars. Quickly, I skimmed the Internet and reserved a hotel room for tomorrow.

IDAHO FALLS, IDAHO to LIVINGSTON, MONTANA

WE CHECKED OUT of that disappointing hotel eager to turn the page and begin a new chapter in our journey home. I was delighted to see beautiful, sunny, clear skies. As Oscar and I traveled north on I-15, we passed familiar spots: the opal place and the lava rest stop. In between were different possible locations to try. The first was Lima, Montana, a town of about two hundred and fifty people.

While searching for a snack, I noticed a little one-room structure: Samantha's Lasso Lattes. There was a "Coffee Shop Open" sign, so we stopped to check it out. I peeked inside, and when the young woman saw me, she came over and slid open the take-out window. I looked at the list of beverage choices and ordered a drink for a morning snack. I like supporting local businesses, especially in small towns. After paying, I asked, "Are you Samantha?"

"No," she smiled. "But, I do know her." Then, she pointed toward a display. Next to the building, there was a plaque mentioning its history. The structure was originally a girl's playhouse in Nebraska.

After many years, it was dismantled and shipped to Lima. Then, after several years, the playhouse was converted into a coffee shop.

Our next portion of road was going to be mountain passes, and part of me wanted to race through while the other part of me wanted to take in the views. I decided to take it slow to minimize any effects on Oscar. Plus, it eased the strain on the car's transmission while going up and down the steep passes. When the mountains were in the rearview mirror, I looked at Oscar. He seemed fine. Then, he dropped his jaw and his tongue popped out. He seemed to be enjoying himself. "That's my boy!" I cracked open the windows, and we kept cruising.

Just after lunchtime, we approached Livingston, Montana, located north of Yellowstone National Park and Grand Teton National Park. A few weeks ago, we had passed this area while traveling west, and I made a note to stop on the way back. In the distance, I recognized the scenic mountains and ranches. As we walked along the finished wooden hallway of our hotel for the night, the Livingston Inn, there was an endless row of wonderful photos from Yellowstone—very cool. There were more photos of wildlife and animals inside our room. All of them were taken by the owners. It was an impressive exhibition.

We dropped our stuff off in the room and headed outside to find a comfortable spot. I found a bench where I could surf the web while Oscar relaxed in the shade underneath. *Wow, this is relaxing.* Then, I noticed a sign indicating there was a place for horses in the back! Not only was it dog-friendly, apparently this hotel was horse-friendly, too. In fact, under the Livingston Inn sign, it read "Horses Welcome."

Following our afternoon break, we went to the Livingston Historic District to explore. I tied Oscar to one of the iron tables in front of the Pickle Barrel and headed in to order a sandwich. Oscar still wasn't out of the woods from his illness, so I gave him some Dramamine hidden within some sliced cheese from my sandwich. While watching the people go by, I kept an eye on Oscar. He seemed OK. He finished his dry dog food and drank water. He looked up at me with his tilted head. I shared some of my sandwich until there was nothing left. His appetite was a good indicator of his continued improvement. "Nice spot we picked," I said to him.

LIVINGSTON, MONTANA to BEACH, NORTH DAKOTA

THE SUN SHOT through the crack between the curtains. I opened my eyes. Oscar was sitting and looking at me. "Dude, are you stalking me?" He tipped his head, came closer, and put his face against the bed. When he was younger, he'd jam his paw into my back or jump on top of the bed. Now he was more subtle.

I looked at the clock: 6:45 a.m. "Alright. I gotcha." I grabbed his leash, and we headed out into the sunny day with a cool breeze off the mountains. Although staggering a bit, Oscar seemed to enjoy the walk. He was smiling and alert. I hoped the burst of energy would last. When we returned to the room, I jumped in the shower, and of course, Oscar poked his head through the curtain. Little bits of water and shampoo splashed on him. He shook his wet head and left the bathroom. After leaving a note and tip for the housekeeper, we were out the door by 9:00 a.m.

We drove east on I-90 to Billings. Just past the city, the road split, and we turned onto the I-94. Thirty minutes later, in the distance, a huge flag flying at half-mast appeared. I saw a "historic site" road sign and decided to take a closer look. I discovered it was a national monument called Pompeys Pillar. Similar to Devils Tower in Wyoming, it appeared to be a rock mass that pops out of a flat area. But, this sandstone butte also has a historical significance: it contains physical evidence of the Lewis and Clark Expedition. William Clark discovered the mass, and he engraved his name in the rocks. "W. Clark July 25, 1806." It was a strategic location, because from the top, one could overlook the surrounding territory.

Since Oscar wasn't permitted, we didn't go to the top of the monument to view the etchings. Instead, we walked along the border of the Yellowstone River. While I looked at historical markers, took photos, and admired the scenery, Oscar sniffed bushes, looked for critters, and explored random scents. The view from six feet above ground is truly different than the view from two feet high!

The stopover was a nice surprise: educational and pleasant. We met other travelers, including two bikers pedaling across the country and a few older couples who were touring the site. They were fond of Oscar, especially because they missed their dogs at home. Overall, Pompeys Pillar was worth the visit.

Oscar did well as we proceeded through beautiful Eastern Montana. He sat in the front seat for a long stretch, enjoying a better view and a back massage. We stopped in Glendive to see Makoshika State Park, Montana's largest state park. Makoshika, which means "bad land" or "bad earth," offered incredible views of the Badlands. From above, it looked like a mini Grand Canyon. Yet, nobody was there. Possibly because it was in the middle of nowhere; probably because it was blazing hot among the open dirt and rock paths.

Oscar and I went through some trails, but it was too hot. It got to the point where I was carrying Oscar half the time. It became exhausting, so we cut the hike short. We got back in the car and continued east toward the Montana/North Dakota border. Forty-five minutes later, we reached Beach, North Dakota. Mile Exit 1. "North Dakota, Oscar!"

I wondered why it was called "Beach." No ocean. Maybe the long open area appeared to be an expansive beach? Or, maybe someone just liked the name, because who wouldn't want to visit a beach? We exited I-94 and pulled into our hotel, the Buckboard Inn. Beach turned out to be a very small town, with a population of about one thousand people.

I decided to take a chance on dinner at a Chinese place, J&J Chinese Cafe. The guy who prepared the food was Asian and barely spoke English, so odds were the meal would be authentic. When I returned to the car and placed the bags down, Oscar started sniffing, of course. "Hang on, buddy," I said to him as he poked his nose into one of the bags. Back in the hotel room, I divided the dinner. Meat, pill, some sauce, and dog food for Oscar; veggies and rice for me. Also, I mixed in some of Oscar's canned green beans.

When Oscar started to get less active and added some weight, the vet suggested adding green beans to his meals. It would be filling for him, satisfying his appetite, without putting on weight. The downside: some dogs don't like the taste. But, Oscar did eat the green beans, so it worked! Funny, because when I tried to give him pills—even sticking them in meat—he'd discard them. I would watch him eat the meat and food in his bowl, then I'd look into the empty bowl and see two pills sitting there! The green-bean strategy lasted for a few years. Then, when he was fifteen years old, Oscar struggled to keep weight on! So, I fed him whatever he wanted without any concern for weight. His weight went from fifty to sixty-three, back to fifty-five, then eventually, a frail thirty-seven pounds.

The meal from J&J turned out to be very good. Who knew you could get quality Chinese food in North Dakota?! After Oscar finished, I looked into the bowl. Not bad. There were a few green beans remaining, but he ate the chicken, crushed pill, and rice. I walked over to check him out.

"How are you feeling?" His eyes were responsive. He looked back at me. "You wanna do a quick walk?" He stood up. "Let's go outside," I suggested. "I can set up tomorrow's itinerary later."

After our walk, Oscar settled onto his blanket. Meanwhile, I uploaded photos and typed notes about our trip through Montana.

Good drive today. Scenery, history, and we covered a lot of miles. Oscar had a tough time getting into the car. (So, I just lifted him myself. Then, to get out, I lifted him down.). But, Oscar did well in the front seat. He got a little bit tired. But, overall, the long night's sleep and the pill seemed to help him.

I listed North Dakota attractions we saw: Lewis and Clark, Glendive, Makoshika, Pompeys Pillar, Yellowstone River, Beach. Then, I added people we had encountered, the dinner in Beach, and descriptions to go along with the photos. Another chapter completed today.

BEACH, NORTH DAKOTA to FARGO, NORTH DAKOTA

I ANTICIPATED AN easy navigation day. We would start at mile 1 (Beach) and drive across North Dakota on I-94 straight to mile 348 (Fargo). The sun was shining, and Oscar was feeling the joy of riding in a car. His head was out the window. Then, up through the open sunroof. There were plenty of sites to see.

In Western North Dakota, the scenery around Medora was very cool. It had an outer space look, with green-covered mounds everywhere. Sort of like bumpy grasslands. Nearby, we made a planned stop at Theodore Roosevelt National Park. We pulled off the highway, and following the routine, I grabbed Oscar's bowl, poured some water from the old plastic juice bottle, and set it in front of him. He lapped up a bit of it, stopped, then poked one paw in the water. Then, he dipped the other paw and started rapidly splashing in a digging motion.

I rolled my eyes.

Meanwhile, a family walked by and laughed at the messy spectacle. I bent down to pick up the bowl. "OK, you're done." I put it back into the trunk.

We walked across the parking lot to the scenic overlook. Suddenly, Oscar collapsed to the ground, and he sat on his rear end with his paws in the air.

"Oh, my bad." I pressed my hand to the pavement. It was blazing hot. "Let's get your tootsies off the ground." I lifted him to a small shady spot, relieving his paw pads. He stood up and resumed walking along with me.

We weaved along the shady spots, and scampered over any hot spots. When we reached the view, I guided Oscar to the dirt path. Meanwhile, I went on the sidewalk to read the information plaques where I learned Theodore Roosevelt had passed through these areas in the 1880s. And, this park itself was established in the 1940s.

Oscar found a cool spot to sit while I took in the beautiful panorama. Among the rough terrain were hiking paths and grasslands. I put it into historical context and imagined crossing this in the 1800s in a rickety covered wagon. That must've sucked. There was no dirt path, let alone a smooth road. There was no bottled water or spots to stop for lunch. Everything was tough and took time. However, it was spacious, clean, and undisturbed, with animals and grasslands.

Oscar chillin' in the Badlands of North Dakota

While there was less to see in the middle of North Dakota, I was glad we took this route. We passed several small towns, and it was interesting to see random oil wells sprouting up everywhere, taking advantage of the North Dakota shale boom. In one place, I saw a drilling rig in front of a church! That's a great way to raise money; much easier than passing around the hat. When seeing an oil well in someone's backyard, I wondered if it were like winning the lottery or finding treasure under your property. The tremendous oil presence contrasted the enormous windmill farms in other parts of the country.

We passed countless tankers, and I considered the truck drivers. It seems like a tough job, driving miles and miles. In many cases, the route is the same. Is that better or worse? It gets monotonous doing the same route; at the same time, the familiarity and being able to establish friends or consistent acquaintances along the way would be nice. There was a rest stop in the middle of nowhere that was loaded with dozens of tankers. They must've known each other.

I tried to put my road trip into the context of a truck driver, pounding out two hundred and fifty or three hundred miles at a time. That's rough.

After a few hours of driving and breaks, we approached lunchtime. Stopping for meals was a treat for me. Excluding vacations, I rarely ate out. Cooking at home is less expensive and more convenient. On the road, trying a restaurant was new and enjoyable. As we entered Bismarck, the capital of North Dakota, I didn't spot any local restaurants with easy access.

"Let's go Taco Johns," I said to Oscar. "We know that place." We used the drive-through then searched for a spot to eat. Meanwhile, Oscar was climbing onto my lap, sniffing the bag of chicken fingers (for him) and the salad and fries (for me). All the while, I was trying to balance the soda in the cradle. Suddenly, I saw an open park. Perfect. Then, I saw a sign, "No dogs permitted." *Keep driving.* I spotted an open field, but there was no parking area or shoulder on the side of the road. The food was getting cold, the drink's ice was melting, and Oscar was impatient. At this point, I considered eating lunch in the car—anywhere.

After fifteen minutes, I pulled into a Walmart parking area. We found a space toward the back of the crowded lot next to a tree with a small patch of grass. I grabbed the bag of food, my drink, and Oscar's leash, although it was probably unnecessary—Oscar was sticking with me and the bag of chicken fingers. After pulling his water bowl from the trunk, I sat with Oscar in the shade and began a picnic in the parking lot! Oscar gobbled up the food in his bowl while I scooped up my taco salad with the plastic utensils.

A few minutes later, a guy came over and offered us a hot dog. *Huh?*

"I finished lunch," he explained. "It seems a waste to throw it out."

I reluctantly said OK and took his extra hot dog. Then, he drove off. The hot dog seemed edible. It smelled fine. I guess he got it from the Walmart concessions? Regardless, after I handed it to Oscar, he buried it next to the tree.

We spent twenty minutes enjoying our picnic at Walmart, trying to be inconspicuous.

A lady in a truck, pulled up, and rolled down her window. "Looks like your dog is enjoying himself!" she said with a smile. I was startled when I saw this truck pull up. Were we doing something wrong?

"What's that?" I asked.

She repeated, "Your dog seems to be enjoying himself!"

"Yep, he's sharing my lunch," I pleasantly agreed.

"Well, he is a handsome and lucky dog." I just smiled as she drove away. We enjoyed the rest of the picnic.

Bring Oscar

An improvised summer picnic in the shade

Before getting back on the highway, I picked up a dessert shake at a drive-through. For the next two hundred miles, we followed I-94 east through more open area of North Dakota. We saw roaming buffalo, cool background scenery, lakes, trains, and more. I remembered being told that "South Dakota was the place to see. There wasn't much in North Dakota." Not the case. We had a chance to see notable parks, and mostly, an opportunity to go through a variety of landscapes. Overall, North Dakota was worth the drive.

By late afternoon, Oscar and I reached Fargo. We grinded through two miles of construction—ugh—exited the interstate, winded through town, and reached the Candlewood Suites. It was in a great location near the FargoDome, the Fargo Air Museum, and a variety of shopping plazas.

After checking in with reception, we both settled in and took a nap. When I woke up, Oscar was leaning over the couch. He reached his front legs to the bottom and then slid onto the ground. The old dog wandered a few steps toward me. "Dude, you have a good nap?"

He paused and turned his head up toward me. He was contorted, legs in awkward positions to maintain balance. Head tilted. "Oh, man, you're a mess," I said in an encouraging voice. He lifted his head, and dropped his jaw, tongue popping out. It looked like a smile. He seemed delighted, like a toddler standing up on his own. "I think you need to relieve yourself, yes?"

We walked across the street to the Fargo Air Museum. Unfortunately, it was closed, but at least we could see the Minuteman intercontinental ballistic missile located in the parking lot. It was definitely an eye-catcher. After our walk, we went in search of dinner. I settled on a sandwich place about a mile further down the road where the employee with a Northern Wisconsin-Canada-*Fargo*-movie accent was nice enough to make grilled chicken special for Oscar. As we ate our dinner back at the hotel, I was skimming maps and attractions and noticed the "famous woodchipper." First thought: *Fargo*, the Coen Brothers' movie. It's the woodchipper from the movie—I had to see it!

There was still daylight, so I helped Oscar in the car and followed the directions to the Fargo-Moorhead Visitors Center. In front of the building, we found a Celebrity Walk of Fame consisting of people who had visited Fargo and left a concrete impression. There were over one hundred from actors, politicians, and other famous people like Kiss and Alice Cooper, Bill Gates, and Dr. Ruth. Then, I saw a yellow woodchipper. So cool! I took photos from different angles. While looking at the details, I noticed a message at the bottom: "This is a copy of the movie woodchipper. The original is inside the building." *You're kidding.* A replica doesn't count. I wanted to see the real one.

We walked over to the building, but it was closed. "We'll have to come back tomorrow," I sighed. "I've driven thousands of miles, so I'm not going to let this go by."

I curiously peeked through the window and saw someone inside moving. Then, luckily, the young man inside the tourist center noticed me. He walked to the entrance and unlocked the door. "Hello?" he said.

"Hey, I was passing through town. I'm in Fargo for one day, and I wanted to see the original woodchipper and—"

"Well, come on in," he said with an inviting Fargo accent. Perhaps, he felt sorry for us? Or, maybe the kid liked company while he cleaned up? I think it helped that we were the only visitors standing outside.

"Wait here," I said to Oscar, who was loosely tied to an outside bench.

Inside the shop, to the left of the entrance, there was an entire section dedicated to *Fargo*. There were photos of the film, and the original woodchipper with a leg sticking out of it. I read about the movie and the history of this woodchipper, signed by Joel and Ethan Coen. Then, I took a few photos.

The kid came over. "You want a picture with the woodchipper?"

"Definitely," I answered.

"Wait, one second," he said. He put down his broom and brought out a *Fargo* prop. "Put this on." Then, he took a few photos of me wearing the flappy winter hat, standing beside the *Fargo* woodchipper. Afterward, he handed me the camera. I viewed the digital pictures—brilliant. I looked through the window to check on Oscar. He was waiting patiently by the door, so I browsed around the shop for a few more minutes.

"Hey, thanks for letting me in," I yelled out to the young man as I left. "You saved me an extra trip tomorrow." He waved and continued his work. People in Fargo were very nice. On the way out, I passed a bench with a sign that read, "Is this the end of your quest to visit all 50 states? Welcome to the Club." It was my forty-first.

FARGO, NORTH DAKOTA to EAU CLAIRE, WISCONSIN

MY WALKS WITH Oscar have evolved over the years. It used to be that as I shut the front door, he would scamper down the driveway. The twenty-five-foot retractable leash would run out of slack, and down the street we would go! He would race around the block, dragging me along. Now, he will trot twenty feet, stop to smell the flowers, lift his leg, and mark his spot, then yawn and meander down the road. The Candlewood Suites we were staying at had an enormous open lawn. In an earlier time, I would've run with Oscar and thrown his ball. Instead, we just strolled along, took it easy, and had a breakfast picnic.

As we sat on a bench across from the hotel entrance, an old guy wearing a Vietnam vet baseball cap slowly rolled up to us in a wheelchair. He was gray-haired, disheveled, and weathered. It didn't bother Oscar; he curiously waddled up to him. He gave Oscar a pat on the head and asked us where we were from. He said he was from Fargo. I didn't ask, but I wondered what he was doing at the hotel, seemingly hanging out by himself. After a very brief conversation,

Bring Oscar

I used DogFriendly.com to get a hotel room in Wisconsin for the evening. It was the last reservation we would need. After that, it would be home sweet home!

We easily found I-94 east, and within minutes, crossed into Minnesota. What a contrast to North Dakota. The miles of fresh, newly paved roads turned into a mess once we crossed the border. There was a lot of construction, yet I didn't see anyone working. There were patch-up jobs and uneven roads. Plus, there were aggressive drivers. Fast is one thing, but there was serious tailgating. Smooth open road was scarce.

We drove the next stretch alongside lakes and ponds, over hills, and through grassland. We stopped for lunch in Clearwater, Minnesota, at a place called D&L Taco Gringo in a shopping plaza with one outside table. A friendly, cute young woman took my order, and an older lady, who may have been the owner, offered cold water for Oscar. While waiting for our food, I offered Oscar some water. He took a sip. Then, he stopped to put one paw in the water.

"Oscar! No, no." Then, he put the other paw in his water bowl and started splashing the water. A moment later, all the water was splashed in our seating area. "Nice!"

A few of the other diners were laughing as they watched the spectacle from inside the restaurant. A couple of minutes later, Oscar looked up at me. "What? Now, you want a drink?" I pointed at his nearly empty water bowl. "Ah, wasn't a good idea to make a mess and waste your water, was it?" He continued to look at me, anticipating that I'd read his mind. I poured some of my water into his bowl. "Try to drink it this time."

I peeked inside the window to see if my order was ready. I saw the young woman carrying a tray with my food, so I went over to open the door and help her out.

"Look at him," she said admiringly as she went for a closer look. "What a sweet dog." She gave Oscar some love, and he enjoyed the attention. "It's hot out here." She looked at his bowl. "Does he need more water?"

Well, he had water until he splashed it everywhere. "Maybe a big cup of water with ice?" I suggested.

"Yeah, I'll get that for him." She gave Oscar a kind massage on the face and then went inside.

These friendly people gave me a good impression of this part of Minnesota, and I was grateful for their kind service. After lunch, I cleared the table and went inside to throw out the trash. I said goodbye to the cute young woman and the older lady. They wished us a successful trip.

The lunch was up to the mark, but I left room for dessert. We drove through Dairy Queen, and then, energized, we got back on the road.

We continued on I-94 east and survived the dreaded road in the heart of Minneapolis-Saint Paul. After grinding through construction, bottlenecks, and irritated drivers, we reached open road again. An hour past the Wisconsin border, we arrived at Eau Claire, Wisconsin, and followed the directions to the Econo Lodge with plenty of time to relax before dinner.

In the hotel room, I uploaded photos from my camera to my laptop. Then, I typed up a few notes to help remember the day's leg of the trip. It was my second to last entry for our journey. I added it to the other folders filled with photos and typed notes of observations, sites, thoughts, and places we had seen. I wanted to have a way to go back and recall the journey. Also, if I returned to any of these places, I'd know where to return. Who knows, maybe I'd write about it all later?

EAU CLAIRE, WISCONSIN to HOME

IT'S OUR LAST morning! We woke up to the first rain we encountered since South Dakota a few weeks ago. After a quick walk, I lifted Oscar into the backseat. He assumed his position on the armrest. As we drove out of the lot, he gave me appreciative licks on the face. "Thank you," I said to him as we made our way to the interstate.

Oscar is ready to take the wheel

The final day of our road trip was rather uneventful. Instead of seeking attractions, the goal was to drive straight home and complete the journey. We retraced our way back through Wisconsin past Black River Falls, the Dells, and to the Madison turnoff. By mid-afternoon, we neared the Illinois/Wisconsin border. Instead of east on I-94 to Milwaukee, we tried south on I-90. That was a mistake. The Illinois part of the drive was awful. There was a brutal combination of traffic, construction, and congestion. *Over four thousand miles; you can suck up the last fifteen*, I reminded myself. *Finish strong.* Oscar stood on the armrest, looking out the window.

As we drove down I-90, I began to recognize the landmarks and could count down the miles until we completed our road trip. Eventually, we turned off the expressway and drove through the residential areas of our town. It was an anticlimactic finish to a wonderful journey. We were home. I looked at the odometer: 4333 miles.

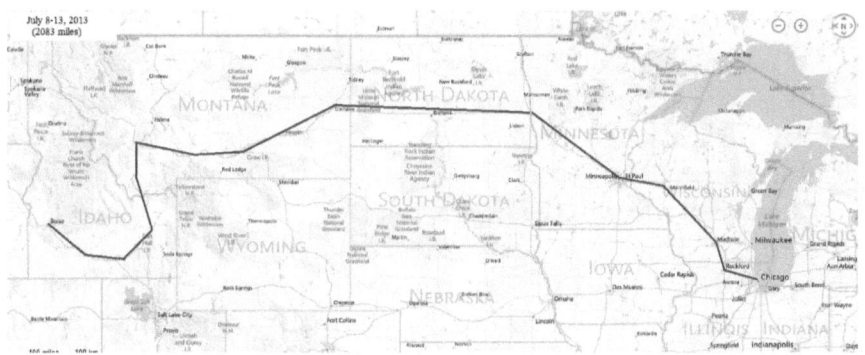

I pulled out the map and traced the last stretch of road with the yellow highlighter. Then I looked at the expanded map of the United States. "That's a long way," I proudly said. "But, we made it."

Oscar and I climbed out of the car, went inside, and found a pile of mail on the kitchen counter. I inspected the basement. No flooding. Then, I peeked out the window into the backyard. The garden was stocked with vegetables. There were a few weeds and growth, but the garden had plenty of ready-to-eat, ripe tomatoes, zucchini, and cucumbers. I found that water and dirt—without my help—does wonders.

When I went outside to start unpacking the car, the neighbor kid, Miguel, who was looking after the house while I was away, came over to say hello.

"That was fast," I told him.

"I saw you pull up." He leaned down to pet Oscar. "How was the trip?"

"It was an adventure. Saw tons of stuff. And Oscar had a good time." I omitted the emergency trip to the vet in Idaho. "The house looks good," I went on. "Thanks for taking care of things."

"Any time," he said.

The conversation was brief. I had unpacking to do, and conversations with a twelve-year-old tend to run short.

"Let me pay you the balance."

"I lost the key," he confessed.

"Oh. Well, it's gotta be somewhere," I said matter-of-factly. "If you find it, just let me know."

"My mom said you'd be angry."

"Not really." It could be replaced. And, I doubt someone would find the key, know it's my house, and break in. Mostly, I was so thrilled to have made it home that the key was a small issue. "How did you get into the house?"

"I crawled through the doggie door."

"Ah, I've done the same, reaching my arm inside." Then, I repeated, "Don't sweat the key. I'm sure it'll show up." He seemed relieved. Besides, two weeks later, he found the key in his room and returned it to me—the day after I had finally bought a replacement.

I handed him the rest of the money, and he was delighted. It was his first job, and the payment was plenty to buy some video games. After he ran off with his cash, I continued unloading the Nissan. Meanwhile, Oscar just sat next to the car, watching me unpack. When I finished, he stayed in place and just looked at me. "We're done," I told him. "End of road trip."

Finally, he trailed me into the house.

I skimmed through the pile of mail. Over ninety percent went right into the garbage. Meanwhile, through the living room window, I watched Oscar sniffing around his backyard. Then, I turned on the computer and did some work. I found an email from my mom.

Glad you made it home. You're back to the reality of city life...work, traffic, construction, etc.

I looked at some of the photos from our trip: Sioux Falls, Mount Rushmore, Fargo, Devils Tower, and Shoshone Falls. *Wow, we really did see a lot of cool places.* Thoughts of all the work ahead just drifted away…

PART II

SOUTH

I got the phone call from Jim. "Your car is ready." I grabbed Oscar's leash from the kitchen counter, and we walked one mile to Supreme Auto Repair to pick up the Nissan.

For years, I regularly visited the local Acura dealer to service my car. While waiting, I'd sit in their comfortable lounge and watch TV, read a book, or listen to music. The dealership even had snacks. And, when I got my car back, it was washed clean. Then, I'd put the bill on the credit card and drive off.

The car ran well, so I accepted paying a premium for the consistent maintenance. When my finances tightened, and the Acura aged and started falling apart, I attempted to fix the simpler items on my own. Otherwise, I'd go to the local tire place or brake shop, or rely on a local mechanic. One day, the manager at an auto parts store suggested trying a guy in Skokie.

"Ask for Jim at Supreme Auto. Nice guy, no nonsense, and reasonable prices," he assured me.

I left the store and met Jim. First impression: slick hair, veteran mechanic in an old-school garage. Instead of beautiful furniture and TVs, his little waiting area had a few old auto magazines sprinkled on worn-out furniture. Plus, the sweet smell of cigarettes. I had worked at a machine shop, so I was familiar with greasy surroundings. Besides, I reminded myself, at the nice dealerships, you pay for that overhead! On the walls were old pictures of muscle cars, classic autos, and personal photos of Jim at other shops.

I learned about his past history, working at dealerships, and listened to his stories about mechanics who took advantage of unknowing customers by recommending not-so-important maintenance or unnecessary replacement parts.

"I've seen a lady overcharged by eight hundred dollars. She showed me the bill. These guys don't care because they figure the customer ain't coming back anyway." He pulled out a cigarette. "I used to work at these places. It was unreal. Eventually, I left the bullshit and went on my own."

"So you like it better?" I asked him.

"Yeah, but it's tough. No vacations. Work a lot of hours." He shrugged.

I concluded Jim was a neighborly mechanic: build a loyal customer base instead of bleeding a one-time visitor. His work was forty percent cheaper. Plus, he could do welding and bodywork, which was useful for my rusty Acura. Mostly, he seemed like a sincerely hardworking, honest guy. After I bought the new Nissan—following one pricey dealership oil change—I left all its maintenance to Jim.

Jim was working on another car when he saw us approach. "Hey, your car is all set. Gimme one minute." Oscar and I stood in the waiting area beside the counter. Jim walked in while wiping his hands with a rag. "You're all good," he said, sitting behind the counter to print up the receipt.

Oscar yanked on the leash and crept around the counter. Jim leaned over and pat Oscar on the head. "Hey, pup! How ya doing?!" Oscar looked up at him. "So, where are you headed this time?"

"We're trying for the South: Alabama, Mississippi, around to the Carolinas. As much as we can see in ten days," I told him. "Have you been?"

"Nah, I've never been down there. Not much further than Indiana. Sounds like a great trip."

"I'm just happy that he likes to ride along." I pointed at Oscar. "Just hoping he can get through another trip. And, that the car can make it."

"The car is fine," Jim said with certainty. "These things can go for well over 100,000 miles. No problem."

I paid and grabbed the key. "We'll be back after the trip."

"I'll see you then. Have a good one!"

Since last summer, I had been craving another road trip. I had ten days off from teaching, so this was an opportunity to go somewhere. I just had to create a doable route—something new that would require less than two weeks. I considered places I'd yet to visit and decided on a cluster of Southern states for our next adventure. It should be warmer, right?

EVANSTON, ILLINOIS to ST. LOUIS, MISSOURI

ON FRIDAY MORNING, I loaded up the car with my bag, a cooler, blanket, and Oscar's stuff. Geez, he has as much stuff as I do! Dog food supply, treats, blanket, and a small box full of medication for his joints. While filling up the backseat, I found Oscar already sitting in the driver's seat. "Ready to go road trip?!?!" He wagged his tail. Evidently, he was craving another road trip, too.

After loading the last item into the car and locking up the house, I reset the trip meter to 0, and we were off. We left at 9:30 a.m., hoping to avoid traffic. No such luck. As the Edens Expressway (I-94) merged with the Kennedy Expressway (I-90), the cars slowed to a virtual standstill. The dense, bottleneck traffic lasted through downtown Chicago. "This is not the express-way. It's the long-way. Where are these people going?" I groaned out loud. "It's ten o'clock. Doesn't anyone work?"

Oscar didn't mind. He was in his "Washington Crossing the Delaware" pose, standing on the arm rest in the front seat, dipping his head under the rearview mirror and looking out the window. A lady in a Honda caught sight of Oscar and smiled, amused by his posture.

We suffered through the congestion, eventually connecting to the I-55 on the way to St. Louis. After two and a half hours, and roughly one hundred miles, we needed a break. There was a turnoff into Pontiac, Illinois. After a five-mile drive around the turns and winding streets, I stopped at a gas station. I put gas in the car and checked with the cashier that we were headed in the right direction. "Yes, this road leads to downtown," she pointed.

We continued down the street and spotted a sign pointing to downtown "Historic Pontiac, Illinois."

"Historic. Never heard of it," I joked. "Good marketing, though. We're here, aren't we?"

As we ventured into the town, I noted a Route 66 Museum. Then, I saw a car theme with murals and a variety of painted mini cars spread around the town. Colorful. Charming curb appeal. "This looks promising, Oscar."

A few blocks away, there were distinct large buildings, which I sensed could be a public courthouse or city hall. I drove in that direction and found a large, open parking lot. After helping Oscar out of the car, I grabbed the leash, my camera, and a sweatshirt. "Let's check out this place."

We started at a bronze Abraham Lincoln statue that stood next to the courthouse. Then, we continued exploring the adjacent streets. I took a bunch of photos of the painted cars, wall sketches, and statues—so far, so good. Any time I could find a scenic spot for me and open space for Oscar was a bonus. It was chilly and overcast, but it was nice to walk around and stretch a bit.

We did a second lap through the town, looking for a lunch spot. I paused to take another photo of a mural. Oscar dragged on his leash. "Wait, Oscar. I want to get this photo." He pulled on the leash. I quickly shot the photo of an old soda fountain painted on the side of a building then followed him around the corner to a terrific souvenir photo op. It was an enormous Route 66 Pontiac, Illinois mural on the side of a three-story building. While stepping back to get a full view, a nice electrician packed up and moved his truck to give us a less obstructed view of the mural. At the same time, a guy leaving work agreed to shoot a picture of us. Perfect. The guy handled it like a pro. First, he moved his car twenty feet over.

"There," he said. "Now, you have a wide-open photo of the mural." Then he positioned us and himself to get maximum area of the mural in the camera view. After a few shots, he handed the camera back to me. "Does it look OK?"

"I'm sure it does," I answered. "He never takes a bad photo," pointing at Oscar.

"I'll bet," the guy agreed.

I looked at the digital images of Oscar and me. "That's a keeper. Thanks!"

Oscar and I cross paths with Route 66

Pontiac was a good one. I was delighted to discover a pleasant place just over a hundred miles from my house. Future day trip? That's what road trips are about: one moment you're stuck in wretched traffic, the next moment you make a cool discovery.

On our way out of town, I started flipping through the XM radio choices. "How 'bout some Hair Nation?" Mötley Crüe was playing. Oscar looked at me from the passenger seat.

"70s on 7?" A Captain & Tennille song. "Or, talk radio?" Oscar didn't care.

A buddy of mine, Mickey, was the first person I knew who subscribed to satellite radio.

"You're out of your mind," I said to him. "Who would actually pay for radio?"

He described the original programming, no commercials, and better reception. "There are so many stations," he told me. "It's totally worth it."

I wasn't persuaded.

Years later, when I bought the Nissan, it came with three free months of XM Satellite Radio. After one month, I realized it was a necessary alternative to local radio. I became accustomed to the minimal commercials and lots of choices. And, there were stations that I would miss. That three-month offer was all it took. I was hooked. During road trips, the subscription was definitely worth the price. In remote areas, the XM signal could reach locations without radio options.

The best part of having a canine companion: he was thrilled to come along for the ride. While Oscar road shotgun, he'd listen to anything—although he cringed a bit when I blasted Alice In Chains. I found an Oingo Boingo song on First Wave, and we cruised along. I think Oscar liked it. He certainly didn't bother to change the channel!

A few hours later, the outline of St. Louis appeared in the distance. As we approached the city, the notable Gateway Arch grew larger. The Drury Plaza Hotel was located walking distance from the Arch and a few blocks from Busch Stadium where the Cardinals play baseball. Without directions, I just continued down the I-55 until I found an exit that led to Busch stadium. Eventually, I spotted our hotel's entrance—as we passed it, on a one-way street. I followed the street to the next light, where there was another one-way turn, the wrong way. "We're in one-way hell," I said to Oscar. He was scanning the new surroundings through the passenger window.

I figured out the maze and reached the parking garage across the street from the hotel entrance. I grabbed my laptop and two dog bowls. Oscar and I headed into the lobby area, which was rather posh, seemingly designed for business meetings, weddings, and other special events. There was a comfortable lounge seating area near a water fountain. This seemed a bit nice for a dog.

We wandered inside, passing groups of people meeting around the water area, dressed in suits, business attire, and evening wear. Yeah, we were a bit underdressed. *Who is more out of place: Oscar or shabby me?* I was wearing old jeans, a faded sweatshirt, and a baseball hat. Oscar stood out more, but it was a close call. He received the common reactions. Some were surprised to see a dog inside the hotel. Most seemed OK with it, and a few didn't notice. I carefully went around the crowd, keeping Oscar close to my side, and approached the front desk. The receptionist checked us in, explained the amenities, and gave me the key.

After a day of driving and with the parking being across the street, I considered restaurants within walking distance of the hotel. After browsing some menus, I defaulted to the restaurant in the hotel, Angelo's Taverna. I ordered take-out over the phone, explaining that I had a dog and wanted all the chicken on the side. Once we had our food, we went back up to our room. I prepared Oscar's meal and set his bowl of food and bowl of water on a white hotel towel in the middle of the room. Meanwhile, I ate off of the Styrofoam container.

After dinner, we toured the area, walking by Busch Stadium, the Arch, and the Old St. Louis County Courthouse, site of the Dred Scott case. It was Friday evening, but the downtown area was quiet. It was windy with chilly late-March temperatures. The Cardinals wouldn't open their home season for another week or so. I could hear faint music from a bar at one of the hotels, but overall, not much was going on. Not a big deal. Oscar's not much of a late night partier, anymore.

ST. LOUIS, MISSOURI to BRANSON, MISSOURI

I WOKE UP and saw Oscar sleeping on his blanket spread over the carpet in the middle of the room. Excellent. I was pleased he had slept straight through the night. After breakfast, we turned toward the Gateway Arch National Park. I wanted to get another look. I remembered visiting St. Louis ten years earlier, going inside and to the top of the Arch. The design and engineering of the massive structure still amazed me.

On Day two of our trip, we switched from southbound I-55 to I-44, heading southwest. We stopped at the Route 66 Diner near the Army training center Fort Leonard Wood. As I went inside to order lunch, I noticed the entrance had a sign that read, "Army, Navy, Air Force, Marines: We serve those who serve." I like that. I remembered the time my brother had spent at the nearby military base.

There was a chilly breeze as we ate, but with the shining sun, it was a bit warmer than St. Louis. We listened to music on my MP3 player and watched a few diners pass in and out of the restaurant.

Bring Oscar

After Oscar polished off his chicken fingers and some of my fries, he was ready. I grabbed his bowls and we returned to the car. Good stop.

We stayed on I-44 southwest, straight to Springfield, Missouri. Then, following the street signs, we changed to US 65 south. During this leg of the drive, Oscar sat in the front seat. I drove with one hand on the wheel, and one hand rubbing his back. He seemed to enjoy that moment. It's up and down with him. Sometimes, the fourteen-year-old looks tired; other times, he seems interested, curious, and motivated. We were headed to our destination—Branson, Missouri. I prepared myself for the possibilities: entertainment and attractions? Or, cheesy schlock?

We went past billboards and music places, reaching the La Quinta Inn without much trouble. While we waited to check in, a few nice people eyed Oscar.

"What's his name?" a little girl asked.

"Oscar."

"Oscar," she repeated and pet him.

Her mother kidded, "Like Oscar the Grouch?"

"Oh, he's no grouch," I smiled.

"No, he's not a grouch," the girl giggled. She knew her mother was teasing.

Then, the father joked, "Maybe, he's Oscar Mayer."

"A wiener dog!" said the brother.

"Nope, just Oscar Madison."

"*Odd Couple*, right?" the father said.

"Good memory," I told him. "Yep, *The Odd Couple*."

The lady at the front desk gave me the room number and keys. Two keys. Just before I left, I asked if there was a specific place to walk around and check things out. They recommended Branson Landing. After a break in the room, we headed over to the Landing along the waterfront of Lake Taneycomo. It had a nice promenade to walk through, and there was a nifty water light show with music at the fountains—a worthwhile attraction.

We meandered up and down the spacious walkway through the open mall. Oscar tried to veer me toward the door entrances. "Sorry, pal. No dogs inside." We could feel the cool air conditioning drifting outside. Then we found Buster's Old Time Photos, a retro photography place. It had a good online write-up, and it accommodated pets. Winner!

Oscar and I went inside to investigate. I noticed the Old West costumes and background scenery for the photo shoots. Then I saw some of the past customer portraits, including a few with pets. The prices were a bit high, but sometimes you just have to go for it. Plus, the place was air-conditioned with seating, so we were content to sit and rest for forty-five minutes in the cool lobby watching the other tourists pose in 1870s outfits.

Eventually, it was our turn. The photographer started discussing options. What sort of background? What type of costume? Where should the dog go? A wardrobe person put me in an old outlaw costume. Then, the lady offered some options for Oscar. "He's not a fan of being dressed up," I warned her. "But, be my guest." Years earlier, I had tried to dress him up for Halloween. Five minutes later, his hat and costume were in pieces in the living room.

"Maybe a bandana?" she tried.

Oscar let her tie the bandana around his neck. Either he was taking one for the team, or he was too old and tired to fight the accessories anymore. We posed for several photos with different backdrops and costume variations. Afterward, the photographer took the digital images and did some editing and cropping. Not bad! I carried the wooden framed picture and a couple of individual prints out of the store, pleased with my purchase.

Bring Oscar

Wanted: A framed photo of an outlaw and his sidekick

During the drive back to the hotel, I took care to observe the surroundings: Ozark Mountains, touristy and quaint streets, theaters, and billboards showing local attractions. I was fascinated by traveling. Two days ago, I was sitting in my house, and forty-eight hours later, I'm driving around a completely different, randomly picked area in Missouri.

BRANSON, MISSOURI to MEMPHIS, TENNESSEE

AFTER A GOOD night's sleep—with the air conditioner cranking—I woke up Oscar and took him for a quick morning walk around the premises. In the parking lot, an elderly man was stuffing bags into the back of an over-packed car. A couple from Illinois was arguing about something. And, a mother standing beside a car with Tennessee plates was gathering her excited kids. They saw Oscar and stopped in their tracks.

"We like your dog," one of the little girls said.

"He's a good one," I answered.

"It's a gorgeous dog," her mother added.

I responded, "Well, on his behalf, thank you." After waving to the kids, Oscar and I went past the other travelers—a mix of methodical, frantic, stressed, and happy.

We were back on US 65, traveling south into Northern Arkansas. I wasn't sure what to expect. When I think of Arkansas, I think of Bill Clinton, moonshine, and Walmart. So, I just followed the map, drove along the Ozarks, and headed toward a site called the

Natural Bridge, which was located outside of Clinton, Arkansas. I had no idea how this excursion would fare. At best, I'd discover a tremendous place. At worst, it was a stop along the way. But I was optimistic. These types of attractions were usually good ones. Scenic, dog-friendly, less crowded, and/or inexpensive. Mostly, it was a chance to walk Oscar, which meant a beneficial activity for both of us.

We reached a large sign: "Natural Bridge of Arkansas" with "Entrance!" printed inside a white arrow. I slowed down and followed the arrow, gently turning off the main highway. As we descended along a winding road, I was intrigued by the adventure. Then, as we got deeper into the wilderness, and transitioned onto a dirt road, I started to wonder if this was a bad idea.

"It's too late to turn back now," I mumbled as we continued through the surrounding woods.

Oscar sat in the passenger seat without any concern. Eventually, we came to a parking area at the end of the road. There weren't many cars or people. This was either a good sign (no crowds to deal with), or a bad omen (it was a crappy tourist spot).

I scanned the log cabin main building and a decorative, old covered wagon on the side of the parking lot. Oscar and I passed through the building and then trotted along a groomed, dirt trail. Twenty minutes later, we reached the Natural Bridge. It was kinda cool. Basically, it's an enormous arched rock that looks like a bridge. It reminded me of an overpass on a highway, but it was made of solid rock. I'm not sure how unique it was. Nevertheless, it was a worthwhile stopover, especially taking into account the nature walk.

After a few photos, we backtracked along the trail, returning to the log cabins and other novelties. There was a collection of authentic items—stoves, furniture, tools, dishes—from the nineteenth century. A wooden sign above a fireplace caught my eye: "Chop your own wood; it makes you warm twice!" It was such a simple life.

An elderly gentleman who worked at this tourist spot asked about us and took a liking to Oscar. He offered some interesting history about the trail, the bridge, and the cabins along the way. He was a native of the area and quite knowledgeable. Plus, he had a welcoming tone of voice and Southern accent. As we spoke, Oscar sprawled out and napped in the middle of the floor! "Sorry that he's hogging the floor. I think he's a bit tired; just takin' a break."

"That's OK," the gentleman said. "The old fella is just making himself at home." The other visitors kindly sidestepped Oscar and smiled.

Our drive through Arkansas was uneventful, but it was interesting. At Little Rock, the road merged and became the I-40 east. I followed the map and anticipated smooth sailing into Tennessee—until we hit construction. When the car slowed down, Oscar opened his eyes. "Not part of the plan, Oscar." He looked around through the windows. "No, we're not there." He placed his head on my shoulder and sighed.

The construction delayed the trip by an hour. After pressing through the bottleneck traffic, we drove across the Mississippi River toward downtown Memphis. Since the weather was nice, and Oscar was due for a break, we stopped to walk along the Mississippi River. There were others on the riverfront path, walking or sitting on benches. In the distance, I could see a huge pyramid. It was a curious structure in the Memphis cityscape.

We got back in the car and searched for the hotel. I followed my written directions to the Super 8 hotel. Turns out it was in an industrial area. Oh well, it's only one night. The room was fine, but when I walked Oscar outside, it felt like a drug deal was ready to go down in the shadows. The enormous lawn area with a massive tree in the middle was nice. But, in the distance, it was an industrial area bordered with tons of construction. This was about as far from vacation scenery that we could get. Then, I saw four shady looking folks smoking and loitering around the entrance. Good thing I had a fierce, intimidating dog for protection. Well, maybe not.

I was too tired to drive into downtown Memphis, so Oscar and I settled on Wendy's. Slim pickings on a Sunday evening. We returned to the no-tell hotel, and I brought in the envelope of cash that was stored under the car seat.

Oscar and I walked briskly down the dim hallway. When we were inside the room, I latched the extra lock on the door. Now, we were ready to sit in our bunker and watch TV.

Bring Oscar

I opened up one of Oscar's cans of wet dog food and put it in his bowl. He gave it a sniff. Pass. "I know," I told him. "None of the good stuff tonight. I don't have much, either." I handed him part of a potato fry. He chewed on it for a while. So, we had some salad, potato fries, and a chocolate frosty. Bon appétit.

MEMPHIS, TENNESSEE to HUNTSVILLE, ALABAMA

BIG DAY AHEAD—AND we were certainly ready to get out of that hotel. We departed early and began the *tour du jour*: downtown Memphis. Oscar and I spent an hour walking up and down the streets. We started at the Elvis statue in the Elvis Presley Plaza then strolled along Beale Street to the B.B. King's Blues Club and the Beale Street Brass Notes Walk of Fame, which had brass music notes, instead of stars, embedded in the cement sidewalk. Along the way, I enjoyed reading the signs and plaques about this Mississippi River town and its entertainers, singers, and historical figures.

While pausing to look at music memorabilia displayed in a club window, an officer interrupted. "Sorry, but dogs are not allowed here."

"Really? I didn't know that." I hadn't seen a sign.

"Sorry, it's true."

Although the block was almost empty, we had to leave. So, Oscar and I walked around the surrounding area, passing the

FedExForum where the Grizzlies played basketball, the Gibson Guitar Factory, and the AutoZone AAA ballpark.

When I outlined this trip, I considered taking time to see the Gulf Coast. Visiting any sort of beach was very appealing. However, that would leave less time for other places. We could go deeper south or east, but we couldn't do both within our time limit. You need time. If you have limited time, you have to make choices. Nonetheless, I was excited that two new states would be checked off today: Mississippi and Alabama.

We passed into the northern end of Mississippi and aimed for Corinth. Oscar and I stopped in front of a large diner storefront, Borroum's Drug Store. I peeked inside to check out the one-hundred-and-fifty-year-old pharmacy and noticed the soda fountain. It looked like a good lunch choice. As we strolled around the block, I noted the license plates attached to the row of parked cars: Georgia, Mississippi, Alabama, and Tennessee. "Not likely to see Illinois plates in this area."

We finished our walk around the town and returned to Borroum's. The pharmacy itself stretched back to the post-Civil War era. I kept imagining this town after the Civil War. This drug store was there among old shops, horses, and dirt roads! I thought about how everything has changed: the streets, technology, restaurant chains, world events, and more. But, the one-hundred-and-fifty-year-old drug store was outlasting all of it—historical. We ordered outside and enjoyed a quiet lunch of fries, a sandwich, and a Coke with a view of the courthouse and statues across the street.

As we were finishing, the young guy who prepared the meal came outside to talk to us.

"Nice dog," he said. "Where y'all from?"

"Illinois." I explained our journey and how I travel with Oscar during holidays. This was our first trip to "The South."

"What do you think of Mississippi?"

"Seems nice," I answered. "We just got here. It's different." Not better. Not worse. Just different. And different is interesting to me. Regardless, it was all about discovery and the journey. And, at this moment, I was having a conversation with a native Southerner who looked like a surfer version of Brad Pitt. He had a slight accent, but mostly he reminded me of a kid from Southern California.

"You all think we're racist, huh?"

He knocked me a little off balance. His tone was harmless, yet the question was abrupt. Was he serious?

"I don't," I tried to answer. "But, I'm sure there are people back home who do." I knew plenty of folks who had stereotypes about the South. *The best part of driving through places is to see for yourself.* And, this twenty-year-old surfer kid was definitely no hillbilly.

"Ah, I'm just kidding," he laughed and went back inside.

Oscar and I capped off lunch with an ice cream sundae for dessert, just like the old fountain sundaes I had as a kid, in a classic glass with whipped cream and a cherry. The surfer kid came back outside to check how the meal was and chat with us again. "Where ya headed?" he asked.

"Not sure. Just driving east toward South Carolina."

"Cool," he said.

"Are you sure you're not from California?"

He just laughed then mentioned being from another town in Mississippi. "Well, I hope you enjoy your stay."

"So far, so good."

Moments later, a crowd of people arrived wearing SEC jerseys. Two of them had orange shirts. There was no game, but they sure looked like Tennessee fans grabbing lunch before a football game. They said polite accented greetings as they walked past us to the doorway of Barroum's. Goodbye, Midwest and Big Ten. Hello, Deep South and SEC!

We continued east on US 72, crossing the Alabama border forty-five minutes later.

"That's another state, Oscar." The drive through Alabama was pleasant. Open road and colorful hills with blossoming trees. I kept wondering about "crimson tide" and "roll tide," Alabama football, and even Steely Dan's "Deacon Blues." The scenic hills did have a reddish coloring. Is that what they meant?

We followed the highway into Huntsville, Alabama, home of the NASA Space Camp and two old friends from Chicago. So, I chose this for the next overnight stop. I easily spotted the La

Quinta Huntsville from the highway, and after settling into the hotel room, I made arrangements with my friends.

Oscar and I made the fifteen-minute trip to Liz and Anthony's house. We met their daughter, who immediately was attracted to Oscar. Also, they had a little dog that was pleased to have a canine guest. Liz and I caught up, talking about old times, what our mutual friends were doing now, and their jobs, kids, and adjustment to moving from Chicago to Huntsville. It seemed like a good move for them. Anthony's chiropractor and physical wellness business was thriving, and I learned that Liz had a terrific job in marketing and advertising mailers.

When Anthony came home from his office, we had drinks and dinner from a nearby Chinese restaurant and spent a comfortable evening reminiscing. Sitting in a home with a family was such a contrast to the hotel room. It was a nice change of pace.

It was interesting to compare their daily lives as a family and mine as a single guy with a dog. I had extra time to pursue other interests and fewer responsibilities; at the same time, they enjoyed the life of having a family and kids. At the end of the evening, we took a few photos, and Liz and Anthony suggested places to visit.

HUNTSVILLE, ALABAMA to KNOXVILLE, TENNESSEE

I SAT DOWN beside his blanket and pillow on the carpet in the hotel room.

"Happy Birthday, Oscar!" He looked up at me as I gave him a hearty hug and pat on the head. Fourteen years old.

I didn't know Oscar's actual birthday. When I adopted him in July of 2001, the vet estimated his age at one year. I picked April 1st to be his birthday. Lighthearted choice? Perhaps. Bad humor? Maybe. But, April Fools' Day was easy to remember. To celebrate, I handed him a dog treat and shared some of my breakfast. Friends would say, "The way you treat him, every day is his birthday."

That morning, we checked out the Madison County Nature Trail, a recommendation from my friends. The scene around the lake was stunning. It was a clear, mild day, so there were beautiful views of the water, streams, covered bridges, and surrounding trees and wildlife. Since it was a weekday, there was virtually nobody using the trail. It was Oscar, me, and nature. While ambling along the gravel and dirt trails, Oscar enjoyed the smells and cool air. I took pictures and was delighted to think, *I'm in Alabama.*

At the car, I gave Oscar water and a snack. I took out the map and traced yesterday's path with the yellow highlighter then looked over the interstate routes leading to South Carolina, a state I'd never visited. Yes, it was worth stretching our drive farther. And, since we're going to South Carolina, how could we not go all the way to Charleston? I mentally recalculated the number of miles and days left. "Yeah, this is doable." I put the map back in the glove compartment, and we started racing east.

Alabama US 72 evolved into Tennessee Route 27, which eventually turned into I-24. At one point, we went from Alabama to Tennessee, then left Tennessee, briefly passed into Georgia, then back to Tennessee—all within about thirty minutes. I think the time zone changed as well, so we could've been going back and forth in time. It was confusing and amusing.

Outside Chattanooga, there were billboards advertising Rock City on Lookout Mountain. Last night, my Huntsville friends had mentioned that their family loved it. So, I decided to see for myself. We parked in the large, mostly filled lot. It seemed rather crowded for a Tuesday, although it was spring break. At the entrance, I hesitated for a second. I couldn't see if this was a suitable place for Oscar and me, and the admission fee was a bit pricey sight unseen. Nevertheless, we were there. I paid the admission.

From the front area, we walked and hiked from scenic view to scenic Tennessee Valley view. There were narrow pathways, unique rock formations, and natural attractions. There was Fairyland Caverns for kids, which contained handcrafted gnomes and colorful dioramas that glowed in the dark rooms. Oscar walked along the flat parts, and for the most part, he could go up and down the rock surfaces. But occasionally, he'd just stop and wait for me to lift him either up or down. Eventually, we got to the top area with a spectacular view over the horizon from which you could see seven Southern states. It reminded me of how close all of these states are.

*Hiking around Rock City and Lookout Mountain,
Chattanooga, Tennessee*

It was seventy-five degrees, sunny, and wonderful. At the same time, Oscar's dark black coat heated him up in these kinds of conditions, so we rested in the shade to cool off. Unable to find a drinking fountain, I bought two bottles of water and grabbed a hot dog cardboard holder from the concessions for a makeshift water dish. Oscar sat on the ground lapping it up. Water splashed on his face and everywhere on his paws. I poured more, and he resumed drinking and splashing. For fifteen minutes, he was delighted to just sit with water in front of him.

A boy and mother walked over to us. "He wants to pet your dog. Is that OK?"

"Of course," I said. "He's just resting, but he likes people."

The boy gave him a few strokes. Then, he amusingly held up his hand with hair. "He's shedding," the mother told her son. "He's hot." She turned to me. "He must shed a lot, huh?"

"Yeah, all the time." I reached my hand down. I gripped Oscar with a tight massage and came up with a clump of black hair. "See? It never stops. But, it's OK. I have wood floors at home."

"Well, he's a sweet dog." The mother turned to her son. "Isn't he nice?"

"Yes," he said. "Good dog!" The boy gave one more pat on the head then they walked away.

Oscar looked cooled off. "Really to roll?" I gave him a gentle tug, and he popped up. "This was a good stop."

After lunch, we drove one hundred and twenty miles to our stopover for the night. Once again, I pulled out the map and traced today's route with the yellow highlighter: Huntsville, Alabama to Knoxville, Tennessee. I looked down at the odometer: *We've gone one thousand miles.* It's astonishing to think how quickly you can go from Illinois to St. Louis to Arkansas to Memphis to Alabama to Eastern Tennessee.

As we get into a rhythm, the miles go faster—and time passes faster.

KNOXVILLE, TENNESSEE to MOUNT PLEASANT, SOUTH CAROLINA

THE SUN WAS slipping through the curtain when I woke up. I looked at the clock. 7:30 a.m.

Well, at least I managed to get ninety minutes of sleep. I looked down at Oscar. He was sound asleep next to the air conditioner. "Oh my gosh. What are you: a vampire?" After sundown, Oscar spent most of the previous night roaming the room. At times, he started to yelp and bark. Nightmare. Fearing he'd wake up others in the hotel, I took him outside. When we returned to the room, he started to pace again. Then he barked again, so we went back outside. This occurred on and off until just before the sun came out. Then, like a vampire, he retired.

I checked email and skimmed over today's route. It required minimal navigation: I-40 east through the Smoky Mountains then onto I-26 east straight to Charleston, South Carolina. Simple.

Oscar got up and began his routine. A few sips from his water bowl. A sniff of the leftover food in his dinner bowl. Dismissed. He was waiting for something better. When I went into the shower, he poked his head through the curtain. After getting dressed, I ran down the hall and rounded up breakfast: orange juice, banana, apple, and bagel for me; scrambled eggs for Oscar. Afterward, we packed up, checked out, and hit the road.

The weekday drive was terrific. We stopped at a North Carolina Visitors Center near Ashville where it was pristine with rolling green hills between the woods; a wonderful spot for a rest break. We walked around the enormous open grass area with picnic tables, surrounded by an untouched wooded area. The grounds were clean with appealing landscaping and rock bed, probably for water runoff, as well as aesthetics. Forty-five minutes later, we returned to the car where I offered Oscar more to drink. I pulled out a treat, and he grabbed it and went into the backseat.

When we entered South Carolina, we took another break at an I-26 rest stop near Kinards. There was a big welcome sign that made for a great photo op. "South Carolina: Smiling Faces, Beautiful Places." We strolled along the shaded sidewalk, and I was delighted to find a stack of free South Carolina maps. They would be helpful, and it was a welcoming gesture to provide detailed state maps for visitors.

For lunch, we took a random exit into Columbia, South Carolina. I drove up and down the commercial area, hoping some place would appear. Eventually, we settled on a Chinese restaurant in a shopping plaza next to a Piggly Wiggly. It offered a shaded wrought iron table just outside the restaurant. The meal was so-so, but the cool concrete in the shade was good for Oscar. So, overall, mission accomplished.

Cooling off in South Carolina

We returned to I-26, and one hundred miles later, we reached the coast—Port of Charleston. At last! We were met by a picturesque view of the US 17 Ravenel Bridge and the Charleston Harbor, which leads out to the Atlantic Ocean. The pleasant breeze off the water, mixed with temperatures in the low 70s, gave me the vacation weather I'd anticipated. It reminded me of San Diego and the Coronado Bridge. San Diego mixed with Southern history: Port of Charleston, Gadsden's Wharf, slave ship history in Liberty Square, Irish Memorial, Fort Sumter National Monument. After ninety minutes of walking through Charleston along the waterfront, we went to the hotel.

The Red Roof PLUS+ in Mount Pleasant was just over the bridge. The location was fine, and the price was significantly less than the Charleston hotels. The room was upstairs, and there was no elevator, so I would have to lift Oscar up and down.

We walked into the room, and I dropped a bag on one bed. I opened up the laptop to check email, look for a restaurant in the neighborhood, and eventually, make tomorrow's itinerary. I logged in to find the Wi-Fi icon had two bars. That's not good. I tried loading a page, and it took a while. Now the icon only had one bar. I tried repositioning by the window, then by the door, and other parts of the room, hoping a different location would get a better connection. It didn't work. "This is like a dot matrix printer!" The hotel was surrounded by trees. Perhaps, that was disrupting the reception? I gave up.

I used my old flip phone to send a message to a past college friend, Mikie. Within twenty minutes, she responded and suggested meeting for dinner at Red's Ice House off the water. It was dog-friendly with outdoor seating. On cue, Oscar stood up and wandered to me. I grabbed his leash, and we headed outside. When we reached the staircase, he just stopped and waited. "Got it." I picked him up and trotted down the steps, then gently set him on the ground. "Lance's escalator service."

When we went through the lobby, I asked about the restaurant. I wanted to double-check the directions. I hate getting lost, especially at night. The guy at the front desk told me Red's was no good. Instead, he gave me a coupon for a nearby place. It seemed fishy. Did he get a kickback?

I ignored the guy's opinion and drove to Red's to meet my friend. We parked in a crowded dirt parking lot next to the waterfront restaurant. There were plenty of people, so it seemed like a good place to me. We approached the restaurant and could hear the music and crowd. Listening to the voices and accents, it felt like an SEC tailgate or post-golf outing party.

We wandered past the bar and found Mikie sitting at a table on the patio.

We ordered some drinks and appetizers. While catching up about mutual college friends and life in general, I looked around the bar. This was a treat, since we hadn't had an opportunity in Chicago to comfortably eat outside in months. It was a relaxing atmosphere.

There were two dogs at nearby tables. Oscar didn't seem to mind. He was on the floor sleeping. The waitress politely walked over him.

Mikie offered suggestions for sites to see before we leave. "Are you free tomorrow? I could show you around after work."

I explained how we only had a few hours tomorrow. Then, we had to race back home.

"But, someday, I'll have to come back for a longer visit."

MOUNT PLEASANT, SOUTH CAROLINA to BUCKHEAD (ATLANTA), GEORGIA

FOLLOWING MIKIE'S SUGGESTION, we went to Fort Moultrie on Sullivan's Island. It was a great idea that offered something for everyone: walking for Oscar, history for me, and a beautiful view for both of us. Plus, there were no crowds on a Thursday morning. In fact, I think we mistakenly walked into the empty fort where no pets were allowed, but nobody was there to say anything. I guess no one was guarding the fort!

The coastal weather was pleasant with clear blue skies. Oscar and I roamed around the grass area surrounding the cannons, fortifications, and structure, then followed the series of illustrated plaques, presenting a brief history of the fort and events since the Revolutionary War. We continued toward Sullivan's Island Beach to get a glimpse of Fort Sumter. I had read about its significance following the War of 1812 through the first shots of the Civil War fifty years later. In the distance, I could see the harbor island in a military strategic context, and in the other direction, I could see the Atlantic Ocean. As we stood on the shore, a cargo ship suddenly passed through the harbor, capping off our tour of the area.

A Patriot standing at the entrance of Fort Moultrie in South Carolina

Now, we turn around!

Oscar and I backtracked on I-26 and stopped for lunch at Fatz Café in Columbia. A few miles earlier, I had spotted a billboard that read, "Fatz: last food for 90 miles (just kidding)." Any place with that sense of humor and marketing strategy seemed worth a try! The menu was filled with classic comfort food. I ordered a chicken pot pie, rolls with cinnamon butter, and a side salad. The food was very good for a Cracker Barrel type of place, with nice, polite service.

While eating three benches from the doorway, we watched families and seniors stroll in and out. It was comfortable in the shade. Oscar lay with his chest on the cool concrete. Fifteen feet away, big hornets were buzzing around the yellow flowered plants, but they stayed in their area and we stayed in ours. Pleased with our lunch choice, Oscar and I returned to the car. I lifted him into the car, and he plopped into the front seat. "Hang in there, buddy," I said. "I'll get you some air con." I started the car and cranked the air conditioner, pointing all the vents into his direction. He soaked in the cool air as we drove off, connected to I-20 west, and headed toward Atlanta.

I remember visiting Atlanta in 1997, following the Summer Olympics. More than fifteen years later, it was stunning to see how much Atlanta had grown and changed. There must've been five lanes filled with cars, going each way. What a mess. Weaving through traffic, we eventually arrived at the Microtel Inn & Suites. I learned that pets were limited to twenty-five pounds, but they didn't seem to care when we checked in. I suppose two twenty-five-pound dogs equal one fifty-pound Oscar.

Once again, we were met with an internet connection that sucked. The signal said "strong," but the pages didn't load well. Too many users? I tried holding the laptop and walking around the room. It didn't help. Instead of searching, we defaulted to dinner across the street at a sports bar called Montie's Public House. It had outdoor seating, so I had a hunch it would be dog-friendly. It turned out to be a terrific choice: beautiful evening weather, good music, and a view of sports on television through the window. Nice. Plus, they prepared a side of pulled turkey for Oscar.

We walked back to the hotel and made it an early night. Tomorrow was another three-hundred-mile driving day, so relaxing in the room sounded good. While Oscar fell asleep on the bed, I wrote some notes and uploaded the day's photos. Then, I took a look at tomorrow's Nashville hotel options. The Friday night rates were too expensive, so I explored places just outside of the city. After thirty minutes of searching, I was unable to find an appealing, dog-friendly hotel room to reserve. *I'll try again in the morning.* It wasn't the only time that I would book a room the day of our arrival.

BUCKHEAD (ATLANTA), GEORGIA to BRENTWOOD, TENNESSEE

WHEN I REACHED down to pick up my shirt, the muscle flinched. I knew I had tweaked it. I tried to rub out the tight muscle in my lower back. I tried to stretch and manage the backache. Damn.

A few years ago, I pulled my back playing basketball. I reached down to my right for a loose ball, and when I straightened up, the muscle had twisted. It touched a nerve, and the pain shot up and down my lower back. I left the court, got in my car, and drove home. By the time I got there, my back was stiffer, and any slight movement led to a nerve jolt that was excruciating.

I didn't know what to do. I tried lying on my back. No relief. Lying on my stomach? On my side? No help. Any slight change of position, and the nerve fired up. This caused my back to stiffen further, which pinched the nerve. And the vicious cycle worsened.

After paralyzing and sweating pain, I dragged myself along the wood floors and pulled the phone off the table. Lying on my side,

I dialed for help. An ambulance picked me up, since I was unable to unfold myself and slide into my car, let alone drive a stick shift. Oscar, eight years old at the time, stood by me, watching this whole spectacle.

At the hospital, the emergency room doctor recognized the problem. She gave me the magic of muscle relaxants, and ten minutes later, I felt brand new. God bless the drug companies! The doctor explained that I needed to rest, and she prescribed additional muscle relaxants, as well as pills for inflammation. "No heat," she reminded me. "Instead, ice will work better." Slowly, I recovered.

A few months later, I was working out at the gym. All good. I reached down to pick up my sweatshirt, which was laying down and to the left. When I stood up, I felt my back twinge. Uh-oh. By the time I got home, my body was contorted. I dragged myself into the house and dropped on the floor. After an hour, it got worse. Then, I crawled to the bathroom like a wounded animal. Climbed up the toilet, reached the sink, and strained to open the medicine cabinet. With pouring sweat and painful back spasms, I grabbed the bottle of old muscle relaxants. I dropped to the bathroom floor and downed one. Again, Oscar was watching this whole episode. While I waited on the floor, he sat sympathetically beside me until the medicine took effect and I could walk around.

So, I had pulled my lower back again, but this time I didn't have any pills for instant relief. The best thing I could do was stand straight up, or be upright on my knees. The worst thing for my lower back issue was sitting, especially in a car. After driving, I'd climb out of the car like a pretzel. Then, painfully force my back straight as best as I could. I often ended up crooked, walking like an old man, hunched over and leaning one way. So, that's how the day started for us. Walking out of the hotel room, looking like two crooked tinker toys: Oscar hobbling with his crooked head, and me, walking slowly with my stiff, crooked back. What a decrepit pair!

We had three more days of driving to make it home in time. Instead of Birmingham, Alabama, I chose the more direct route toward Nashville. We headed north on I-75 out of Atlanta then veered northwest through a sequence of state highways out of Georgia and into Alabama. Oscar was sitting in the passenger seat,

Bring Oscar

looking out the window. He seemed to be alert and enjoying the moment.

Midway through the drive, we took a detour back to Huntsville. We stopped to have a quick lunch with my friend, Liz, at Panera Bread. Her daughter was at school. "She'll be so jealous that I got to see Oscar." After lunch, Oscar and I took an hour walk around the Space Camp campus. Although we could not go inside, the two of us got a firsthand view of the Space Shuttle and a rocket on the side of the main buildings. *Are those actual NASA space crafts or replicas?*

Following our exercise, we returned to the car. I opened the map, pulled out my yellow highlighter, and traced the route we had covered during the last two days. Then, we looked at the remaining area of the trip. "Goin' north, Oscar." I put the map back in the glove compartment and gave Oscar a pat on the head. Then, we left the Space Camp parking lot, and found our way to Alabama State Route 53.

We crossed into Tennessee, merged onto I-65, and within one hundred miles, we arrived in Brentwood, just south of Nashville. I contacted my college friend and arranged to meet after he finished work. With a few hours to spare, Oscar and I took an excursion to Two Rivers Dog Park, perhaps the best free dog park I'd ever seen. There was an enormous amount of space, and it was clean. Oscar led me to the fence, eager to get inside with his furry friends. Eventually, he went off by himself and started digging a hole in the dirt. When he got a bit tired and thirsty, he came over to me. "You diggin'?!" I said to him. He seemed pleased with his activity.

I poured some water into one of the park bowls left for the dogs. Oscar took a sip and then started splashing with his paws. "What's he doing?" a lady asked, half-laughing and half-curious.

"He's drinking, splashing, making a mess."

Two other dogs wandered over to watch Oscar's little game. They seemed half-interested and half-confused by Oscar's antics. Now the fresh bowl of clean water had become a small puddle of dirt water. Oscar looked up. One paw was in the bowl, and the other wet paw was beside it. "So embarrassing," I joked. "I can't take you anywhere."

I walked over and dumped out the dirty water then refilled it with clean water for the other dogs. Oscar took a sip, and just before he dipped his paw in again, I stopped him. "You're done. Let the other dogs have some. Let's go walk around."

At 4:15, Oscar and I returned to the car and started toward the hotel in Smyrna, twenty-five miles outside of Nashville. On the way, I got a message from my friend, Erich; he had gotten off early from work. So, instead of the hotel, we turned to his home in Brentwood.

During the next couple of hours, we walked around his neighborhood and caught up. Then, Oscar and I had dinner with him and one of his teen daughters. We ordered take-out from The Tin Roof 2, a local bar and grill. Back at his house, we ate and watched a basketball game on TV. At 8:30, the day was winding down, and Erich offered his place. "With the dog?" I asked.

"Yeah, he seems mellow. We have an extra room."

I didn't want to mess up the room. Plus, they had a cat upstairs. "Maybe we can just take this spot around the couch?"

Erich handed me some blankets. While the hotel room would be more spacious, we would've had to drive twenty-five miles east and south to get there. Then, after checking in and leaving tomorrow, we'd have to backtrack twenty miles north to head home. With five hundred miles in front of us, I didn't mind saving forty-five miles of driving. So, Oscar and I crashed in Erich's living room.

BRENTWOOD, TENNESSEE to HOME

THERE WERE FIVE hundred miles between Nashville and home. The last leg of the trip would be broken into three parts: one third to Louisville, one third to Indianapolis, and one third to Chicago. It was a long stretch through Indiana, but I reminded myself, twelve hours from now, we'll be sitting in our living room at home!

We said goodbye to my friend in Tennessee and headed north on I-65. In a short time, we crossed the Tennessee/Kentucky border. "Whoa, there's a sign for the National Corvette Museum!" I doubted we could go inside, but it might be worth a stop. *You never know what you'll find.*

I took the proper exit and followed the local road signs to Corvette Drive. We reached an enormous parking lot, which included Corvettes with various license plates. Corvette enthusiasts making their pilgrimage to Bowling Green, Kentucky. We walked around the enormous buildings and peeked inside the windows, getting a glimpse of the museum and displays. Very cool. As expected, Oscar was the only canine. Some people looked over in curiosity as he walked along with me. A few kids pointed or came over to pet Oscar, but most just ignored us and went along admiring the cars.

Along the sidewalk, there were engraved bricks dedicated by countless Corvette groups around the world. There was a huge mural along the wall, which was a perfect photo op. I guided Oscar in front of the mural. "Wait here." I took a few steps back. "Ready?" He looked at me, and I took the picture.

Yes, living the dream

We continued past countless banners, representing Corvette clubs around the country, which decorated the walkways around the main building. There was a picnic area, outside statues, and tons of Corvette stuff. Heaven for the 'Vette fan. And, nice for us. It was a cool, sunny day, with lots of places to walk around.

In the distance, there was another huge warehouse with cars displayed on the outside. Hmm. We walked closer, where I could read the sign: "Art's Corvette." There was a Model T and two other classic cars under the building overhang. Inside was a showroom of antique cars, as well as a few Corvettes. As I stared through the window, an older guy waved at us. I cracked open the entrance door. "You wanna come in?" he said with a friendly southern drawl.

"I have my dog with me."

"Well, bring 'em in! I love dogs." It was Art himself, inviting us inside.

I gladly paid the five-dollar entrance fee, and we spent forty-five minutes walking around the enormous space. It was quite a vast car collection. I took photos and noted all the cool cars from a wide variety of eras: antiques to muscle cars to modern sports cars. Art walked over and pet Oscar, and he offered to take photos of us in front of his cars.

A couple of Classics in Bowling Green, Kentucky

Considering we had a lot of driving ahead of us, Oscar and I kept the visit brief and left Bowling Green. Along I-65 north were stretches of construction which diverted us. At one point, there was a spot that took us entirely off the interstate, onto Kentucky Route 61, and into the backwoods of Kentucky. It was inconvenient and time consuming. Given that today was our five-hundred-mile leg, I wasn't thrilled with any delays. But, on the upside, we did see some new things off the beaten path, including the Jim Beam Distillery. "I'll bet there were bootleggers and bourbon on these roads." While sidetracked, we met some helpful people along the way, particularly a train conductor who confirmed and clarified our written directions. Route 61 to 245 and back to the 65. Ultimately, we ended up going around Louisville, crossing into Indiana. Once we were back on track, we started making good time on I-65. Still, it was another couple of hours of driving, so we needed a rest.

Our last meal for the road trip was at a Subway next to a gas station. It was comical: the glory of our trip ended with Oscar eating his dinner next to the car, while I stood eating a sandwich and chips.

Dining at the gas station in Indiana

"Let's get rollin'!" Oscar looked up, satisfied with his dinner mix of dog food and Subway turkey. I lifted him into the car, threw his items into the trunk, and we headed onto the interstate. We drove along the two-lane highway, through endless flat land in Indiana.

As we passed an occasional billboard to turn off into a farm, diner, or tourist spot, I counted down the miles to Chicago. There was a huge windfarm. At first, it seemed sort of cool with the futuristic look, but after a while, it got old and just wrecked the otherwise open scenery with the sunset.

At the northern end of Indiana, we connected from I-65 to I-90. Then, we approached Chicago from the south. I kept counting miles and anticipating our arrival home. *Nearing the end of another successful road trip*, I happily thought as Oscar sat next to me in the passenger seat. The skyline of the Sears Tower and John Hancock Center was appearing and becoming recognizable from the distance—the last stretch.

After over four hundred and fifty miles of driving, we still had to pass through downtown. I hoped it wouldn't be too congested. Suddenly, I was cut off! "What the fuck!" I slammed on the brakes, and reached my arm to the right to protect Oscar. But, it was too late and didn't extend far enough; Oscar went shooting into the dashboard and glove compartment.

He ended up lying on the floor on his back, facing up with his paws dangling in the air amongst my laptop, sweatshirt, and other items on the floor.

Like a bulky prize fighter, he picked himself up, a bit stunned. I grabbed his collar and helped him climb up. He resumed his position in the passenger seat, looking outside the window. One ear was sideways; one ear was back. "Ridiculous." I pulled alongside the oblivious guy, talking on his cellphone. Then, I watched him zigzag ahead of us. It was an omen. Ten minutes later, we ran into traffic congestion on the I-90. The last twenty miles would be a ninety-minute grind home.

I turned off the engine in the driveway. "Well done, Oscar!" I looked down at the odometer: 3031 miles in a week and a half. Road trips are amazing. One day, we were at home, then Missouri, Arkansas, Tennessee, to South Carolina. Then, seventy-two hours we were back home with Oscar lounging around the backyard.

PART III
EAST

During dinner with some relatives, a cousin asked about my sister living and teaching in Bogotá, Colombia. Then, she asked about my summer vacation plans. I explained that I was taking another road trip. "Such a trip!" she said with amazement. "You're all so adventurous. I wish I could do that."

Actually, you can, I thought to myself. It just takes money, which she had, and an extended period of time, which she had. Granted, she would have to travel alone. But, it was possible. It may seem intimidating to venture into the unknown. But, traveling now versus thirty years ago is less complicated. The Internet provides maps, hotels, and tourist information. Even without GPS, it's rather easy to drive around. Plus, if you want effortless contact, then you can bring a mobile phone.

"We're headed to Maine and the Northeast," I told my cousin. "Assuming the dog and car can make it."

The Nissan had about seventy thousand miles on it. And, Oscar had over fourteen years on him. There were the same risks: Would we have to turn around? What would we encounter? How would we handle the travel? But, any apprehension disappeared as soon as I booked the first hotel.

I had a macro-plan to drive through Rhode Island, Delaware, New Hampshire, Vermont, and Maine—states I had never visited. But, to be honest, the micro-plan didn't exist. I had no idea how much time we'd spend in each place. I suspected a long break somewhere on the East Coast before returning, but I didn't know.

I anticipated a contrast to last year's trip. Going through the West offered space and vast distances between big cities, which seemed better for a traveler with a dog. At the same time, smaller states and denser areas in the East would make it easier to connect more places of interest.

Before departure, I bought an Eastern United States map, double paid my bills, polished off the perishable food in the refrigerator, and packed a week's worth of clothes. I collected Oscar's stuff, including his pain meds, tramadol, fish oil, dog food, and green beans. We were still using the green beans to curb his appetite without adding pounds.

I made the same summer arrangement with Miguel, my thirteen-year-old neighbor. He agreed to collect the mail, watch the house, and email me if something went wrong. I liked having someone who played outside watching the house. Plus, his grandmother liked giving him responsibility.

EVANSTON, ILLINOIS to PERRYSBURG, OHIO

ON A TUESDAY morning in June, I walked through the house to check the lights were off, the refrigerator was empty, and the desktop computer was shut down. Oscar trailed behind me. No running water in the sinks or gas from the stove. "Good to go," I said to him. "Going road trip!" I lifted him into the backseat next to Froggie, Sylvester, and his familiar blanket. By the time I got into the driver's seat, Oscar had maneuvered over the arm rest and into the front seat.

"That's what I thought." I started the car, cracked the windows for Oscar, and we pulled out of the driveway. My mind cleared away the travel preparations, work, and responsibilities—vacation.

The beginning of the journey went along the Edens Expressway to the Kennedy through downtown Chicago, a drive I had made hundreds of times. At 9:30 a.m., there was a moderate amount of traffic and construction, which was expected. There is always construction in Chicago, a city that will never be finished. It's a city that can squeeze a two-year road construction project into five years.

By the middle of the afternoon, we had traveled two hundred and fifty miles, reaching the Maumee/Perrysburg/Toledo area in Ohio. We turned off I-80, followed the side roads, and stopped at the Side Cut Metropark. There were walking pathways and river sites. And, the canal locks presented an interesting view of the waterway that had been an extension of the Miami and Erie Canal. I imagine this place gets filled with fishermen, kayakers, and hikers, but today, it was rather peaceful. At one point, I spotted some birds up high and deer in the distance. Oscar just watched. His days of chasing animals were over. We finished near the "Side Cut Locks," reading the history and engineering of the river locks.

Following our afternoon walk, we got back in the car and headed to our hotel. The La Quinta was solid as anticipated. Easy check-in, pet-friendly, and the room had great internet, nice air conditioning, and easy access outside. Through the window, I could see the enormous front lawn. It was also a quick fifteen-minute drive to Toledo. Oscar and I made the trip and walked around Fifth Third Field, home of the Toledo Mud Hens. Along the way, I looked at the baseball memorabilia in windows of the adjacent sports bars and peeked through the iron gates to view the inside of the ballpark. It's a terrific hometown facility. Throughout the time, I kept thinking M*A*S*H's Maxwell Klinger was its number one fan. Also, who picked the Mud Hens' name and why?

We took the interstate back to Perrysburg and found an ice cream place called the O-Deer Diner. We'd return there for dessert. First, we headed to a Mediterranean place called Zingo's. "Can you give me a 'stay'?" I asked Oscar.

A few years ago, Oscar would get excited and want to follow me. One time, I went inside a bar and asked for a dinner menu. As I waited for the bartender, I heard a clanging sound at the entrance. I turned, and with horror, I saw Oscar laboring while he dragged the entire table behind him! "Oh, my God," I reacted.

"Looks like he's rearranging the furniture," the young bartender told me jokingly. "Or, he wants a beer?" Oscar kept plowing forward, trying to join us. "I'll have a waitress bring out some water for him."

Bring Oscar

I checked the outdoor tables at Zingo's. They were wobbly and unattached, but they seemed heavy enough. "I'll be right back." He watched me go inside the restaurant. I anxiously waited in line, regularly peeking out to check on him. I stepped outside twice and waved to him through the doorway. When it was my turn, I quickly ordered falafel and chicken sandwiches then returned outside. "Good job, buddy." He was lying on the ground, watching people walk by—easy.

After our food arrived, I pulled out the chicken and put it on top of his dry dog food. I squeezed some of the flavored juice on top. He gobbled it up, finishing just after I started on my dinner. He looked up at me, so I handed him some of my falafel. I alternated: one bite for me then one piece for Oscar. Damn, he eats his piece faster than I eat mine! We sat in the patio and enjoyed the meal and scenery as people went by.

Before getting ice cream, we walked up and down Perrysburg's main streets. We continued along the Maumee River, looking at the large statue of Commodore Perry and other monuments. Ah, Perrys-burg. I made the connection. Also, I learned a bit about the War of 1812 and its prevalence in Ohio.

We made our way back to the O-Deer Diner for ice cream. I ordered a regular cup of ice cream with a topping. It was enormous. Oscar eagerly followed me and the ice cream. I started digging into the sundae mountain that was spilling over. "If this is a regular, what the hell is a large?!?" Oscar listened and waited for a taste. I scooped some of the cherry topping for myself then picked at the soft serve ice cream with the back of the spoon handle and gave Oscar a lick.

A couple next to us watched. "Lucky dog," the lady said.

"Yes, he is," I agreed. "You have no idea." Oscar just had a chicken sandwich, now ice cream—a happy dog, indeed. Although, I'm not sure what his vet would think.

We sat for twenty minutes, watching the townspeople stop at the ice cream shop for a summertime snack. This was small-town summer living at its best. Around 9:30, the sun was finally setting, so we returned to the La Quinta Inn. I was pleasantly surprised by Maumee, Perrysburg, and Toledo.

PERRYSBURG, OHIO to MONROEVILLE, PENNSYLVANIA

ON OUR WAY out of town, we drove past downtown, along a side road to Fort Meigs, built in 1813 to defend Ohio during the War of 1812. It was a good spot for another brief history lesson, and the open view and large lawn made it a perfect place for a morning walk. After walking around the fort and monuments, I handed Oscar a few biscuits and we were back on the road. Oscar was adjusting quickly to life on the road again. He had some extra enthusiasm that was good to see in him.

Following the map, we remained on the I-80/90, passing through Ohio towns just south of Lake Erie. Eventually, the road split where I-90 east went up through Cleveland to the northeast. Since I had been to Cleveland on two other occasions, we took I-80 east and cut to the I-76 south toward Pittsburgh. We stopped for a driving break and to get gas. As I stretched and filled up the tank, I noticed the substantial gas tax. *What's that for?* I'd likely spend over one hundred dollars extra just to drive on the toll roads and pay the high gas taxes. Doesn't that pay enough for road maintenance?

In the afternoon, we arrived in the outskirts of Pittsburgh. Since it was a larger city, the layout made it tough during rush hour to get into the downtown and find the sites. Instead, I decided to check into the hotel, get Oscar a replacement ID tag—his had fallen off at some point—and grab a light dinner.

Petco was a welcome site for Oscar. He sniffed the aroma of dogs and treats. I kept a close eye on him because he had a habit of suddenly lifting his leg and marking a corner of an aisle. He gave a pause once, but I yanked him along before he could start. Otherwise, there were no incidents or accidents. We went to the machine and printed out a dog tag with his name, my phone, and email. On the way home, we stopped at Penn Station East Coast Subs to pick up dinner. Back at the room, I mixed some chicken with his dog food, green beans, pain pills, and joint medicine. Tasty.

MONROEVILLE, PENNSYLVANIA to EXTON, PENNSYLVANIA

IN THE MORNING, we checked out and found our way back onto another toll road.

"Gotta pay to play," I mumbled as I grabbed the next toll ticket. Our next big stop was Gettysburg, which was two hundred miles away. While Oscar napped in the back, I passed the time by listening to talk radio and a variety of music. We exited I-70/76 and took Lincoln Highway 30 through the rural areas. Although it was slower than the Pennsylvania Turnpike, I preferred winding through the towns, looking at the people, shops, and homes. Also, I could hunt for a lunch spot.

Around one o'clock, we ended up at Pat and Carla's Italian Eatery in Chambersburg. Pizza sounded good, and it proved to be a good choice. There was a wonderful pizza aroma and pleasant people. Outside, there was plenty of room to relax. Mostly, two big slices and a drink for under five bucks was a great deal.

Bring Oscar

We continued along Lincoln Highway 30 into Gettysburg, a remarkable place, full of history. I especially liked seeing first-hand the battlefields and notable areas that are described in Civil War accounts. I had read detailed history books full of facts and events, featuring battle strategies, locations, and notable officers: Lee, Grant, Longstreet, Pickett, Buford, and countless other names. Now, I was standing there and seeing it before me! In many ways, the entire town is a museum. Unfortunately, it began to rain, then pour. On one occasion, I left Oscar in the car for fifteen minutes while I ran out in the pouring rain to see the site of Lincoln's Gettysburg Address, a spot that is not open to pets. Otherwise, we quickly passed through other historical places.

That day reminded me how much the Civil War sucked. It was muggy and humid. Then, it was raining and miserable. Imagine being a soldier in that crap. When I got into my car, I turned on the air conditioner. In the 1860s, there was no air conditioning, not to mention heating in the winter time. Oscar placed his face in front of the air vent. "Yeah, it would've sucked," I said to him.

Oscar at Gettysburg just before it started raining

In just a few hours, Gettysburg made a great first impression. I knew someday I could return to catch parts I missed.

We drove toward Southeastern Pennsylvania, aiming for West Chester, just outside of Philadelphia. The plan was to have dinner and catch up with my old college roommate, Andrew. Beforehand, we checked into the Hampton Inn. While exploring the cable TV listings, I found a message from Andrew. He was delayed at work and asked for a later dinner. The extra time sounded good to me. I skimmed the cable channels until I found an episode of Discovery's *Dual Survival.*

The show features two survival experts who recreate a dire situation—their goal is to get out and find help. This episode involved two hikers who got lost in the Rocky Mountains. The experts were placed in the Rockies with the same supplies as the lost hikers: half a bottle of water, an energy bar, and a small backpack. Then, with a personal knife, the two experts spend a few days (a one-hour show) surviving and attempting to get out of their predicament. The survivalists emphasized the biggest mistake these hikers made: they didn't tell anyone where they were going!

When traveling, I kept these survival tips in mind. Every night, I emailed my mom with the upcoming hotel reservation, so she had a paper trail. If she didn't hear from us in a few days that would be a place to start. In the car, I kept a few bottles of water, some snacks, and energy bars, plus Oscar's treats and dog food. We could easily wait it out for days. Plus, it was summer time, so the temperature would never get too cold, although I did pack a few blankets.

While watching the show, I re-checked email. Andrew left another message with a time and address to meet. When I arrived at his house, his wife and kids were not home, but I did get to see where he lived and the sort of life he's led. We had dinner at a nearby outdoor eatery. It was in a nice, upscale neighborhood. While we spent time catching up, Oscar sat comfortably under the table. Every so often I handed him some scraps off my plate, but mostly, he just rested or eyed the dogs passing by. Overall, it was a pleasant evening for all.

After dropping Andrew back at his home, Oscar and I returned to the hotel. I changed clothes, brushed my teeth, and got ready to go to sleep. Ten minutes later, I heard Oscar wandering around the room. Then, he stood by the door. "Really?" I sat up in the bed, and Oscar seemed to perk up. He needed to go out. I changed clothes, put on shoes, and grabbed his leash and bags. We moved briskly down the hall to the elevator. Ugh, staying at a hotel on the third floor left us at the mercy of the elevator.

"Come on," I urged the elevator. I looked down at Oscar. I looked up at the elevator arrow. Then, I heard the elevator ring. The door opened. As we got into the slow elevator, I could sense Oscar needed to go. I tried to keep him moving. "Hold on, buddy." Second floor.

"Two more to go." First floor. The door opened, and I quickly led Oscar through the lobby to a patch of grass in the front. He stopped just outside the door and relieved himself on the sidewalk. Oh well, he got close. At least, it wasn't in the lobby! I quickly diluted the puddle with some water, and we returned to the room. "Nice job."

EXTON, PENNSYLVANIA to NEW CASTLE, DELAWARE

WE GOT UP late and checked out. At the reception desk, they offered complimentary "breakfast on the go" bags. This was a convenient, thoughtful timesaver, especially with a dog. We were on the road, headed for Delaware.

The previous night, Andrew recommended Rehoboth Beach, mentioning he took his daughters down there from time to time. I love going to the beach, and here was an opportunity. It would be a roundtrip. Drive all the way down there then turn around and drive back the same way. The bad news: It meant driving almost the length of Delaware and back. The good news: Delaware isn't a very large state.

The distance to Rehoboth was about one hundred miles. Halfway down the state, the Air Mobility Command Museum was an aviation museum on the grounds of Dover Air Force Base. We pulled off Route 1 to visit. Outside the museum, there were various memorials, plaques, and aircrafts. Then, at the entrance, I noticed that dogs were permitted through most of the museum! Oscar and

I wandered inside and walked around the displays and exhibits. Then, we went outside, where a variety of retired aircrafts were sitting. It was neat going around the airfield, getting an up-close look at these aircrafts, which included cargo planes, a bomber, and fighter jets. Also, I noticed a plane that looked like the presidential Air Force One.

Since the concrete was hot, we hopped from shaded area to shaded area, pausing under the wings. We couldn't go inside the planes, although I did climb up the stairs and peek into one of them while Oscar waited under the wing. Back inside the museum, there was a bunch of cool exhibits, photos, additional planes, mementos, memorabilia, and history. Also, there was a flight simulator.

Flying high in Dover, Delaware

We returned outside to view a huge fighter jet. Oscar posed in front of the plane, and I shot a few photos of my copilot. At last, we walked over to some 9/11 pieces, POW tributes, and other military items along the lawn area outside. This proved to be a worthwhile excursion.

Oscar was doing fine, so I stuck with the plan to go all the way down Route 1 south to Rehoboth Beach. We walked up and down the boardwalk and watched the people on the sunny beach. I bought lunch, and Oscar picked a sidewalk bench in the shade to eat our meal.

Next, we headed four miles up the road to check out Lewes. This town, pronounced "Lewis," just off the Delaware River, was originally a 1600s Dutch colony. There seemed to be a lot of history, as this location was part of an important waterway flowing from over five hundred miles away. It was interesting to see buildings that were hundreds of years old, starting with the Cannonball House, which was a tourist area and maritime museum. Built in the eighteenth century, the building still had the original cannonball in its foundation from the bombardment of Lewes during the War of 1812.

We stopped briefly at a homemade ice cream shop before retracing Route 1 back north. As hoped, it only took an hour and forty-five minutes to travel from Rehoboth Beach to New Castle where we would be staying for the night. There was a mix-up at the front desk about whether or not I reserved a room that was OK for pets. Fortunately, it got cleared up relatively quickly. I was glad I didn't have to scramble to find another hotel. I was tired and relieved to avoid the hassle. Disaster averted.

I went outside and could see Oscar sitting in the passenger seat in front of the blasting air conditioner. When I reached the running car, I looked through the window. Disaster. During the fifteen minutes it took to clear up the reservation mix-up, Oscar unfortunately lost his bowels and crapped over the entire front seats. F%#k. I had pet cleaner and paper towels, but there was diarrhea in the seat belt and behind the seats. Oh. My. God. There was crap between the seats.

I felt bad for Oscar because he had a solemn look on his face. Poor guy.

I quickly drove the car to the back of the hotel, near our room. Then I frantically started trying to clean up the mess. Scoop up crap. Put it in a bag. Walk sixty feet to a garbage bin. Dump. Then, go back to the car and scoop up some more. (It was like slopping up chunky paint.) Put in a bag. Repeat. I spent forty-five minutes trying to sop up as much as I could. Oscar sat near the car and waited.

I cursed myself for not walking the dog before going into the hotel.

I cursed the online reservation for not confirming the right room.

I cursed the hotel for its mistake, causing the delay.

I excused Oscar. He had a look of guilt, curiosity, and nausea as he watched me work.

What a mess.

I had gotten most of it. But, I jammed my hand with the paper towel in between the seats and came up with bits of brown. It was impossible to get it all. Then, I leaned over to smell the seat. "EWWWW." It smelled like Simple Solution mixed with shit. I began liberally pouring the Simple Solution between the leather seats rather than using a damp rag.

As I was finishing up, I noticed something: "Oh. My. God." Bits of crap were caked on the side of Oscar! I guided him carefully into the hotel room, away from the furniture. Then, I picked him up and put him in the shower. Shit, there was some of it on me now. I cranked on the spigot and started giving him a bath. Then, I dumped my shirt in the tub with him. Eventually, he was clean, I had a clean shirt on, and the car was about ninety percent. I had to accept that some of the stuff was between the seats and impossible to completely wipe out. Oh, shit—literally. I hoped a power vac car wash could get rid of the rest later.

Exhausted, we still had to grab some dinner. We headed outside, and I opened the car door…and, OH MY GOD…it smelled like a sewer. A sewer with a disinfectant scent mixed in. It was gross. I started the engine, rolled down the windows, and went back inside the hotel room to check for a nearby auto place or car wash. Online, I found two possible places.

We drove ten minutes, with the windows wide open—desperate to drown out the smell. Out of habit, Oscar stuck his head out the window, enjoying the wind. And, part of the ride, I tried sticking my head out the window. Then, I put my shirt sleeve over my mouth and nose. Eventually, we reached the address of the auto place. It was closed.

I skipped the other place in order to make this drive as short as possible. I found a fast-food place and ordered the greasiest, smelliest meal imaginable. When I received the chicken and fries from the drive-through, I opened the bag, hoping the chicken aroma could drown out the foul smell.

We returned to the hotel and ate dinner. Fortunately, Oscar seemed OK. This was certainly a full day—full of highs and lows.

NEW CASTLE, DELAWARE to EDISON, NEW JERSEY

I OPENED MY eyes and looked up. Then, I looked down, preparing for the worst. Fortunately, Oscar was lying on his blanket in the same position as last night. I guess we had both slept well. We missed the 9:00 a.m. breakfast deadline. I considered picking up a bag of smelly, aromatic fast food. Instead, I went directly to the auto parts place. I told my story, and the guy recommended "Ozium, to get that new car smell." I followed the can's directions and sprayed a bit inside the car's front seat and backseat areas. While the product worked its magic, Oscar and I went for a walk around the shopping center's parking lot. When we returned, the car smelled remarkably better—a miracle.

We visited a historic district of New Castle where there were cobblestone streets. It was cool to see taverns, inns, and buildings from the 1600s and 1700s. There was the Delaware River and spot where William Penn had landed, and we found a marker citing the point of one of the first railroads—New Castle to Frenchtown—in the 1830s.

After lunch, we made our way to I-95 and headed northeast toward New Jersey. Years earlier, my brother and I had played tourist in Philadelphia: Liberty Bell, a trip to the Vet to watch the Phillies, a cheesesteak. Perhaps, a quick visit with Oscar? We started cruising—for about ten minutes. Then we slowed until we reached standstill traffic, on a Saturday no less. What a mess!

The thirty-mile stretch took two hours longer than expected due to an accident, construction, and traffic. The clear view of the Philadelphia skyline was appealing, but I lost any energy to navigate the city. I just wanted to get out of the bumper-to-bumper traffic. Eventually, we passed Philadelphia; however, the rest of the drive was a long haul as well. Thankfully, Oscar seemed OK, lying in his spot in the backseat.

At last, we reached the outside of New York City, where the skyline of lower Manhattan appeared.

Oscar's first view of New York City

I spent twenty minutes figuring out which exit to take from the several crisscrossing highways: I-95 crossing with I-287 crossing with a local Route 440. What city planner designed these roadways? I circled back, eventually reaching our hotel's town.

Bring Oscar

We parked in the lot of the New Jersey Extended Stay. Like everything else in the east, the room was rather pricey, but much less expensive than New York City. Mostly, after a grinding day on the road, I was delighted to take it easy. Maybe we'll head to Manhattan tonight? At the moment, Oscar was sleeping by the door. "Good idea. Today was a long driving day."

After doing laundry and lounging around the room, I woke up Oscar and rallied. After all, we're a few minutes from New York! We got in the car and went to Manhattan. I took the tollway to Holland Tunnel because it was the closest place to enter NYC. Also, it emptied into Lower Manhattan, a somewhat familiar territory, where I had visited cousins two years earlier.

It cost almost twenty-five dollars in toll fees. Years ago, my friend joked, "You have to pay tolls to get out of Jersey, but you don't have to pay to get back in." After emerging from the tunnel, I drove up and down a few main streets, looking for a pizza place. I'm a big fan of New York slices. But, after driving around for twenty minutes, I lost track of my location and was empty-handed. I found an empty street with free post-6:00 p.m. parking. Incredible. Open street parking in New York for free. After we parked, I saw a guy walking his dog. "Is there any place we can eat around here?" I asked him.

He suggested a restaurant around the corner, "Westville Hudson at 333 Hudson." Oscar and I wandered over there. When we were seated, there was a couple next to our table.

"Hi. Sorry to interrupt. Do you mind the dog?" I asked.

"No, not all," they answered. "That is nice of you to ask."

"I always try to find a spot away from everyone. You never know if someone doesn't like dogs. Or, maybe has allergies." The couple thanked me for asking, and even though he had allergies, the distance was fine. Then we got to talking, for basically the entire meal.

"Are you from around here?" I asked.

"New Jersey," they answered. "We're in town to watch our son's soccer game. It's a big tournament, and he is playing nearby." They decided to grab a quick meal. I learned he worked for Oracle and she was a physical therapist.

"I'm a math tutor," I told them. "I work one-to-one with all ages."

They described their three boys in high school and college. "And, all three are good in math," the lady proudly mentioned. (I get different reactions. Sometimes people recall how they were terrible at math, and sometimes people will say how their kids love math.) As we chatted, Oscar shared some of my meal. Then, he napped next to my chair.

"You have a nice dog," they mentioned. "He's very well-behaved."

"Yes, he's a good one," I answered. "He's probably tired. We had a long day. But, he likes these road trips."

"Where have you been?"

I listed the states we had crossed. Then asked, "Any suggestions? We're driving up to Maine and back around." When you strike up a good conversation and seek information, it's a great opportunity to get places to visit, restaurants, and lesser-known options. Besides Central Park, they suggested Newport, Rhode Island. Then, unexpectedly, the wife said, "you know what place I really like? Lake Placid. It's one of my favorites."

"Hmm, I never considered that."

"Yes, it's beautiful. Mountains in Upstate New York." The evening's chain of events would shape later parts of the trip. *The journey evolves.*

EDISON, NEW JERSEY to MILFORD, CONNECTICUT

"WE'RE HERE." OSCAR'S ears perked up as we pulled up to Central Park West. He could see the activity through the window. The plan was to meet my friend, Jill, and her dog at Belvedere Castle in Central Park. Oscar and I walked around the park, spending about an hour going from 87th to 81st streets. It was a terrific summer day. Not too hot or humid. I've always been amazed by the size of Central Park; miles and miles of valuable, unexploited real estate. And, when you walk into the greenery, it's an escape from the city concrete and noise. As we wandered, I realized there were many sections I had never seen during past visits.

We found the Belvedere Castle, where hundreds of people on blankets were socializing, reading, spending time with their friends, families, and pets. I spotted Jill and her little pup, and we sat amongst the others. Oscar gave Jill's dog a friendly sniff. Then he slid toward Jill's picnic basket and gave a nosey probe of the snacks inside the basket. We caught up on news about common friends in both New York and Chicago.

Afterward, Oscar and I met another friend, Rachel, at 94th Street, where the three of us went to nearby Gabriella's Restaurant and Tequila Bar. They did not allow dogs in the patio dining area, but there were tables lined along the wide sidewalk, so we sat inside the restaurant boundary and Oscar sat just on the other side.

Special reserved seating and eating in New York City

After a particularly nice day in New York, we got back on the road, headed toward Connecticut. Following an exhausting stint of driving, we were greeted by an unfriendly guy at the front desk of the hotel. On top of that, our room was mediocre, and the Internet network was peculiar and untrustworthy. *You get what you pay for—sometimes less.* A road trip has ups and downs, so I just accepted this down part. In the end, it was just one night, a matter of hours.

MILFORD, CONNECTICUT to NEWPORT, RHODE ISLAND

THE NEXT MORNING, we checked out quickly. Time to move on from this bummer hotel. Oscar and I drove to Starbucks to connect to their Wi-Fi network and book a hotel. I selected an inn directly in Newport, Rhode Island, without checking online reviews. It was more expensive than I usually paid, but beggars—in a Starbucks parking lot—can't be choosers. We had a place for tonight.

We left Starbucks and took I-95 toward Rhode Island. Two hours later, we reached the bridge into Newport. Then, as we turned onto Bellevue Avenue, I thought, *Now is the moment of truth: what kind of place did I pick for tonight?* The front entrance looked appealing. As it turned out, the Inn on Bellevue was a charming little place. The young lady at reception was very helpful. After checking us in, she patiently escorted Oscar and me to the second building and pointed out the entrance. While she returned to the lobby, I grabbed my bag from the car. Then, Oscar and I walked into the unlocked room—and saw two cats! We returned to the front desk.

"I'm sorry to bother you again," I said. "I think we got the wrong room. Any chance you could show us again?"

"Of course," she said. "Sometimes it can be confusing."

She kindly walked back to our building and showed me room number one in the "red building." Behind the door was a quaint room with a pseudo fireplace and classic antique furniture. There was a flat screen TV and great Internet. Among the wood floors, Oscar found a comfortable patch of carpeting next to the air conditioner. I placed his blanket next to him. The space was tight, but that didn't matter to us. I posted a five dog-bone rating in my BringFido review.

The Inn on Bellevue was a terrific starting point to explore Newport. We walked out front and started down the main road toward the Touro Synagogue, the oldest synagogue in the US—two hundred and fifty years old. I read the displayed information and history, and then we went through Patriots Park, which was filled with blooming flowers. We continued up the road to an old cemetery. Through the iron fence, I could read some of the Jewish tombstones. Nearby, a placard mentioned Newport's colonial history of religious tolerance. It was fascinating to see US history through preserved items dating back to the 1600s.

It was a pretty hot day, so I decided it was best for us to return to the hotel room. It was also a good time for me to check email and look over Newport sites. In the background, the TV was on a business channel. *Where did he go?* I looked around for Oscar. Not on his blanket. *Where is he??* I leaned over and found him under the bed, sleeping on the cool floor. After our break in our room, we drove down to nearby Easton's Beach, which was recommended by the front desk. It was a beautiful, sunny afternoon, with a clear view of mansions, the beach, and cliffs. Although dogs were not permitted on the beach, they were allowed on the Cliff Walk trail!

We made a short drive to one end of the trail where there was plenty of parking. I collected Oscar's water, the camera, and my MP3 player. Along the three-and-a-half-mile paved path, I could see the Easton Bay and beach below on the left and the large back lawns of the mansions above us on the right. Occasionally, Oscar would take a break to rest or sniff the plants. Sometimes, I'd stop

Bring Oscar

to take a look at the breathtaking view of the water. After walking a little more than halfway, we turned around. "Good walk, huh?" I said to Oscar. Fortunately, most of the path had been in the shade. He seemed pleased.

We returned to the inn, and I struck up another quick conversation with the reception lady next door. "We're looking for dinner. Is there a place nearby?" I asked. "Something that's light."

She suggested a natural foods store, which was a basic market with sandwiches and salads. "It's straight down Bellevue Avenue next to the creamery." Then, she added, "Mondays are buy one shake, get one free." So, that was the plan for dinner—small salad or healthy sandwich for dinner. Then, two milkshakes for dessert!

After dinner, Oscar and I walked to the creamery and joined the outside line. I noticed lots of people carrying two shakes, one in each hand. Some couples split them, one each. And, others were two-fisting. Through the window, I watched the young workers cranking out shakes for the families and teenagers waiting outside.

I asked if I could order two juniors. The girl quickly replied that the two-for-one deal was only good for the large "Awful Awfuls." Yes, that was the name of the shakes! Two was much more than I could finish—but that didn't stop me. I ordered two large Awful Awfuls, one strawberry and one chocolate. The girl handed me the two big cups. "Awful Awful" was printed on the side. (Awful Big. Awful Good). I drank half of each, while offering Oscar sips of the strawberry shake. We agreed: it was awfully good!

We returned to the inn, and on the stairway toward our room I realized I had lost our room key. *Where was it?!?* It wasn't in my pocket. It was an old-school key too, not an electronic card. It had a big tag with #1 attached to it. We retraced our steps in the lobby and back to the car. Eventually, I decided to go back to see if I had left it in the...and yes, there it was...the key was still in the door! Nobody took it or went into our room. Wonderful.

NEWPORT, RHODE ISLAND – Day 2

I LIKE THIS spot!
Whenever we found a nice, comfortable place, I considered adding another day. It was a great way to take a driving break and slow down to enjoy a particular part.

The receptionist looked at the written list of incoming guests and noted there was availability. Even better, we got the same room and no second pet fee.

Oscar and I had breakfast out front on a small wooden table in the middle of the brick sidewalk. It was a beautiful, clear morning. The young lady from the reception desk brought a bucket of ice water for Oscar. I had French toast, fruit, and a cookie.

"You want some of this French toast?" Oscar continued staring at me. After we made eye contact, he stood up, getting excited. "Alright, alright," I told him. "Can you give me a sit?" Oscar paused and then sat for me. "Nice." I tore off a corner of the French toast and gave it to him. He chomped a few times and swallowed. Then he stared at me with anticipation. "That was fast," I said to him.

Then I put out my hand. "Gimme five!" Oscar lifted his left paw and put it into my hand. I rewarded him with more French toast. "You still got it."

Truth be told, I barely trained Oscar, but he picked up and maintained the basics: sit, down, stay (most of the time), and shaking my hand. Most of all, he understood the doggie door and where to do his business. He was a smart dog with untapped potential, but he had a lazy owner who spent little time training him.

"We should take your show on the road. The crowd will love it."

After breakfast, we played tourist, starting at Touro Park, including the Old Stone Mill and the Matthew Perry Monument. Then we visited the Arnold Burying Ground. I didn't see his grandson, Benedict Arnold, the infamous traitor, buried there. After a walk around town and the waterfront, we drove down Bellevue Avenue, looking at all the mansions. Big money...

We reached Brenton Point State Park, located on the southwest tip of Aquidneck Island in Newport. It was a sunny, clear day with a breeze off the water. A few kids in the distance were climbing along the rocks near the shore. Across the street, there was a family flying a kite in the huge grass area. We walked along the rocky, dry lava-like shoreline, watching the water crashing.

I wanted to get a photo of Oscar and me, so I asked two teenage girls who were laughing and skipping by. "Hey, could I trouble you for a photo?" I interrupted them.

"Sure," they said. "You have a cute dog."

"Yeah, he's a good one. But, he doesn't know how to use the camera." They laughed. I handed them the camera, and they followed me along the rocks.

"Thank you so much," I said to them. "I have lots of pictures of him, but every so often I want to get one with both of us."

"Glad to help." They were quite polite.

Brenton Point State Park, Newport, Rhode Island

After a few shots, they handed the camera back to me. "That's a pretty view."

"Yes, and he never takes a bad picture," I added. "Thank you again."

"No problem." They gave Oscar a friendly goodbye and wandered off.

We drove around the inlet and briefly stopped by Fort Adams, a coastal fortification built in the 1790s (and named for President John Adams). We skipped the walk through and went back to Easton's Beach to get lunch. I ran inside a snack bar and ordered lobster rolls and fries. It would be the first meat I had eaten in months, but I wanted to find out if lobster rolls lived up to their delicious reputation. They did!

After lunch and a nap, Oscar and I went for a late afternoon walk. We toured another part of town where there were several quaint shops along a red brick sidewalk. Ahead, I noticed a large green awning with the words "International Tennis Hall of Fame."

Bring Oscar

We crossed the street to get a closer look. Above the entrance, there was a large banner promoting an upcoming tournament. On the sidewalk, there was a sign about the sixtieth anniversary, the Rolex Hall of Fame Enshrinement Weekend, and congratulating the newest inductees, which included two names I recognized: Lindsay Davenport and Nick Bollettieri. In the windows, there were some memorabilia and exhibits.

I learned another piece of trivia today. "Sports cities for 1000, Alex," was the category. "This pleasant town is the location of the International Tennis Hall of Fame."

"Where is Newport, Rhode Island?"

NEWPORT, RHODE ISLAND to STOWE, VERMONT

THE DOWNSIDE OF East Coast driving is the density and traffic, but the cool thing about the East Coast is the ability to blow through multiple places in no time. Today, the plan was to leave Rhode Island, pass through Massachusetts, and make a stop in Nashua, New Hampshire. Then, after lunch, continue to Stowe, Vermont.

We wound our way north past Providence, Rhode Island, and into Massachusetts. Then, we traveled across the state, reaching the border of New Hampshire. After one hundred and twenty miles of driving, we stopped in Nashua. At one of the intersections, I saw a bright, colorful mural of Roy Campanella and Don Newcombe from the 1946 Nashua Dodgers, a minor league baseball team of the Brooklyn Dodgers. *Hmm, I learned something new today.*

I followed the directions to my college classmate's house. I saw Neil and his two kids playing in the backyard. After a tour and introduction to his boy and girl, we drove to a nearby pizza and sandwich place. It was a pleasant day to eat lunch outside. I enjoyed reminiscing about our mutual friends and getting a firsthand look at Neil's Nashua life.

Afterward, we took a walk through part of Mine Falls Park. During the walk along the wooded path, his sweet eight-year-old daughter insisted on holding the leash as we strolled over a bridge and down the way. Oscar had a moment of confusion as I walked eight feet away while the girl held his leash. But then he just went with it, walking with her. After an hour, we emerged at the entrance by the high school, where Oscar and I left our friends to continue to Vermont.

While winding through the mountains on I-89 north, I admired the scenic views—until it started to rain. And, rain. Then, pour. And, pour. I kept cranking the windshield wipers to higher speeds until they were whipping back and forth at the highest speed. It just barely exposed the road ahead of me. This was like someone constantly pouring buckets of water on the windshield. I turned the bright lights on so other drivers could see us. I had no idea if there were cars behind or ahead. There was no space on the road shoulder to pull over. On one side was the edge of a mountain, and on the other side was the traffic going the other way. It was a white-knuckle drive.

After a few minutes, faint bits of lights appeared. Cars and trucks were slowing to 30 mph and flashing blinkers and bright lights. Without anywhere on the road to pull over, we just drove and hoped for the best. Suddenly, there was a turn-off to a scenic view. It was a relief to get off the road. In the parking lot was a sign about free Wi-Fi. I pulled out my laptop. Incredibly, the site had tremendous Internet Wi-Fi, even during the bad weather. As I finished checking messages, Oscar climbed into the front seat. He looked anxious. "You want out, don't you?" I grabbed his leash, and we stepped into the pouring rain. We trotted over to a picnic area with an overhang. It was only twenty yards, but we were soaked. Oscar sniffed, found his spot, and then released a long stream.

I tried to dry Oscar off with one towel I'd packed and put the other on the front seat. After quickly helping Oscar into the passenger seat, I raced into the driver's seat. I took off my wet sweatshirt and changed into a dry shirt. As soon as I finished putting on dry clothes, Oscar shook his body, spraying water all over the place! "Now you do it?!?!" He looked at me, climbed off the towel in the front seat, and climbed into the backseat. "And now you're going to mess up the back seat?" I laughed. He plopped down and started to close his eyes. "Nice." Despite the mess, there was an upside: I just got a free power wash for the car. However, the car also now smelled like wet dog. Hey, maybe that'll be the new scent of the day. We've gone from Oscar's diarrhea in Delaware, to Ozium new car smell in Rhode Island, to wet dog aroma in Vermont. I cracked open the windows and resumed driving.

Within an hour, we turned onto Route 100 and reached Stowe and the Commodores Inn. It had a classic ski resort interior that was welcoming. Nice guests staying at the inn walked past us, looking kindly at Oscar. And, the staff was very friendly, mentioning they had dogs at home. After checking in, the lady gave me a big key. Down the hallway was room 201, conveniently next to the elevator and a soda machine. Despite the possible noise, I didn't mind rooms next to the elevator or vending machines. It's helpful for going in and out with Oscar or for making quick trips to get a snack.

While in the parking lot retrieving our belongings, I made eye contact with a guy unloading his car. He looked like Philip Seymour Hoffman. He nodded. "How y'all doing?"

"Good. Just got here."

"Nice dog."

This was an opening to ask a few questions, natural curiosity and for information. "Are you visiting or from around here?"

"I grew up here," he answered. "I live in Virginia now."

I leaned over and noticed the Virginia license plates.

"Visiting a few friends. Gonna do some fishing," he continued. "How about you?"

"Just driving around the country," I started. "First time in Vermont; planning to check out Stowe, and hit Burlington tomorrow. Any suggestions?"

He recommended places in Burlington: Church Street Marketplace, the waterfront area, and Battery Park. "All of them are fine for the dog." He added, "Try Beansie's Bus. The locals eat there."

I wrote them on a piece of paper for tomorrow. He reminded me to try the maple syrup too. He informed me that real maple syrup has no sugar and should be frozen. Plus, he mentioned that Vermont permits only local syrup to be sold. You learn something new every day.

During our conversation, he mentioned owning a B&B. I wrote down his information. Perhaps, we'll need a bed-and-breakfast in Virginia? "Thanks for the ideas," I said as we headed to the inn's lobby. Stowe, Vermont, was off to a good start.

Next, we were off to check out the Commodores Inn's restaurant, Lighthouse Bar & Grill. It had sort of a casual dining/pub/yacht club atmosphere. There was a patio, but since it was wet outside, I did some investigating inside the bar. Graciously, Pierre, the bartender/manager, invited Oscar in with me! We sat at a table near the bar. We encountered a dad and two kids eating dinner, but they all liked dogs, and I spotted our Phillip Seymour Hoffman friend sitting at the bar with his wife. Otherwise, since it was off-season, and rainy, most of the room was empty.

Dinner was quite good, especially the cream soup. And the chicken was a winner for Oscar. The cook even cut the chicken into strips for Oscar. All in all, this was a terrific place. Afterward, we walked past the bar's popcorn machine, skipped the dart board, and returned to our room.

STOWE, VERMONT – Day 2

THE ROUTE TO Burlington was direct, and we were headed somewhere unique—the "World's Tallest Filing Cabinet." I thought it would be easy to find a towering structure, but it took a bit of perseverance. After driving back and forth, and then asking someone, we found it. It was in a side neighborhood, on an empty lot, surrounded by shrubs, weeds, and vegetation growth. The attraction was definitely one-of-a-kind, and weird. Thirty-eight filing cabinet drawers stacked on top of each other, reaching about fifty feet into the air. Yet, it was an interesting photo op. I took a few shots from a distance. Who thinks of this stuff? Was it some random artist making a statement about the office workplace? Or, was someone just trying to unload a surplus of old filing cabinets? There must be some significance.

Oscar and I strolled through the brush to the base of the tower. The drawers seemed permanently shut, and the cabinets had a bit of rust on them. It was certainly not a maintained exhibit. After sniffing in the weeds, Oscar joined me at the large concrete platform. Then he sat and waited while I took photos of him next to the tower base.

Just another day at the office...

We continued to Lake Champlain, stopping in a perfect space next to Battery Park. I started looking for Beansie's Bus, and thankfully it didn't take long to spot the bright yellow bus. I stepped under the shade of the awning to look at the basic menu. Grilled cheese, French fries, and a soda seemed suitable. As we waited for our order, I peeked at the clever set-up inside the bus. The seats were removed and replaced with kitchen items, a sink, refrigerator, and other cooking features found in a typical restaurant. A very efficient use of space. It reminded me of the food trucks in New York.

After our delicious lunch, we walked up and down Waterfront Park. It had a beautiful view of Lake Champlain, as well as some monuments and memorials. A plaque read "Battery Park: Scene of British Attack in War of 1812." *Wow, the War of 1812 again!* That conflict extended over a large territory. We had seen it referenced our first night in Perrysburg, Ohio, then in Lewes, Delaware, and now in Burlington, Vermont. *I need to retake US history.*

We continued along the pleasant streets around Burlington Center, leading to the Church Street Marketplace. Just outside of town was the Ethan Allen Homestead Museum. Allen was an early inhabitant of Burlington and a folk hero of Vermont. During our brief visit, Oscar and I passed a cool wooden bridge, the restored farmhouse that Ethan Allen built, and other parts of the property. I learned that he was a farmer, writer, and politician, as well as a soldier during the Revolutionary War. "Ethan Allen is more than a furniture store!" I joked to Oscar. Our family had some Ethan Allen pieces in the living room. In fact, there were German Shepherd chew marks in a few of the table legs.

On the way back to the inn, we made a quick detour to the Ben and Jerry's Factory. It was unlikely that Oscar would be allowed inside, but it never hurts to see if there are photo ops, statues, information boards, or other outdoor items. Plus, it was just off the highway. We could be in and out in no time.

We parked in a giant lot and ended up walking around Ben and Jerry's Flavor Graveyard, a place memorializing retired ice cream flavors. The discontinued flavors on tombstones included Turtle Soup, Wavy Gravy, Tennessee Mud, and White Russian. Near the entrance, I took advantage of a photo op with Oscar sticking his head through a Ben and Jerry's ice cream board. Although we couldn't go inside the factory, it was worth the quick visit to this notable Vermont spot.

Hoping for a dog flavor

Our last stop was the Cold Hollow Cider Mill, which was advertising "legendary cider donuts."

"Hmm, I've never had those before," I thought out loud. "And, if they're 'legendary,' then they must be good!" Since the place was large, I assumed there were other Vermont items. I browsed through the bakery, maple syrup, cider, and other specialty products. I came out with donuts and the best apple cider slushy. (OK, I'd never really had one before, but this frozen treat was delicious.) We checked out the old cider presses and looked at some of the items for sale. Then we sat at a bench outside and enjoyed the snacks. "What a day!" I said to Oscar. "We saw a lot of stuff, huh? You and I would kill it on *The Amazing Race!*" We had zigzagged through a variety of niche spots, and we did it in a rather short amount of time. I imagined Phil Keoghan greeting us as we checked into the Vermont pit stop.

When we returned to the Commodores Inn, Oscar and I took a quick stroll near the pond in the back. Several canoes stacked next to the calm water added to the serene atmosphere. Back inside, cookies and refreshments were waiting for us in the lobby—I liked this place. So, I requested another night.

STOWE, VERMONT – Day 3

TODAY WE HEADED out to find the Sterling Gorge Falls. Following the one-hour morning hike, we drove around the Stowe area. I found the Vermont Ski and Snowboard Museum and Hall of Fame. I wasn't sure if I'd recognize any of the inductees, but I appreciated the niche and the nifty bits of history and trivia. In the late afternoon, we stopped at the Pizza Joint at the Schoolhouse Store. Yesterday, we were eating lunch from a yellow school bus. Today, pizza from a converted schoolhouse! Decorations included a few classroom desks in the waiting area. The pizza was OK, but the view from the porch, and the conversation, were terrific. The nice owner had been in Stowe for twenty-five years. He had an old dog and provided an extra bowl and water for Oscar, as well as the chicken I purchased.

We returned to the Inn and were greeted by the lady at the front desk. I picked up complimentary lemonade and fresh baked cookies on the way to the room. While I watched TV, Oscar worked on his chew treat. The end of an easy reset day.

STOWE, VERMONT to BANGOR, MAINE

ALMOST TWO WEEKS into our journey, we had checked off several states, including new ones: Delaware, Rhode Island, Vermont, and New Hampshire. Today, we would reach Maine, my forty-ninth state, and using a rough estimate, Oscar's thirty-fifth. While leaving the hotel, I grabbed two more fresh cookies for the road and looked down at Oscar. "Commodores Inn was a good one!" He wagged his tail as we exited.

After an hour of winding through countryside—and passing antique stores, maple shops, and ice cream stops—we arrived at St. Johnsbury. I had read an article about a "dog mountain" with a "dog chapel." This was a must-stop.

We took a gravel road through a residential area, ending at Dog Mountain. Then, we drove up the steep hill to a parking area. At first glance, Dog Mountain and Dog Chapel could be described as a mecca for canines and sanctuary for dog lovers. There were statues of dogs, plenty of space to run around, and outstanding views of the Vermont green scenery.

Oscar and I wandered into the chapel, encountering wooden pews (with dog carvings) in front of decorated stained glass. On the side, there was a board describing the site's history and mission of its late founder, Stephen Huneck. On the walls were hundreds of pinned notes and posted letters. Mixed in were countless photos and tributes to dogs that had passed away. I looked down at Oscar and was thankful that he was still around.

Oscar inside Dog Chapel, St. Johnsbury, Vermont

I proceeded into the sanctuary for a closer view of the stained glass dog images and other colorful mosaics. Meanwhile, Oscar seemed interested in a three-foot wooden dog statue sitting at the entrance. I stopped to read a few dedications and considered leaving my own handwritten tribute. Instead, I just fondly remembered the many dogs our family had had over the years. Outside, there were several animated dog statues next to a "No Dogmas Allowed" sign, an opportune place for a souvenir photo. This was truly a one-of-a-kind place.

As we drove across upper New Hampshire toward Maine, we saw all sorts of pretty scenery. That's the great thing about road trips: it really is about the journey as much as the destination. There are plenty of little bonus places between the main attractions. An hour later, we reached a terrific scenic shot of the Androscoggin River, just before crossing the state border.

A quick stop along Route 2

We resumed the drive alongside the river, searching for a snack stop. I was hungry again, and Oscar can always eat. We pulled into a Gulf gas station next to an Italian market that sold pizza, pasta, and subs. *That should work.* "I'll be right back. Going to get us some vittles." I ran into the market and bought a sub sandwich, ice tea, chips, and a whoopie pie—a popular Maine treat. I skipped their blueberry pastries, having learned the ripe blueberries were one month away. After our snack break, we continued driving on US 2. Just ten minutes down the road, I found Rumford Falls, with picnic tables and a view! That would have been a pleasant place to eat outside. Oh well, it happens when a trip is improvised. We looked around and found a dedication to former Secretary of State Edmund Muskie, an enormous lumberjack statue, and a tribute to a native tribe from the region.

We followed US 2/ME 100 east all the way to Hammond Street in Bangor, Maine. I followed my written directions and laptop screenshot maps to the Motel 6. After dinner, I noticed there was a washer and dryer. I had a roll of quarters and a leftover mini-box of detergent in the car. This will work.

In the room, I began to outline travel around Maine. I skimmed over attractions and hotels in every surrounding area, but I couldn't find an economical option for us. Maybe we'd use Bangor as a base and just drive back and forth? After searching the Internet, I decided to delay my decisions and book another night at Motel 6. I was buying some time at a cheap price.

I expanded the online map on my laptop. Oscar and I had just about reached our turnaround point!

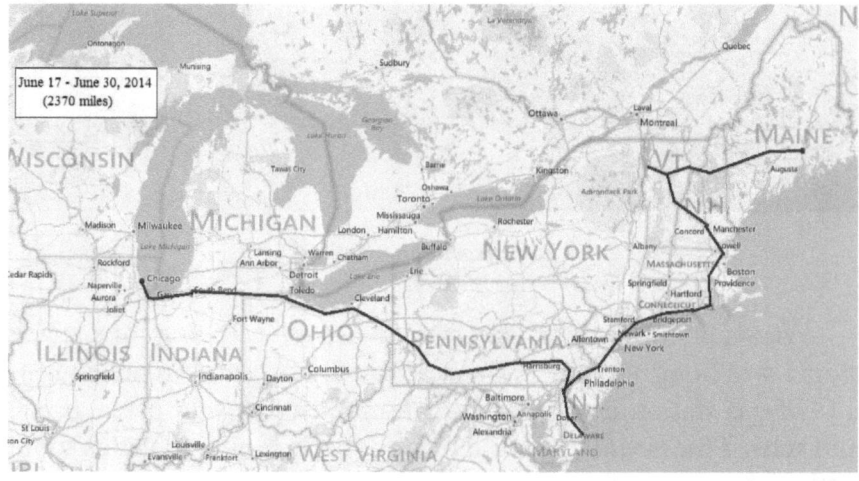

BANGOR, MAINE – Day 2

IN THE MORNING, we headed down the road to find Stephen King's house. It was a weird, touristy thing to do. Part of me felt a bit intrusive going to the guy's house. But, part of me felt it was OK, because the residential address was published, and the house itself was far back from the street. In the end, we weren't the only ones. Random people parked in the residential area, came down the sidewalk, and peeked at the famous house. Most took a picture at the entrance, an iron gate with spiders and creepy adornments, which verified it was the horror author's residence.

I asked a mother and daughter from Virginia to take a photo of Oscar and me, then I returned the favor. Not much else to see. No chance Stephen King would come out in his robe and slippers to say hi. So, we walked back to the car, cranked up the air conditioner, and headed for the highway.

Bangor to Bar Harbor was one hour by car. The town of Bar Harbor can get filled with visitors. It gets especially crowded when a cruise ship or the tour buses arrive. But, there is plenty of open hiking around Acadia National Park. And, I found simply driving around the surrounding area was easy, with plenty of spots to pull over and get a terrific view.

We drove up the winding road to Cadillac Mountain, the highest point on the East Coast. That makes it the first spot in the United States to see the sun's first light appear each day. At the top, Oscar and I got out to see the spectacular viewpoints overlooking Bar Harbor and Frenchman Bay.

View of Frenchman Bay from Cadillac Mountain, Acadia National Park, Maine

We returned to the main town, parked, and started looking for a place to eat. I fully expected the meal to be expensive—market price for lobster—but hey, I was saving a bundle on the cheap hotel room. We were ready to splurge. We ate lunch at Stewman's Lobster Pound, which served some of the best lobster I'd ever had. Two pounds steamed in a pot with melted butter, corn on the cob, and fries. Best of all, they seated us in a terrific outdoor location. We had a view of the harbor and pleasant temperatures from the cross-breeze. On the way out, I took a few pictures to capture the moment, including a touristy shot with Oscar sticking his head through the Stewman's cartoon lobster board.

Following a fantastic lunch, Oscar and I walked around the town a second time, peeking inside the shops. At the end of Main Street, we reached a large grass area facing the harbor and picked a shaded spot to take a break and enjoy the breeze off the water. We watched the tourists walking, eating ice cream, and sitting in the park. Suddenly, I noticed an older lady and her twenty-five-pound black dog: It looked like a mini-Oscar!

"Oh, my gosh, look at your dog. It looks like mine!"

"They're like brothers," she agreed.

"What kind of dog is that? I've always wondered what the exact breed is."

"It's a Schipperke." It was half the size, but the face and mannerisms were exactly the same as Oscar.

"I see some gray under his chin, like my dog. How old is yours?"

"He's sixteen years old."

"You're kidding," I said. "I hope my dog gets that far. He's fourteen." Since Oscar was part Shepherd and Lab, and larger, I recognized his life expectancy. But, you never know.

"These dogs can get up there. Our last Schipperke was eighteen years old."

"Wow."

A moment later, the lady's husband showed up and introduced himself. He, too, noticed the dogs' similarities. "It is remarkable." We observed the two dogs, sitting side by side. They literally were looking in the same direction, with the same gaze. Identical, like a little brother.

BANGOR, MAINE – Day 3

WE STARTED THE day off going to the Paul Bunyan Statue. That made two giant lumberjacks in three days. Oscar and I walked up for a photo and closer view of the thirty-one-foot-high attraction. It was erected in 1959, Bunyan's 125th birthday. Apparently, Paul Bunyan and the logging industry may have been born in Bangor. But, with folklore, other towns are making the same claim.

Next stop was lunch, but first I had to find Oscar some more water. Every so often, I would stop to pour water into my cupped hand, giving Oscar a drink—until the bottle was empty. Now, he had to gut it out during our unexpectedly long trek. At last, the Penobscot River appeared in front of us. And, along it was the River Walkway. Best of all, there were food trucks in a parking lot by the river. Yet, no water fountain in sight—strange. We went down to the first food truck. They had sandwiches and sodas, but no water. Really?

"Don't worry," I said to Oscar. "We're getting close." His tongue was hanging out, but he pushed on with me.

We walked to the next one. There was more food but only expensive bottled water. "Someone's truck must have a running water hose." I tried a kettle corn guy, but no luck. Then we went over to a wood-fired pizza truck called Pompeii Pizza. "You have any water?"

"Bottled water?" the lady asked.

"Any chance you have tap water for my dog?" I showed her my empty bottle.

"We do. Nice dog." The lady filled the bottle. Then she came out with a plastic bowl of water. Oscar immediately dropped his face into it. Heaven! "It's a hot day for him," she said. "Let me get some more."

Lapping up water from Pompeii Pizza

To repay them for the water, I ordered a margherita pizza and a Coke. We sat in the grass and had our picnic lunch. The pizza was delicious. Meanwhile, people wandering by the river came over to greet wet-faced Oscar.

"Hot day for him," they would comment.

"Yes, the black coat isn't helping," I said. "But, he's a warrior."

After thirty minutes, Oscar was alert. Replenished with water and pizza, he was good to go. Plus, getting attention from people around us provided an added boost. This area proved to be a pleasant oasis.

When the folks at Pompeii Pizza finish serving the lunch crowd, I walked over to give them a quick compliment and to thank them again for the water. They asked about Oscar, where we were from, and our journey. Then, I learned about their business, the family's investment in this mobile pizza oven, and the other brother's truck in another part of town. These were likable, down-to-earth, hard-working people.

Following a stroll around the waterfront, we bought some ice cream and sat near the pizza truck. One of the sons from the pizza truck asked if we wanted a ride back to our car.

"Really? You don't mind?"

"Glad to. I'm heading home. I'll drop you off on the way."

"And, it's OK if the dog goes in the backseat?"

"Not a problem. I'll bring the car around."

A few minutes later, the kindhearted guy drove up. Oscar and I got into his two-door Honda. I explained that we were parked near a bakery and bagel shop in the Main Street area.

"I know exactly where you're at."

After two miles and a shortcut through side-streets, we spotted the Nissan. "This is very nice of you. We're definitely grateful. You saved us a long walk back!"

Two days later, I left glowing online reviews. "Pizza was terrific. Service was outstanding. Red carpet treatment from the people at Pompeii Pizza in Bangor." I hoped their family business would become a smashing success. Since then, I have returned to Bangor. The brick oven place was in the same spot. The son who gave us a ride was still there, and he remembered Oscar and me!

In the hotel room, I cranked up the air conditioning. While Oscar rested, I gathered a bag of dirty clothes and dropped them in the washing machine down the corridor. Then, I checked email, booked the next hotel, and started exploring possible places to visit. Meanwhile, we still had a few hours of daylight. I decided to try the Rock Solid Disc Golf and the Big Bang Boom Fireworks shop in nearby Holden.

Bring Oscar

The disc golf was cool. The course ran through the woods with receptacles and markings. I paid the five-dollar greens fee to try it out. It had been many years since my days of ultimate Frisbee and Frisbee golf in college. I heaved the Frisbee into the calm air, and the toss sliced hard to the right. I trotted over to the terrible landing. I threw the Frisbee for my second shot, and it overshot the other way. I jogged to my next position. Meanwhile, Oscar just watched me running around. Then, he went back to sniffing the trees, grounds, and whatever past critters had left. Then, my third shot. Then, fourth shot. Eventually, I closed in on the first hole. Oscar was wandering behind me. At last, I landed the disc inside the basket. On to hole number two.

The second hole was deeper in the woods. My second score was slightly better than my first. As we began the third hole, I realized we were going deeper and deeper into the woods. There was no way we were doing all nine holes. Between the wandering in summer temperatures, lack of a breeze, and carrying Oscar, thirty minutes of disc golf was enough. I returned the Frisbee to the shop then took a quick look at the fireworks next door.

Inside the fireworks shop, I got a bit of Maine militia flavor. The place was filled with fireworks of all types, prices, and sizes. Damn, the stuff was more powerful than the old days of bottle rockets and sparklers. Plus, the shop had videos, so you could see what the firework would do when lit. Pyros in the twenty-first century!

BANGOR, MAINE to LINCOLNVILLE, MAINE

MAINE IS A tremendous place to drive, whether it's along the coast, or winding through quaint towns. It's appealing, with lots of temptation: it seemed every ten minutes there was a turn for ice cream or a stop for lobster rolls or a candy shop. It's tempting to try them all! But, there's only so much room in my stomach.

One notable place was Red's Eats in Wiscasset. A few people had mentioned it having the best lobster rolls. "Worth the drive and worth the wait," they told me. So, I saved my appetite, and we drove out of our way to find out. The US 1/Maine 27 passed over the Sheepscot River and became Main Street, entering the middle of Wiscasset. On the right side, there was a line of people wrapped around a small building. Red's Eats.

We joined the line next to some easygoing people. "Nice dog," the couple said to me. "He's so well-behaved."

"Yeah, he's a good one. A bit old, so he's mellow."

"How old is he?" they asked. "Fourteen years old."

"Oh, my! He looks like a pup." Oscar looked up at them, enjoying the attention.

"Nah, he's getting up there in age." I gave Oscar a friendly massage on the face and ears. "See, he's got the white whiskers on his chin."

It was around eighty degrees. A young woman from Red's Eats came over and asked if we wanted a bowl of water. I showed her the bowl in my hand. "Can you pour some in here?"

She did, and Oscar gulped it up. She offered snacks to the people in line. I took the garlic bread, but passed on the other items, saving my appetite for the good stuff.

As the line slowly moved, I noted the food people were eating in the patio area. Damn, it looked good. Also, I read several news articles and awards posted on the wall.

"How long is the wait?" I asked.

"It takes about an hour," they conceded. "But, it's worth it. Best lobster rolls anywhere."

I looked across the street. There was another lobster shack, probably with the same menu. Only four people stood in that line. Hmmm.

"Well, we came all this way," probably stating what others were thinking. "So, we're gonna wait." If I had two days, I'd try the other place. But, we were just passing through.

"Where are you from?"

"Around Chicago," I answered. "My pal and I wanted to see the East Coast."

"Wow, that's far. Does he like being in the car?"

"Loves it. And, he's a great companion."

The line inched forward, while a family walked past with their food. The lobster rolls were piled with meat that spilled over, and they had fries and other sides. We had been in line for thirty minutes. To be honest, waiting with Oscar wasn't a big deal. Several people came over to greet us, so the time passed rather quickly. The lady returned with more water and a few more snacks. We were getting close.

Waiting for our feast in Wiscasset, Maine

We rounded the last corner, approaching the menu and ordering window. So close! Oscar sat right in the middle of the people in the shade. Ten minutes later, I reached the window and ordered. Lobster roll with melted butter, fried zucchini (I could tell myself that I was eating a healthy vegetable), and a Coke. It was around twenty-five bucks. At this point, it didn't matter. Two thousand miles, one hour in line, hungry—cost was irrelevant!

Five minutes later, the lady in the window presented our food on a tray. I took our meal and picked up Oscar's leash. We ambled past the line along the back patio. Incredibly, there was an open table in the corner where a family had just left. We grabbed it—a shady spot for Oscar to sit out of the way of the other customers. My mouth started watering as I started setting up the lunch.

At last, we dove into the lobster roll, piled with meat pouring out of the bun. It was outstanding. Also, the zucchini dipped in sauce was tremendous. Yes, it was worth the wait. Oscar gobbled the bits of lobster that I handed him. "Yes, you're a lucky dog! Who in their right mind would share lobster with his dog?!?!" Oscar looked up and waited for another piece. What a life! Just lying there on the ground, not having to move, while I'm handing him lobster and fries. Happy dog. We enjoyed the pleasant weather, great food, and a shaded spot to sit. It was probably the best lunch I'd ever had.

Afterward, we walked around town, viewed the large nearby river, and ended at a local ice cream shop. Why not? Oscar waited by a bench while I went inside to pick out a couple of scoops to try. After the final snack, we backtracked on US 1, heading northeast toward the coast near Camden, Maine. An hour later, we arrived in Lincolnville, Maine. We turned off Atlantic Highway 1 into the Bay Leaf Cottages, which had offered a dog-friendly place at a decent price. The cottage exteriors and grounds were very appealing.

During check-in, the lady greeted us and made a point to go over the rules about leaving the dog alone, keeping the dog leashed, and using dog areas. "And, no dogs on the beds, please," she specified.

"No problem," I said. "He's mellow." We had a casual hotel routine, but could work within strict guidelines of these premises. We just needed a place to relax, check the Internet, and sleep.

In our cottage, the living room had quaint furnishings and a welcome bag for Oscar, which included extra dog treats and a blanket for dog guests. On a card was written, "Please keep pets off the furniture and beds." It was a reasonable request. The linens and covers appeared to be special, homemade quilts. In fact, I think the furniture and bedding were too nice for me, let alone my dog!

LINCOLNVILLE, MAINE to BOOTHBAY HARBOR, MAINE

TURNS OUT WE were perfect cottage guests. There wasn't one stain or dog hair in the entire room. Shortly after that realization, I went online and found an email from Miguel, my young pal watching the house. "There is water in your basement." Oh, no. I opened a weather webpage and saw the heavy rain in Chicago. That's not good. But, there wasn't much I could do; we were over one thousand miles away. I walked outside onto the porch of our cottage. The ground was damp. "Looks like it rained here, too. No wonder we slept so well last night." I caught the smell of the ocean! And, the cool breeze. Nice.

Bay Leaf Cottages was a good spot. It reminded me of going to Grandma's house. She loved having the grandkids—but don't mess up her nice furniture!

Oscar joined me outside. "Your dog cannot be in the room alone," I remembered hearing yesterday. "And, keep him on a leash, so he doesn't disturb any guests."

Bring Oscar

"He's always with me," I assured her. "He doesn't run very far anyway."

During the first month I had Oscar, he ran away three times. Yes, despite the nice home, backyard, and fantastic chicken-filled meals, he slipped out of the backyard three times! The first time, I received a call from a random person saying they had found my dog. I was horrified, as I drove from work to their address as fast as possible. I thanked the lady, who was quite gracious.

"Oh, he's very nice. We were happy to let him run around in our backyard." They lived one mile south of my house. Back home, I inspected the backyard and found a small hole dug into the dirt under the gate. It seemed there would be enough room to squeeze out. So, I poured bricks and dirt to firm up the area. Problem solved...

...Until a few days later, I got a call from a man. "My kids found your dog." I raced to their house, where I discovered that the kids had torn off Oscar's tags. They were hoping their father would let them keep a random dog they had found. Fortunately, the father figured it out and demanded that they give him the tag with Oscar's info on it. They lived one mile east of my house. Back home, I inspected the backyard around the entire fence. How did he get out? I added a few barriers here and there, but I'm not sure it was the solution.

The following day, I got a call from a nice lady. "Did you lose your dog?" she asked.

"Oh, my gosh!" The damn dog ran away while I was working at home! The backyard was empty. "Where did you find him?"

"I'm at the park, and he just ran right up to me," she answered. "I didn't want him to run away, so I'm just playing with him." I grabbed the leash and raced out the front door. This time, he was three blocks west of my house.

Oscar was playing with the lady at the park. She was standing next to her car. She saw me running with the leash and waved. Oscar wagged his tail when he saw me arrive. For him, it was all a party!

We returned home. I needed to figure out how he was escaping. I walked along the entire wooden fence that surrounded the backyard, looking for digging marks. I pushed on the wooden gate, and it popped open from the latch. Aha. I solved the mystery! Oscar was pushing on the gate until it popped open. Then, he would run away. Moments later, when the wind blew, it would push the gate back into the latch and close it! Then, I'd look outside and see an empty backyard with a closed gate. It was quite a disappearing act.

I looked at Oscar standing beside me on the hotel patio. "How 'bout a quick walk?" I suggested to him.

After enjoying the complimentary breakfast, we traveled fifteen minutes along the coast into Camden to visit Mount Battie; in particular, the one-hundred-year-old Memorial Tower. From the parking lot, we walked along a path toward the tower. I could see people standing at the top of the forty-foot stone structure, enjoying the view of Penobscot Bay.

At the bottom, I read a plaque above the entrance, which described the history of this tower dedicated to World War I veterans from Camden. Inside, I saw a concrete spiral staircase.

"Take a load off," I said to Oscar and asked him to sit. He set himself down in the shade. "Here's a treatsie. I'll be right back." I raced up the circular stairwell to get a look from the top. After taking a few pictures, I trotted back down.

Afterward, we took Mount Battie Road to another part of the Camden Hills Park. We found a trail that reached a bench after emerging from the trees. We had a beautiful view of the Maine shoreline. For twenty minutes, Oscar and I just sat on the bench and enjoyed the breeze off the coast. We followed the shoreline trail, getting other glimpses of the rocky coastline. When we were finished, we resumed our journey in a southern direction, traveling along US 1.

"Wait a sec," I said to Oscar. We stopped at the Mount Battie Take Out & Ice Cream along the roadside. Decorated with cartoon lobster images, the snack bar included a menu of Maine coast offerings, burgers, and ice cream. We sat in the lawn chairs, ate their blueberry ice cream, and watched the summer visitors go by.

Leaving Camden, we had a pleasant drive along US 1. At the fork in the road, we turned south onto ME 27. In the afternoon, we reached Boothbay Harbor. We followed the road along the water to our hotel, Cap'n Fish's Waterfront Inn.

It was a pretty location, a tad out of town, away from the crowds. Our room was a bit musty, but that seemed understandable since we were by the coast. Oscar and I headed out to the waterfront to view the harbor, boats, hotels, and condos. We took an old wooden bridge to get there, passing the "Footbridge 1901" sign. In the horizon, I could see a woman paddle boarding. It was a pleasant summer atmosphere.

We did some exploring and browsing. I passed a t-shirt store and saw a fudge and taffy shop. The fudge seemed touristy expensive, but the taffy was intriguing. Through the Daffy Taffy doorway, I asked, "Is this homemade?"

"Yes, it is," the lady answered.

"Let me find a place for my dog. Then, I'll come back and—"

"Well, bring him in!" she said.

Inside, there was a long boat filled with taffy. I was careful to keep Oscar's nose out of everything. I picked a variety of flavors. Although I had no intention to eat it now, I wanted to buy something and support the shop. *Business 101 lesson: inviting a dog can be good for sales.*

Actually, I bought a bunch of candy, partially because sweets are my weakness, but especially because of the lady's good nature and welcoming attitude. "That was so nice of you to invite us inside," I told her. "He likes to browse."

"Glad to have you," she answered while putting the items in a bag. She gave a friendly smile toward Oscar. As it turned out, the taffy did taste good. And, I had plenty to eat during the rest of the road trip.

BOOTHBAY HARBOR, MAINE to PORTLAND, MAINE

I CHECKED THE Internet connection. Nothing. Shipwrecked at Cap'n Fish's. Luckily, last night I had enough connectivity to book tonight's room in South Portland. After some donuts, fruit, and juice in the lobby, we backtracked north on ME 27 to Wiscasset. (If it wasn't 9:30 a.m., I might've done another round of lobster rolls at Red's Eats.) We turned onto US 1, a Blue Star Memorial Highway, and started southwest toward Portland.

The first planned stop was Yarmouth to see Eartha, the world's largest rotating globe. We pulled into the parking lot, and in the distance, I could see an enormous globe displayed in the building. Eartha's shadow was looming in the window. It was massive. I set Oscar on the sidewalk in front of the building for a photo. Although he seemed uninterested, he sat for a few pictures, providing perspective about the size of this globe.

Where's Oscar? Sitting in front of Eartha!

I wanted to get a closer look. Since pets were not allowed inside the map store, Oscar waited in a spot under the shade. "Gimme five minutes," I promised. He didn't seem to mind. I hustled into the map company's building to check it out. I discovered there was a museum about Eartha and the employees who built this fifty-six-hundred-pound item. It was a cool (and free) exhibit that had structural statistics, history of its construction, and the Guinness World Record Award. Yes, indeed, the "world's largest world." *Is that possible?*

A few minutes later, we stopped for lunch. I think if I lived in Maine, I'd be tempted to permanently give up my vegetarian ways and eat lobster rolls and ice cream every day.

I remembered Maine was notable for lighthouses. After checking into our hotel in Portland, we took an opportunity to visit the lighthouse at Fort Williams Park called the Portland Head Light. The area had plenty of dog-walking space. We passed through the Battery Blair, a fortification built in 1903 and manned during parts of World War I and World War II. There were memorials, tributes, and historical information. Then, beyond it, we got our first view of the lighthouse. It reminded me of layouts I'd seen in travel magazines. I took several picturesque photos, including the coastal shore and fog.

Oscar and I walked up the path to get a closer look. I learned the Portland Head Light was the oldest in Maine, dating back to the 1790s. Also, it's one of the most visited and photographed in the country. No doubt, it was a scenic lighthouse view!

PORTLAND, MAINE to MILFORD, MASSACHUSETTS

OSCAR'S COLLAR RATTLED at 5:20 a.m. *He's up.* Sometimes, the summer light comes too damn early. I put on my shoes and shuttled him down the hall. Once outside, he immediately did his business. A yellow stream, followed by three instinctive hind kicks of dirt to cover his tracks.

"Good job, Oskie."

After walking around the hotel lot, we returned to the room. I checked online messages, looked at today's route and attractions, and fell back to sleep. I woke up again at eight o'clock. Oscar was sound asleep, with his tongue sticking out and a funny expression. I crept by him and snuck out to check the breakfast room. The waffle maker was appealing. There were juices, cereals, fruit, and store muffins. However, the hotel was adamant about not taking food out of the breakfast area, so I downed a muffin and jetted back to get Oscar.

Just outside of Portland, we stopped at Len Libby Candies to peek at what was touted as the "Home of the Life-Size Chocolate

Moose." Yes, *moose*, not *mousse*. "Lenny" was a seventeen-hundred-pound milk chocolate sculpture that took four weeks to create and carve. It was a five-minute stop at a candy shop along the road. It may not have been spectacular, but it did satisfy my curiosity.

Two hours later, we reached the Boston area. We passed Fenway Park and weaved by Symphony Hall where the Boston Pops play. After some driving, I parked the car next to a big park with statues. "This will work," I said out loud. "It looks historical." It was raining, so I put on a thick shirt and light jacket. Oscar and I walked around the border of the park, looking at statues and tributes to history figures. The rain continued, which meant no pictures. I didn't want to damage the camera. That was disappointing.

I take a lot of pictures. My dad once asked why I took so many. "What are you going to do with them?"

"I'll look at them."

"You really go back and look at the photos?"

"Actually, I do," I answered. "Not all the trips. But, from time to time, I'll look at a batch of photos. The memories and details immediately flood back to my mind. It's like going back there."

"Hmmm, I never thought of that. Makes sense."

Also, I maintained a brief digital journal with notes and a timeline. I kept receipts and wrote down significant items. If I ever wanted to return to a location or offer recommendations, I'd have it written down. The photos were souvenirs, and I get a kick out of seeing Oscar in front of Rushmore or under the St. Louis Arch, but mostly, I like to capture the memories for a later time.

For this particular afternoon, the weather was bad timing. Without a map, I had found a parking space right next to the Boston Common, parks, and the Freedom Trail. We were exactly where I wanted to be! There was even an off-leash portion of the park for dogs. If only the weather were more suitable.

I called my mom to give her a travel update and to get the Boston forecast. She looked online, and it showed rain all day. "Then, it's time to go find the hotel." We found the La Quinta in Milford, about 35 miles from Boston. I parked in the lot, grabbed my wallet, and reached for Oscar's leash. *Where is it? Damn.* I realized the leash was sitting on the ground by the Boston Common.

I had set it down when I lifted Oscar into the car. Unless nobody touches it for fifteen hours, it won't be there tomorrow. My brother had made that thing many years ago. It was a great tie-up leash that Oscar had had for ten years.

After bringing the bags into the room, I took out the laptop, hooked up the Wi-Fi, and started checking messages. Meanwhile, Oscar wandered around the room. He walked past his water bowl and took a sip from the toilet. He sniffed the curtains and under the beds. Suddenly, I looked up and saw Oscar pause. He was leaning forward on his front legs. Uh-oh. He looked at me with a sly smile, and then he starting relieving himself. "No!"

I leaped out of my chair. Unable to move him without shooting the streaming everywhere, I reached over, grabbed a towel, and threw it under him. He kept peeing. He had a look of sensational relief. How long was he holding it? Why didn't he go when we were outside? At least it didn't happen in the lobby.

When he finally finished, I started my rapid clean-up. I threw the towel into the bathtub, doused it with shampoo and soap, and soaked it in the water. Then, I pressed dry towels and cloths onto the wet carpet. I dried most of it and then threw the washcloths into the sink. Oscar sat and watched me at work. I don't think he realized what he had done, or maybe he did. He was nearing fifteen years old, so maybe he just couldn't hold his bladder like he used to?

"Wait here."

I raced out to the car to grab Simple Solution and paper towels. When I returned, he was sitting in the same position.

"No problem, Buddy." I sympathized with the old guy. "I got this." I sprayed the Simple Solution on the damp spot. The scent in the room immediately changed. "All good."

Since Petco was still open, we made a quick trip. We explored the aisles, reading the boxes, prices, and leash lengths and fabric. I kept one eye on Oscar. He sat and watched—so far, so good. After picking out a leash, we continued through the store, passing toys (Oscar's a big fan) and chew snacks. In the dog food section, I looked for Oscar's normal brand. It wasn't there. I started reading ingredients of alternative bags. Out of the corner of my eye, I watched Oscar sniffing and sniffing. Suddenly, he paused and lifted his leg. I yanked him. Damn, he left a trail of yellow drips on the floor. "You're killin' me." I moaned as I looked at the yellow arc on the tile. "Aren't you dried out yet?" We walked to a nearby cleanup station and grabbed some towels and cleaner. Then, walked back and wiped up Oscar's mess.

"Are you happy?" I looked at him. He didn't care. Marking territory was business as usual. I found a bag of dog food, and we went to the check-out.

"Nice dog," the cashier said.

"Yes, he's a good one," I answered. "Except for five minutes ago," I mumbled.

"Does he want a treat?"

"Maybe," I answered.

The lady reached over. "Can he sit?"

"Oh, yes, he can." I turned. "Oscar, sit." With an eye on the treat, he sat down. I reached out. "Gimme five!" Oscar put his paw in my hand.

"Very good," the lady said as she handed him a biscuit. Oscar dropped it on the floor. I picked it up and put it in my pocket. Oscar rarely ate treats at Petco until after we left the store. We walked out with a new leash and a bag of dog food. Damn, dog items are expensive here.

Back at the hotel, I found out the laundry room was free for guests. And, they provided complimentary detergent. Nice. Milford seemed to be a good choice to dry off, rest, and regroup. Mostly, we were saving over one hundred dollars per night by staying thirty minutes outside of Boston.

MILFORD, MASSACHUSETTS - Day 2

PREPARED WITH PRECISE directions and a map, we went from Milford to Boston. We took I-90 to I-93 north and onto side roads through Chinatown. Then we popped out into Boston Common, near our stop yesterday. One thing I became good at was familiarizing and figuring out areas. After driving through once or twice, I recognize landmarks and surroundings.

I parked, and I did check—Oscar's leash was gone. We revisited areas and monuments that we had seen already; but, instead of pouring rain, it was picture perfect. Oscar and I walked some of the Freedom Trail. Then, we continued to the Holocaust Memorial Park, where six fifty-four-foot glass towers stand. It's an incredible place with history, symbolism, sadness, and aspiration.

Since we only had two hours in the meter, Oscar and I turned around, made a quick pass along Boston City Hall and the Faneuil Hall Marketplace area. Then, we raced back to the car. The meter had expired, but no ticket. After an Oscar water break, I scooped up some coins from inside the car and refilled the meter for another two hours.

We toured around the parks some more and found a place to rest. After a thirty-minute rest, Oscar and I started for the Charles River. It was getting warmer outside, so Oscar took advantage of a puddle from yesterday's rain. He waded through the puddle, sipping some of the water. Then, he stopped and plopped down into the water, submerging his undercarriage. Oscar loved to cool his belly! He just sat there like a swan in a pond.

A family walking by, who watched this event unfold, was smiling and laughing at Oscar's spectacle. "He found a cool spot, huh?"

"Yeah, he does that," I told them. I let Oscar enjoy his spa. After a minute, I gave a slight tug on his leash with an encouraging, "Let's roll!" He popped up with puddle water dripping.

We walked down Charles Street past the restaurants, past the shops, and past a park. After another four blocks, I asked a young woman, "Where is the Fiedler Footbridge where we can see the river?"

"Who is Fiedler?" she asked. "He was conductor of the Boston Pops—long time ago."

"Oh." But, to her credit, she was super-nice, typing the location in her iPhone and pointing me in the direction of the Charles River. "Take the Esplanade along the Charles River."

I looked at her phone. As it turned out, we were near a different bridge. "Oh, my God. We were looking at the wrong bridge on the map."

"That's Boston," the young woman said matter-of-factly.

We walked over the Longfellow Bridge, around the Charles River Esplanade, and reached the Fiedler area. There it was: a cool, giant bust of the acclaimed conductor. The sculpture was interesting because it wasn't chiseled. Instead, it was constructed by layers of concrete. The strata of different sizes created the face of Arthur Fiedler. It reminded me of pin art.

A canine maestro sitting next to the legendary Boston conductor

After a rest, we made our way back to the car. We made it back before the meter expired. I had wanted to see the Boston Tea Party Ships & Museum, but I had already dragged Oscar around for over four hours. That was enough for one day. The Boston Harbor isn't going anywhere. One mile past our hotel, we grabbed take-out from Thai Pepper. Ten minutes after cleaning out his bowl full of dog food, green beans, and teriyaki beef, Oscar was asleep beside the bed.

MILFORD, MASSACHUSETTS – Day 3

"OY, OSCAR. YOU got *schmukis* on your eyes." I took my thumb and wiped the crust around his eyes. He seemed pleased. "Hungry for some vittles?" His ears perked up. I trotted down the hallway and returned with our breakfast. While snacking on the meal, I handed Oscar scrambled eggs and wrote down places to visit. I made screenshot copies of maps and directions from the Internet and saved them onto my laptop.

We started at the Milford Upper Charles Trail, specifically looking for the Vietnam Mountain Biking Trail. I asked a few people, but nobody knew. I guess I should've done better research. I never did find the path. However, we did meet a guy from the neighboring town, Hopkinton. He explained where the Boston Marathon starting line was located and what to look for. "Check out the Hopkinton State Park," he added. "It's a good place to bring the dog."

We drove to Hopkinton and found the Boston Marathon starting line on a quiet street, near the library and civic buildings. I took a closer look at the faded starting line on the street, which, I imagined, they'd repaint for the next race. "Pretty cool, huh Oscar?" He was sniffing the grass by the park. I took photos of the starting line and the life-size bronze sculpture of a man in an overcoat preparing to fire a pistol to begin the marathon. "Remember when you used to race?!" Oscar looked up at me and wagged his tail.

After the marathon starting line, we drove to nearby Hopkinton State Park. After paying five bucks, we entered and learned that the park was indeed enormous. I found the area we wanted: boat loading ramps where dogs were allowed! We stood before the large reservoir. Off to the right was a place to rent paddle boats, and straight ahead, a few dogs were wading in the water. Owners were sitting in the cement area, getting some sun. Farther out, dogs happily swam around. This was a great suggestion!

I let Oscar wade in the water, while I stayed off to the side. Gradually, I let out more slack from the leash, and he went deeper into the water. Soon, he was actually playing in the water! I remembered his years of swimming and running at the dog beach. When he was younger, we would get into the Acura and drive to the lakefront. As we passed through downtown Evanston, Oscar would perk up, sticking his head out of the window, eager with anticipation. When we reached the parking lot near the water, he got ready. As soon as I opened the door, he was off! He would trot and sprint a quarter of a mile, zigzagging around pedestrians, straight to the dog beach entrance gate. I would jog after him, holding his leash and latex ball, until reaching the entrance where he was excitedly waiting. When I opened the gate, he'd sprint on the sand to the water.

We went to the Evanston dog beach regularly. Sometimes, I'd take him in the winter time. I would be freezing my ass off as the wind from Lake Michigan blasted my face, but Oscar loved it. In the summers, he would run up and down the shoreline or chase the ball or swim out in the distance to snatch balls. Aquadog! He was great at retrieving. Whenever I noticed another dog had lost a ball, or there was a ball bobbing in the distance, I would point to it, then Oscar would look and enthusiastically go get it, retrieving the stranded ball in the middle of the open lake. It was impressive.

Oscar's become a bit bigger and stockier than those days, but he was still able to battle. It reminded me of a retired boxer going back into the ring. He clearly recognized the water, swimming, and frolicking with other dogs. At one point, he stood on the deck in the middle of the water, overlooking a yellow Lab swimming back and forth. He debated whether to jump into the water or stay on the deck. He went around.

Oscar enjoying the action at Hopkinton State Park, Massachusetts

The other owners were very generous. One of them, a tattooed guy in his twenties, was swimming with the dogs and happily let Oscar play along, even allowing him to swipe one of their dog's toys. Although he couldn't keep up with the quick dogs and swim out to retrieve the ball, Oscar was truly enjoying himself! I was delighted to watch him and the scene of people paddleboarding, kayaking, and swimming. Very cool spot. This was a terrific moment.

We hiked back up the paved road and got in the car, rolled down the windows, and drove off. As we passed the south end of the reservoir, Oscar had his head out the window, smiling, and enjoying the view—and perhaps, remembering his days long ago when we went to the lake.

Afterward, we aimed for Newton, Massachusetts. I had printed an email my mom had sent last week.

We were back to Chestnut Hill (Newton) in 1971–1973, the address is: 12 Acacia Ave.

It is one house from the corner, and across that street is the football field of Boston College....The corner house was for the Jesuits....We used the swimming pool at the College during the summer....One day, you slipped and fell on the part around the pool, and I think we never went back....Ha-ha!

I remembered the public pool and getting stitches on my head, plus a few other images from my early childhood. But, I was still curious to see where we had lived forty years ago. I found Acacia Avenue. Interestingly, everything seemed small. When I was six years old, the street we lived on was so far to the main road. It was so far to run down the street to my friend's house. But, it was just one block. When I returned to my home in Phoenix, I had the same reaction. The street, which seemed so far when I was young, wasn't that big after all. And, Madison Meadows Middle School had a huge field where we ran laps during PE, but it wasn't as large as I remembered.

We returned to the hotel room with two bags of dinner. Oscar devoured his meal while I ate my salad. I uploaded pictures taken today and sent a few of them to my Mom. I'm sure she was curious to see what the old house we lived in looked like. I looked down, and Oscar was sitting beside me. I leaned over and saw the chicken strips were gone, but the dry dog food remained in the bowl. "That's a weak effort!" I joked. I put a few more strips in his bowl.

"What do you think?" I said out loud. Oscar just sat and looked up at me. "Should we check out Lake Placid?" I looked from there and noticed Buffalo and Niagara Falls. "Why not do all of Upper New York?" Oscar seemed to approve.

I always wondered what Oscar was thinking. He liked swimming in the lake. He liked his treats. And, he enjoyed our walks. I could guess what he thought while staring at my dinner.

What about the big questions? If I had a wish, I'd ask for twenty-four hours to talk with Oscar. He could answer my questions: What do you do all day? Where did you come from before I adopted you? (The rescue had said he was a stray found on the streets.) You walked right up to me at the shelter—did you know you wanted to go home with me? What happened with that vestibular disease? Is it still painful? Did I do a good job with you? There were many unanswered questions. But, during dinner, I knew what he was thinking. So, I shared my meal.

MILFORD, MASSACHUSETTS to ALBANY, NEW YORK

THE SPOT FROM Oscar's accident was completely gone. We departed the La Quinta Inn and drove down the road to the Granite Gulf gas station near the Wendy's and I-495 entrance. They had a free air filling station, so it was worth filling the leaky tire and checking their auto shop. A local who was waiting said the place was good, so I took his word for it. One of the young mechanics checked my car quickly. Unfortunately, it wasn't a simple patch. "It's the wheel sensor. It's corroded, so there's a leak."

"Ugh, this has happened before."

"Yeah, the salt and corrosion from the winters will do it."

"Well, I gotta replace it," I sighed. "How much?"

"About two hundred bucks to replace it with parts and labor."

The cost wasn't too bad. The bigger concern was time. "Can you guys get it done as fast as possible?" I hoped. "I got the dog with me."

"We can replace it in no time," he assured. "We just have to get the part."

"Alright."

Another guy waiting for his car overheard our conversation. "Don't worry," he said. "These guys do good work."

They seemed on the ball, and the cost was reasonable. In the end, it was better to get this fixed now rather than worry about the air in my tire every few hundred miles. So, Oscar and I made ourselves comfortable.

While we sat in the waiting room of the gas station, I recognized the opportunity. I had a brief conversation with a local Boston guy and listened to a few guys talk about the Red Sox with thick Boston accents. It was all part of the traveling experience.

After a couple of hours, the mechanic returned. "You're all set."

"Really?!"

"Yep," he said. "As soon as we got the part, it took no time."

"Fantastic." I was thankful that the car was repaired quickly, and more importantly, it was fixed rather than being stranded on the road somewhere with a flat. Problem solved!

On the way to New York, we were going to pass Springfield, Massachusetts, home of the Naismith Memorial Basketball Hall of Fame. I had been a diehard Phoenix Suns fan, and I loved playing and watching basketball. So it seemed worth a stop, even if Oscar couldn't get inside the museum. Perhaps, there would be notable statues outside?

After an hour, we pulled off the I-90 Turnpike and winded along I-91 into Springfield. There was a big tower with a basketball at the top next to a huge museum, which was visible from the highway. There was a marquee, strip-mall type sign with "Basketball Hall of Fame" at the top. Below it there were a list of places, including LA Fitness, a tavern, a pizza place, a Mexican restaurant, and even a Subway. I thought I'd find an ornate building with monuments in front; instead, it was a large parking lot in front of a mall-like set of buildings. When I was a kid, I dreamed of visiting the Basketball Hall of Fame. Now, as an adult, I just didn't have the same excitement.

I cranked the air conditioner for Oscar and ran inside. I could see large displays and NBA-type banners but realized it was too much to see in a few moments, so I turned around and returned to the car. Oh well.

We searched for lunch, landing in a seedy part of Springfield. Strike one. Then we found an appealing pizzeria, but it was closed on Mondays. Strike two. Then we drove straight to the Quadrangle where the Dr. Seuss National Memorial Sculpture Garden was located. We found a seemingly nice place for lunch, but while we waited for our food a guy came over and said dogs were not allowed on the premises anywhere in the Quadrangle.

"Really?" I looked around and did not see anyone within hundred feet of us. So, wide open park space, not permitted. The guy gave us the evil eye, so I started scooping up Oscar's water bowl. Strike three. "Geez, nothing is easy today," I mumbled. "Springfield, Mass. was a disappointment for our hero and his canine companion," I announced.

Oscar and I moved on to Albany, New York. We got out and started exploring a three-block area. The Egg, a performing arts center that was built in the 1970s, was very cool. It was shaped more like a spaceship-type saucer than an egg. Definitely unique, and it stood out. Also, the New York State Capitol building was impressive, particularly the enormous set of stairs behind the General Philip Henry Sheridan Statue. In Oscar's glory days, we would've trotted up to the top. But, in his golden years, we opted to walk around the building.

After forty-five minutes, we went to The Waterfront on the Hudson River. I scanned the area. It seemed seedy. Great potential, but weirdos were hanging out there. Maybe we were in the wrong section? Oscar had his head peering through the window. "No, buddy," I told him. "I don't think we want to walk around here." So, we left for the hotel.

I followed a screenshot from Google Maps. While navigating through the unfamiliar town, I wondered if relying on the search engine's map was a mistake. It was taking a long time. We were headed into the ghetto, and I sensed it was all wrong. I locked the car doors, stopped on a side street, and called the hotel's 800 number. It went to a corporate switchboard.

"Do you want the direct number to the Best Western?" the guy asked. *No shit! What other number would I want? Why didn't they put the direct number on the website?* I politely responded, "Yes, I'd appreciate that."

After writing down the number, I called the Best Western in Albany. "Hello," a lady answered.

"I think I'm lost or have the wrong address," I started.

"Can you hold on a minute?" After waiting five minutes, I hung up and tried again to find the hotel myself. The neighborhood started to get a little bit nicer, but there wasn't a single hotel in the area. After fifteen minutes of frustration and wasted time, I needed serenity. We stopped at a gas station. I filled up the tank and called the hotel again. "Hello," another lady answered.

This time, I got a person who could help! She asked for my location. I mentioned the corner street sign and the gas station. She recognized it, and then she explained that I was on the right path. "Keep going down the road," she assured me. "The Best Western Sovereign Hotel - Albany is in a suburb of Albany. It's about fifteen minutes from the downtown."

"Ah, it's on the other side of town."

At last, we made it. After fixing a tire this morning, getting kicked out of a park at lunch, and getting lost in Albany, this was not our best day. After checking in, Oscar and I went to our room on the second floor in the back. I was too worn out to hunt for a dinner spot, so we tried the place next door, 1228 Grille. While eating, I recharged the electronics, checked messages, and watched a bit of television. I looked forward to tomorrow's adventure, hoping it would go smoother than today.

ALBANY, NEW YORK to LAKE PLACID, NEW YORK

AFTER A BRIEF overnight stop, we continued driving to our primary destination: Lake Placid. It was a bit out of the way, but it was a must-see recommendation from our dinner companions in Manhattan. At the very least, I wanted to see the location of the 1980 Olympic "Miracle on Ice."

As we drove north on I-87, kilometers and French translations appeared on some of the road signs; also, an occasional Canadian flag. We were close to the border! In fact, one sign indicated that the road to Montreal was about an hour away. Ugh, if I had brought my passport, we could've made a detour to Canada.

Driving through Upstate New York was wonderful. I was reminded that New York is much more than New York City. We drove through miles and miles of undeveloped mountains and forest preserves. Although, during a stretch, a McDonald's Golden Arches sign extended above a tree line. Now that's marketing!

Eventually, we reached the "Welcome to Lake Placid" entrance. Then, to the right, towering in the air, stood the bobsled run. They offered summer bobsled rides! I'd seen these at amusement parks and overseas, but this one was a former Olympic site. I looked at the business hours and price. Then, reality set in. There was no way a two-man bobsled would become a one-man/one-canine bobsled ride. I wasn't going to leave Oscar in the car, so we passed. But, it did leave a lot to the imagination: Oscar and I shooting down the bobsled run!

We arrived in downtown Lake Placid, along Mirror Lake. Great call! It was awesome: pretty views, sports history, and a charming town. We drove past the shops and restaurants, eying potential places Oscar and I could explore. At the end of the main road, I spotted the Lake House at High Peaks Resort. Our room proved to be a perfect retreat. It looked out to Mirror Lake, with an extensive grass area in front for Oscar. On the wall, there was a poster listing the "46 High Peaks of the Great Adirondacks." Our room was named after the twentieth highest peak: Rocky Peak Ridge. I was glad I didn't skimp on price, having selected a more expensive spot with a lake view. The fifty-dollar flat pet fee was steep, but after a couple of days, the average price became quite reasonable. Regardless, I overlooked the cost. Sometimes, it's best to splurge for a one-time trip.

"Ready to get rollin'?!" Oscar popped up, excited to explore Lake Placid. We walked out of the hotel, down the hill—taking in the terrific view of Mirror Lake—and right to the main street. I found The Good Bite Kitchen, which appeared to be a vegan / vegetarian café. The tiny place had a wait of one person, plus a slight view from the counter, so I tied Oscar to a wobbly table and went inside.

I chose a veggie, quinoa, bean, nut dish with a blueberry drink. As I ordered, I could see the passing people give Oscar a gentle pat on the head. He was enjoying the attention. Overall, he seemed quite content to sit and wait and save a seat for me. Our meal was tasty, healthy, and under ten bucks. Perfect.

We continued walking along Main Street, and I took some pretty shots of the Village of Lake Placid. Then we got to the Olympic stuff. No doubt, this was the reason for the visit. We started outside the speed skating oval, where Eric Heiden won five golds in 1980, and the ice rinks that featured Sonja Henie, who won figure skating gold in 1932. Very cool.

There were some great photo ops, including a faceless Olympic skater, where you could stick your head through. I picked Oscar up, and poked his head through the hole as two girls helped us out—one taking the photo, and the other laughing at us!

Oscar training near the Olympic Village in Lake Placid

After clowning around, we continued to the Olympic ice rink, site of the US Hockey Team's Miracle on Ice. We found the entrance to the classic 1980 rink. Of course, no pets were allowed. I looked around and spotted a corner area with a handrail attached to the cement ground. This would work.

I hate leaving Oscar out of my view. What if someone came by and took him? Or, what if the police saw a dog and took him to animal control? Maybe I should have left a note next to him. The road was on the other side of the building. There appeared to be little to no pedestrian traffic. I looked at my watch and gave myself three minutes. "Wait here, buddy. I'll be right back."

I darted inside and ran toward the stairs. I took one last look through the window and saw Oscar sitting in the shade, enjoying the view. Then, I sprinted up the stairs and down a hall where I spotted an entrance to the Herb Brooks Arena with a massive photo of the iconic Miracle on Ice Olympic hockey team celebration. I walked through the painted doors, and there was the rink. Above were banners of past hockey stars hanging from rafters around the rink. Below, there was a group of ten young skaters using the ice. I had the same impression as other observers: Considering how incredible this sports moment was, the actual arena wasn't very large!

After one minute of shooting photos and appreciating the history, I ran back out into the hallway and down the stairs. When I reached the atrium, I could see Oscar sitting and waiting. I went down the last set of stairs, walked out the front entrance, and returned to Oscar. He looked up at me and gave a mild tail wag. "That wasn't too long, was it?" He didn't mind. "Your turn." I got to see the rink; it was time to find something for Oscar to enjoy. "Where do you wanna go?"

We turned around and started heading up Main Street toward the hotel.

Later in the afternoon, we went back into town for live music, a weekly summer offering from the village. The small amphitheater didn't permit pets. Instead, Oscar and I stood above at a spot overlooking Mirror Lake. Nice atmosphere. Oscar enjoyed meeting others and basking in the attention. We met a nice family from Hershey, Pennsylvania. They said they liked Oscar, and as was often the case, they missed their dog at home. It started raining and the crowd scattered. Then, it began pouring. Thankfully, it had waited until the evening!

LAKE PLACID, NEW YORK – Day 2

AT 6:00 A.M., Oscar rumbled around the hotel room. We walked through the sliding door onto the enormous lawn. We had a cool morning and a pretty view of Mirror Lake. Oscar did his usual business: some leaks, some smells, some yawns. Then, we went back inside and back to sleep.

After waking up again, we walked down the hill, along Main Street, to the Crepes place from yesterday. I ordered the banana and Nutella crepes. The food was delicious. In the adjacent deli, there was a sandwich list—forty-six sandwiches matching the forty-six peaks in the Adirondacks area—which looked tasty. We had a lunch plan for later.

Following breakfast, we headed to the Brewster Peninsula Nature Trails. We reached a spot with a long, dirt path. Do we start walking and see what's at the end? Then, we have to turn around. Or, just skip it? After weighing pros and cons, we took a pass. I'd prefer to just go back to town and walk around the shops and lake; lots of dog and people watching seemed better for us.

We went back to the Big Mountain Deli & Crêperie, this time for a sandwich. I looked through the window and saw a line of people. Well, not much choice. I wanted to try this place. Oscar waited on the sidewalk while I went inside to buy lunch. The first customer ordering was excruciating slow. I routinely stepped out of line to peek out the window. One time, a young girl approached Oscar. I shouted from the doorway, "It's OK. He's friendly." Then, I went back to my spot in line.

A few moments later, I stepped out of line and peeked outside again. A few adults were looking at Oscar. I went to the doorway and shouted, "He's good. I'm just getting us lunch." No, I'm not a bad owner who leaves a dog outside while shopping and eating inside.

The lady smiled. "He's a gorgeous dog! So, well-behaved."

"Yes, he is!" I replied. Actually, he's a well-behaved old dog. Ten years ago, he would've ripped out the post holding him in place. Now, he's content to calmly sit and wait.

I went back in line, then out of line for another dog check. Fortunately, the fifth time I looked outside, there were three young girls entertaining Oscar! They saw me in the window and waved. I waved back and smiled.

At last, I reached the cashier, and ordered a sandwich. "And, can I get a side of chicken. I got my dog outside." The guy cut up chicken strips. Then, he labeled it grilled chicken for three bucks. "Three dollars—is that fair?" It was more than fair. It saved me from ordering something else and picking off the chicken.

While waiting for the rest of my order, I watched Oscar through the window. People continued to stop and pet him. Some had dogs, and some didn't. But Oscar was great—well-behaved and making friends!

After I collected my sandwich and "Oscar's chicken order," I asked the guy if he was the owner. He said it was a family business. That makes sense. Great service, nice people, everyone pitching in.

I went outside with lunch and greeted the crowd standing around Oscar, playing with him and taking pictures.

"Sweet dog. What's his name?"

"Oscar."

"He's a cool dog. Friendly."

"Yeah, he loves people," I added. "Thanks for keeping him company." I was delighted.

"Glad to. Bye, Oscar," waved one of the little girls as she walked away with her parents.

I collected the celebrity, and we went across the street to a bench.

After finishing the sandwich, we walked back to the hotel. It was slow going because Oscar had to smell everything. There were tons of dogs here, so the scents must've been everywhere. In addition, Oscar stopped for a drink at every complimentary bowl of water.

"What is this, a doggie pub crawl?"

Following a two-hour nap, we enjoyed our last walk through town, taking in the scenery and picking up dessert. Lake Placid had been a terrific stop. Plus, multi-day stops are fantastic resets, taking a break from driving and using the extra time to relax and explore without any rush.

When we returned to the room, I looked at sightseeing attractions and printed maps for tomorrow's drive. I also skimmed over my credit card account to check hotel charges. After three weeks, we were over budget. But then I uploaded terrific photos and wrote some notes about Lake Placid and realized, yes, it has all been worth it!

LAKE PLACID, NEW YORK to ROCHESTER, NEW YORK

AFTER ONE LAST view of Mirror Lake, we loaded up the car and checked out. Refreshed for another stretch of driving, we began with another scenic tour through the Adirondack Mountains. Green trees, small towns, and although there was only one lane, we moved nicely down Route 3. Bonus: The weather had cooled off, which was a comfort for Oscar. In fact, we drove with the windows down for most of the time. The 4-40 air-conditioning method worked splendidly.

We passed through a succession of towns, starting with Saranac Lake. A few days earlier, I had considered this less expensive option, but I'm glad I decided to spend the extra money and stay in the heart of Lake Placid. Next, we paused in Tupper Lake, which was similar to others with pizza shops, ice cream, a church, and boat rentals. We continued winding through Route 3 until we stopped at Harrisville to see a "scenic spot" that wasn't all that scenic.

Thirty miles later, we neared Watertown. Using my printed maps, we managed to get to our target in the middle of town. There weren't many signs, it was sort of crowded, and weird people were loitering. Yet, at the corner, there was Cam's Pizzeria, an inviting place with typical New York slices. Oscar and I shared two cheese slices while sitting on the bench in front of the shop.

I had vague written directions, so getting to Oswego was, at times, precarious. But we managed to connect to Route 104 and trekked to Oswego. I had chosen Oswego along Lake Ontario rather than Syracuse south on I-81. First, we stopped at a little rest place with a map board of the Lake Ontario area. That's when I realized we were near Niagara Falls! Maybe we would go there tomorrow? Afterward, we went around the Fort Ontario State Historic Site, which offered a bit of history as well as an outstanding view of Lake Ontario. Then, we walked to the nearby Safe Haven Holocaust Refugee Shelter Museum where I learned about the nine hundred and eighty-two mostly Jewish refugees who were invited to stay at Fort Ontario from 1944–46.

Just outside of Oswego, we made a brief stop at Ontario Orchards—a bakery, fruit, and vegetable market. I picked up a few pieces of fruit and a fresh-baked muffin for later. Then, it was a straight drive along Route 104 to Rochester, New York. Ninety minutes later, we arrived at the Hampton Inn. While unwinding in the room, I heard a screeching sound. I sat up and saw Oscar near the corner of the room next to the light cord. He didn't, did he? I took a closer look and realized he had chewed through the cord and shocked himself. "Nice going, Dr. Frankenstein. What are you doing?" *Every day, dogs do things that are funny, stupid, and gross. This one goes under half stupid and half funny.*

During his first year with me, Oscar loved chewing on things— except the eight-dollar PetSmart toys. He ignored those, but he loved my shoes and socks. Plus, I learned months later that he chewed the bar under my wooden coffee table. I always thought, *Wow, I have the best dog. He hasn't wrecked the furniture (like our other dogs used to).* Then, my brother pointed out, "No, look under the table." It was lined with chew marks. It's no wonder Oscar's teeth started to chip away. He chewed on the table, rocks, and tree branches.

Oscar stepped away from the outlet next to the lamp cord, and he timidly sat on the other side of the hotel room. "Yeah, that was a bad idea, wasn't it?" I told him. Fortunately, the light still worked.

ROCHESTER, NEW YORK to SOMEPLACE, SOMEWHERE

DURING A TRIP, I typically take advantage of hotel offerings, such as fruit, snacks, or bathroom items. I don't steal towels, but I also don't see anything wrong with collecting leftover soap or shampoo. After all, the hotel won't reuse my half-empty mini bottle of shampoo. I tried a flimsy toothbrush, which was slightly better than my dead electric toothbrush, and a free razor that nicked my neck. It was a noble effort. The Hampton Inn offered a complimentary laundry facility next door, but I wanted to get to Niagara Falls. Instead of a two-hour delay to do laundry, Oscar and I hit the road. After a ninety-minute drive on I-90, we followed the signs to the waterfall. It was definitely a cool site, but not as great as my first visit. Fifteen years earlier, I went with a Toronto friend to visit Niagara Falls from the Canadian side. It was a better view, and it wasn't as developed and commercialized.

Today, on the New York side, there were touristy shops, a casino, expensive parking, and crowds of people. Across the water, I could see tons of hotels. Maybe Ontario had done the same? Another negative, on the New York side, we couldn't get an unobstructed front view of the falls, except from the observatory. On top of that, dogs were not allowed. Nevertheless, it was worth the tour detour. We got some exercise and photos before moving on.

Top-shelf view of Niagara Falls, New York

Our next stop was Buffalo. We drove along the eastern tip of Lake Erie—quite scenic. When I first think of Buffalo, I imagine cold weather and snow, but on this summer day, it was sunny, warm, and clear. We made a stop to see the "Monty the Therapy Dog" statue. It's a bronze sculpture of an English Setter that served as a therapy dog. Oscar and I found a spot near Monty to take a break. As I snacked on my bagel from the Hampton breakfast, Oscar looked up at me. "Dude, you're not going to like this one." He continued to stare at me, so I broke off some of the plain bagel and handed it to him. After five seconds, he dropped it out of his mouth onto the ground. "I told you."

Years ago, my father visited for a week. After he arrived, we stopped at the grocery store to pick up a few items, among them were two packages of Smart Dogs, a meat alternative to hot dogs. He explained how he had gotten used to the flavor and claimed they were healthier than regular hot dogs. When he left, there was a package of Smart Dogs remaining in the refrigerator. I hate wasting food. The ingredients seemed healthy enough, so I decided to try one. I heated it up and put it on some bread. I took a nibble and it was blah. So, I poured on a ton of ketchup to disguise the flavor and odor. Blah. But I didn't give up. I tried smothering a piece in baked beans.

As I attempted to eat one of these things, Oscar came and assumed his position next to me. He sat and waited for a sample of my dinner snack. I broke off a piece of the Smart Dog and handed it to him. He gave it a sniff and pulled his muzzle back. "No interest?" I said to him. "You're not going to make me eat this thing alone, are you?" I dipped the piece in ketchup and tried again. This time, Oscar let me drop it into his open mouth. He chewed once and dropped the piece of Smart Dog onto the floor. "It's no good, huh?" I said to him. "That's all I got."

I picked up the piece of food and reached over to Oscar again. This time, terrified that I'd force him to eat it, he got up and ran through the doggie door and outside into the backyard! I stood up and looked out the window. Oscar was in the backyard, staring cautiously at me from a distance. I never offered him a Smart Dog again. And, I threw out the remaining package.

After finishing up the bagel, I found my way through the Buffalo side streets to the interstate. We briefly drove along Lake Erie again, continuing on I-90 south. Then, at the fork in the road, we exited to US 219 heading south. After an hour through Western New York, we drove into Pennsylvania. By now, Oscar had migrated across the stick shift and was laying comfortably half on my lap. A few moments later, we made a detour to Bradford, home of the Zippo lighter museum and factory. I had found the Zippo facility among the quirky, nifty places on RoadsideAmerica.com. It seemed like a cool place to visit. Plus, we'd travelled this far, so why not detour another ten miles and take an hour or so.

We passed over some railroad tracks, followed another arrow, made a few turns, then saw a large building with a massive Zippo insignia on the front. Found it! We parked in front of the museum where there were several sculptures and monuments related to the famous lighter and its founders.

I set Oscar next to a bench and took a peek inside. There were no signs regarding dogs. On a whim, I asked if I could bring my mellow, well-behaved fourteen-year-old dog inside. The lady at the Zippo/Case Museum was super nice and allowed Oscar to come in—and proving it never hurts to ask! We walked around the exhibits, carefully keeping a distance from other visitors. While I looked at the displays and information out of one eye, I kept the other eye on Oscar to be sure he didn't step on anything, or worse, suddenly lift his leg to mark something.

I noticed a thirty-minute movie, and the screen room was empty. I suppose, for most tourists, thirty minutes is a long time to sit and watch. However, we had the time, and the room was air-conditioned and quiet. So, I watched the film while Oscar napped. It was a nice break. The movie was entertaining, or at least, interesting.

We did one more lap around the museum, visiting the Bruce Willis *Die Hard* photo, an enormous mosaic American flag composed of Zippo lighters, an exhibit of early Zippos, and other historical displays. Plus, there was a window to the "Famous Zippo Clinic," which was a repair shop that would fix any Zippo sent to them.

After a day that went through Niagara Falls, Buffalo, and the Zippo/Case Museum, it was time to take it easy. We picked up some Stromboli for dinner and called it a night.

SOMEPLACE, SOMEWHERE

(The town and hotel are unnamed, so they don't come after me.)

AFTER A PLEASANT dinner and evening walk, we watched TV until falling asleep in the hotel room. The air conditioner was humming when I woke up at 2:00 a.m. *I hear something.* I listened closely. *It's like an oozing sound.* I leaned over the side of the bed to check Oscar. *What the—?* "Oh shit!" Literally, oh, shit. Oscar was sleeping like a baby, eyes closed—with crap oozing from his ass. It was on the blanket, but it had crept onto part of the carpeting! The carpet had a dark plaid design. Maybe I could clean it and avoid a stain. The last thing I wanted was a massive cleaning fee for damage.

    I ran down the hall and impatiently waited for the elevator. Instead of going through the lobby, I snuck out the side door, ran to the car, and loaded my backpack with clean-up supplies: paper towels, stain and odor removal, and plastic bags. Plus, I grabbed a second blanket from the car. Then, I sprinted back to the side entrance. "Dammit!" The door didn't open. The key doesn't work after midnight, which meant I had to sneak through the lobby.

    I took a peek, and the desk guy was watching TV in the side room. Like a burglar, I scampered by and got to the elevators.

Bring Oscar

"Come on. Come on," I said impatiently until one door opened. I headed back up to the room. Oscar was still sleeping, even as I lifted him up and start cleaning. Then, his eyes opened, but he seemed a bit groggy. I continued using lots of paper towels to lift up the crap into the garbage bag. And, I kept applying the stain removal.

After fifteen minutes, I had a pile of refuse in a garbage bag. It stunk. I needed to get it outside. I ran to the elevator, down to the side door, and outside. I imagine nobody saw me at 2:45 a.m. I put it all into my trunk—like dumping a dead body in the car! I crept back through the lobby with my backpack. The kid in the room noticed me. I just casually waved; nothing unusual at 3:00 a.m. He just nodded.

I returned to the room. Oscar was asleep again. I used the hotel's shampoo and soap to mask the odor with a more common smell. Then, I placed a white hotel towel under Oscar's ass. The room's scent transformed from sewage to shampoo. And, there was no apparent stain in the carpet. "I think we're good," I hoped. Then, I reluctantly went back to sleep.

At 3:35 a.m., I heard more oozing! I jumped out of bed. It was pouring out of his ass onto the white towel. But, Oscar had moved! So some of it was overflowing onto the carpet. Not again!

I ran back down the hall, out the side door, and to the car. I picked up more items, then headed back through the lobby, up the elevator. Cleaning Round Two. Then, back down the elevator, sneak out, dump another bag plus two hotel towels into the trunk. I've never stolen towels from a hotel, but I didn't know what to do. I was unable to wash out the diarrhea in the sink. Where could I stow them in the room? What a mess!

I darted across the parking lot and inconspicuously snuck passed the lobby. Then, I shot up the elevator and back to the room. Oscar was sound asleep. I went back to bed like a returning thief in the night.

At 6:00 a.m., following a couple of hours of sleep mixed with paranoia, I got up. The room's odor was not bad. I made sure to shower with the door open, hoping the scent of shower soap and shampoo would spread into the air around the room. Afterward, I went downstairs for orange juice and a muffin. When I returned,

Oscar was awake, lying halfway on another white towel and halfway on the remainder of the clean blanket. I noticed some dried crap matted in the fur on his leg, so I washed it out. I gave him some solid chicken from last night and a solid, dry dog biscuit. No moist foods for him today.

I sniffed the room. It wasn't fresh enough. Am I imagining an odd smell? "I got an idea," I said to Oscar. "Wait here." I ran down the hall to the vending machine to buy some popcorn. I threw the popcorn bag in the microwave. Ninety seconds later, I took the popcorn out, opened the bag and walked around the room, waving and shaking it around. A minute later, there was a sweet smell of popcorn in the room.

For housekeeping, I ordinarily leave a brief thank you note and money next to the TV remote control. But, for karma, I tripled the tip. In a weird sense of compensation, I considered it a partial payment for the trashed white towels I had taken. And, perhaps, a fallacy that paying extra would somehow make up for the whole mess.

At last, we went to the front desk to check out of the hotel. The night shift guy was gone.

"How was your stay? Everything OK?" the lady receptionist asked as she took the key.

"Yeah, yeah," I responded casually.

"Would you like a receipt?"

"No, we're good. Thanks, though." Then, we escaped. After driving fifteen minutes, I spotted a dumpster. I looked around and waited until there were no cars in sight. Then, I opened up the trunk of the car and dumped the two garbage bags into the dumpster. Ridiculous. I felt like I was secretly getting rid of the evidence. I emptied out a few other trunk contents, and we drove off.

Located just off Route 36/119 is the town of Punxsutawney, Pennsylvania. I'd seen *Groundhog Day* over and over again, so I was aware of the history of Groundhog Day. But, I wanted to see the spot firsthand. At the very least, learn how to spell Punxsutawney.

I recognized the town, passing several groundhog-themed statues. Oscar and I walked around the pleasant town, taking photos of the Punxsutawney Phil animated statues: Phil in a postman's outfit in front of the post office, Phil in an Irish outfit playing the bagpipes, Mayor Phil, Baker Phil, Patriot Phil, and more. There was also a local diner, a novelty shop, and hardware store. I find areas without chain stores and restaurants more appealing.

We went through Barclay Square in search of "Phil's Burrow," the home of the actual critter. In front stood a welcoming groundhog statue, Phil in tuxedo, with "Punxsutawney" etched in his top hat. There was a window viewpoint attached to the public library. Anyone could walk up and peek through the glass to see Phil's home. Today, the little guy was resting in the corner, so it was tough to see him. But, Phil the groundhog was alive and well next to the library!

A photo at Phil's place, Punxsutawney, Pennsylvania

Next, we went to find Gobbler's Knob, where the groundhog ceremony takes place each year. We followed a rough printed map and drove up the main road until we reached the end of town. *Hmm, must've missed the turn-off.* I turned around, and this time, I drove slower and looked more carefully for a road or sign—and ended up at the other part of town. *How did I miss Woodland Avenue? It's a significant tourist spot, so shouldn't there be a sign?*

We spent thirty minutes driving back and forth over a four-mile stretch of road. It was a small area, but I could not find the road! I got directions from the attendant inside a local gas station. I didn't see the turn. I went inside a diner for directions again. He pointed and told me exactly where the street was. When I came back outside, Oscar was sitting in the driver's seat. Maybe he was tired of going back and forth. "Slide." I nudged my way into the car. Oscar popped over to his passenger side. "I'll get us there."

We continued down the road, making U-turns. I was determined to find the spot where Phil emerges to see his shadow on Groundhog Day. *What am I missing?* Oscar was smiling, tongue hanging out, and calm as could be as we drove up and down the road. "I know it's here," I said out loud. "It's on TV every year. We didn't drive two thousand miles to be defeated now!" There is a fine line between determination/persistence and obsessive/compulsive. There is nothing worse than finishing a trip and realizing you missed something that was possible to see. Suddenly, I saw a dirt road—a road I had passed several times. It was unmarked. "You're kidding. That's got to be it." I learned that Clearfield goes north, while Woodland goes south. The Woodland street sign was missing. And, the Gobbler's Knob sign with the arrow was covered by a tree branch.

We turned onto the unmarked road and went up the hill. Then, I spotted the big sign.

"Welcome to Gobbler's Knob: Punxsutawney, PA – Weather Capital of the World" with a cartoon of a groundhog. Getting warmer. We pulled into a big dirt lot. Thousands of people will show up on February 2, but on July 12, it was almost empty.

After Oscar finished gulping some water, we walked to an information board. While Oscar sat in the shade under the board, I read about Punxsutawney and Phil the groundhog, including the town's history, things to do, and pictures of past events. Yes, there are people like me who actually read this stuff. Afterward, Oscar and I walked through the trees to the site of Gobbler's Knob where Punxsutawney Phil sees his shadow, or not. There was a big sign on top of a stage behind a podium and a door for the groundhog to appear—all in front of a huge area where crowds of people can watch. It's definitely unique!

I was pleased that we got to see everything in town. But I wondered, who named this town? That guy must've been drunk when he came up with Punxsutawney. A spelling bee contestant's nightmare! I learned it's a Native American word meaning "Land of Sandflies."

Next, we were headed through the woods of West Virginia. Just past Valley Point, I saw a marking for Old Virginia Furnace and pulled over. We were overdue for a driving break. Oscar and I got out of the car to stretch and look around. We climbed down a steep hill to the towering furnace. There was a faded plaque describing the history of the Virginia Iron Furnace, built in 1854. We continued down the grass trail until we reached a river flowing through rocks. Two photographers were setting up to take a beautiful shot of the river streaming through. I politely interrupted and got the man to take photos of Oscar and me. There was a lot of moss and rusty grime from water runoff, and lifting Oscar over the rocks was a bit tricky, but we ended up with some pretty pictures.

Playing around in West Virginia

I carefully climbed back to the side of the river and set Oscar down. The old man, Cecil, handed back my small camera. My Kodak digital was definitely modest compared to his professional, large lens camera. When I asked where we were, they explained it was part of the runoff from the Cheat River. Cecil offered suggestions for places to see: Blackwater Falls State Park, Morgantown, the university, "and definitely Coopers Rock," he emphasized.

"Damn, we passed that one!" I remembered seeing a sign for Coopers Rock State Forest. "Tomorrow, we'll have to backtrack and visit it."

After a nice break, we walked up the path, past the big furnace, and back to the car. Then, we resumed our ride through the winding road. We reached Kingwood and soon arrived in front of the large lawn of the Preston County Inn. The front had a large, southern-style porch and a University of West Virginia banner hanging amongst the columns. I maneuvered the car slowly through the driveway full of potholes. From the parking lot, Oscar and I walked through the side door and down a hall to the front. No doubt, the halls and some carpeting were a bit rundown and dated. At the same time, it had a thought-provoking, historical atmosphere. There's no doubt this location was off the beaten path, but I've always been intrigued by lesser known spots.

I picked the inn's restaurant for dinner. I ordered veggie lasagna and some chicken for Oscar. The chef, the owner's wife, had thoughtfully labeled one box "lasagna" and the other box "Oscar." While sitting in the porch area, I observed the variety of guests: young hippie types, old couples, black and white—all wearing different attire. I enjoyed listening to the conversations with accents reminding me that I was in West Virginia.

After nightfall, a teen church group had a movie night on the front lawn. They set up a large white projection screen, and the inn had a makeshift concession stand with popcorn and candy.

Oscar and I sat on the lawn and watched the feature, *Scooby Doo 2: Monsters Unleashed*. The movie must've been at least ten years old, but it was suitable for the kids and teens. As I watched glimpses of the show, Oscar napped on the grass beside me. I observed the pleasant summer scene: movies, good sound system, and street cars going by, all under a full moon. I loved the small town atmosphere. After finishing the popcorn, and halfway through the movie, we called it a night.

KINGWOOD, WEST VIRGINIA – Day 2

AFTER A QUICK snack from the continental breakfast, we loaded up for today's adventure in our Mystery Machine. The plan was to explore the area, emphasizing visits to Morgantown and Coopers Rock. The first part went through the green trees to the entrance of Coopers Rock State Forest. In front, I noticed a plaque attached to a rock: "This Property Has Been Placed On The National Register Of Historic Places By The United States Department Of The Interior."

"OK," I said to Oscar. "Let's see what it's all about."

We walked along the rock path through the woods, passing a few picnic tables under a covered structure. Through the trees, I could see the opening. A few minutes later, Oscar and I reached the viewing area. There was a large patio, bordered by a short stone-pillared wooden fence. Unsure of Oscar's footing, we crept down the slanted surface. I kept a tight hold of him as we neared the edge to look over. It offered a breathtaking sight of the pristine West Virginia forested hills.

There were a few other visitors enjoying the panoramic view. In one direction, two people were using the telescopes. Meanwhile, Oscar was watching a family thirty feet to our left, posing for a picture with their two big Golden Retrievers. After finding someone to take a photo of us, Oscar and I returned down the path to the entrance. Along the way, we passed a few animal rock-and-wood structures near extra picnic tables. Also, there was a sign mentioning an old iron blast furnace from the 1800s. Overall, this was a cool park with plenty of hiking trails and great picnic areas with barbeques. A worthwhile visit.

After an Oscar water break at the car, we took an easy twenty-minute ride to Morgantown, home of West Virginia University. We drove through town, including Don Knotts Blvd, and parked in a commercial area. Oscar and I walked around looking for the Don Knotts sidewalk star. After going back and forth three times, I was disappointed to find the star had been removed. There was a square portion of sidewalk missing under an orange public works wood blockade. I read they were raising money to build a statue tribute to Don Knotts, also known as Barney Fife.

Much of the town seemed to be in transition. Several buildings were open for lease. I wondered if the coal regulations were hurting the area. It seemed like there was a lot of potential. It claimed to have won the "Great American Main Street Award," although I had never heard of such a competition. Nevertheless, it looked like Morgantown was trying.

Oscar and I continued under overcast skies, searching for possible lunch places. I picked an open front local place called Chico's Fat. After loosely tying Oscar to a parking meter in front, I went inside the empty restaurant and ordered a large burrito, chips, and drink. During our chat, the young guy working there explained, "Once school starts, the town comes alive." After collecting my lunch, I went back outside and sat in front with Oscar. We ate near the curb; Oscar got the chicken chunks while I took the rest. The burrito was terrific, and we finished just as the rain began.

I noticed the drivers in this area were fearless (or reckless). They must've been familiar with the narrow one-lane highways, which leave little room for error. Even when the rain was pouring down, some still drove like moonshiners fleeing the law. One big pickup truck coming in the opposite direction lost momentum and swerved into my lane! I quickly shifted toward the side, and Oscar went flying. Luckily, the driver corrected his truck in time. *It's the other guy you gotta worry about.*

In the front lawn of the inn was a big sign promoting events, including the weekend's Kingwood Baptist Block Party, a social with food and dessert. I liked the atmosphere around here. I think the reviews underrated this place. The inn had local newspapers, maps, and information. The front porch seating and lawn was a relaxing area for guests. There was even a second floor enclosed porch for breakfast seating. I could see recommending this place to some, yet not recommending it to others. But, for us, it was a solid choice. I'd go back there. Plus, the price was right. I left a review online, offering specific details and trying to put the negative reviews into context. For us, this was a pleasant visit.

KINGWOOD, WEST VIRGINIA to BECKLEY, WEST VIRGINIA

OSCAR WAS SOUND asleep on his blanket in between the beds, his chest slowly expanding and shrinking. While I was busy watching cable news, booking a hotel, taking a shower, eating breakfast down the hall, and packing a few things in the car, he didn't move. The advantage of an old dog: he likes to rest. I finally woke him. "You ready to rally, Oscar?"

We checked out and began today's adventure. From Kingwood, I followed Highways 26, 92, and 11 to Audra State Park. After driving through the backwoods, I found a wonderful hiking and water area where the Middle Fork River cut through. Awesome. We parked in the lot with just two other cars. *Where is everyone? It's Monday, but isn't this a tourist area? Or, maybe the earlier rain changed visitors' plans?*

After locking the car, we walked down the hills toward the river area. Oscar was perking up in the outdoorsy surroundings. At the bottom, we stopped. "Damn, I forgot the camera." *Do I go back up and get it?* (Murphy's Law: If I don't, I'll probably see something and wish I had it, and if I do get the camera, then I probably won't need it.) "I have to go back and get it."

Should I leave Oscar here? Or, drag him with me back up the hills to the car? I looked around, and there were no people and no moving cars. I loosely tied his leash to a hand rail. "Wait here," I told him. "Wait," I emphasized. He looked at me. Then, I started to walk away. He watched. "I'll be right back." I sprinted up the hill about six hundred yards to the car. In the distance, I could see Oscar standing patiently next to the rail, watching me.

I grabbed my camera from the car and raced back to Oscar. He was fine. I imagine it never occurred to him that I would just abandon him at this spot. I unhitched the leash, and his tail started wagging as we walked toward the bridge above the river. Then, we continued lower to the water.

We waded in the slow current for a while. As we surveyed the area, a few people arrived. We took half of the trail to the "caves." It was a rather smooth path, even though I had to lift Oscar from time to time. In the end, Oscar was absolutely delighted to walk in the chilly running water. And, yes, I did take a few terrific photos.

Our next stop was a "little church" in Buckhannon. I had difficulty finding the location, so I went into a Subway to ask for directions. Many think guys are too stubborn to ask for directions. Not me. My GPS is "Gather People's Suggestions." I have no problem pulling over and asking anyone, because I hate wasting time, getting lost, or backtracking. I'll even stop an extra time to make sure I'm on the right trail. The trick is asking directions from the right people. Often a gas station is good or a local restaurant. Also, I like asking a small group, following the theory that the "wisdom of the crowd" can provide the best information.

"Hi," I said. "Sorry to trouble you. Any chance you know where the little church is? It's supposed to be near Route 20?"

"I know what you mean." She nodded. "Yes, it's down that road a couple of miles. It's off Route 20, just to the left. There's a big grass area."

Her directions were better than the online instructions. I found that personal directions in these small towns worked better than some of the search engine maps. I went full tourist and continued. "And there's supposed to be a miner's memorial in Sago?"

"Yes, behind the church. If you follow Sago Road off Route 20, it'll lead you there."

"OK." I didn't ask details about the Sago Mine Disaster. I considered the possibility she knew the miners and families involved.

With more specific directions, we resumed our drive. The rain stopped when we reached the Sago Baptist Church at the southern edge of Buckhannon. It was a little one-room chapel amongst the trees just off the road. It was a memorial to a young boy who died over sixty years earlier. The small church was interesting and a nice dedication.

We continued down Sago Road to the Sago Mine Disaster Monument, which was placed near the site of a 2006 tragedy. I had a vague recollection of the incident being shown on TV, until the lady at Subway reminded me that one kid survived. That story I did remember.

Winding through the area, I was struck by the poverty of Appalachia. I suspected the closed mine, or anything related to coal that's under pressure from government regulations, wasn't helping. Driving by small houses in disrepair and foreclosure presented a vivid picture. The road through the neighborhood to the memorial was sad in more ways than one.

After a ten-minute drive through the side streets, we reached the memorial. Imprinted in the large granite stone were the names and faces of the twelve victims. "We'll see you on the other side." In front of the dedication, there were lots of flowers and mementos left. The images of a mining hat, coal cars, a cross, and a flag carved into the granite were artistic and moving. One bench had a portrait of the lone survivor etched into the seat. Oscar and I were the only ones standing at the memorial; a peaceful moment of silence. Before leaving, I stepped back to view from a distance. The decorative monument stood in a lawn area, beneath a waving US flag, beside a Baptist church. It was definitely worth the detour.

We went back to the Subway for lunch. Then we continued on the Mountaineer Scenic Expressway US 19 until we reached a scenic overlook on Powell Mountain. The rest area wasn't much.

However, there was a terrific view of the West Virginia hills. I pulled some items from the trunk and gave Oscar his early dinner. Oblivious to any cars that went through the rest stop, Oscar dined al fresco. Meanwhile, I walked over to read the historical marker for Young's Monument. I learned Henry Young was a Confederate soldier or sympathizer, killed early in the Civil War. Nearby, there was a solitary grave. I recognized that organized battle in this mountain area was impractical. Instead, there were skirmishes, raids, and small-scale warfare. A single burial wouldn't be uncommon. Also, the marker mentioned the divided loyalties in this area, which mirrored the split of Virginia in 1861.

When Oscar finished, we resumed our drive down US 19. West Virginia had been enjoyable, and it's unmatched. In addition to the landscape, you could sense the work ethic and conservatism. I saw a shop with a huge "We did build this" sign in front. There were lots of churches. And, a billboard with the word "Abortion" where the "b" and "r" were crossed out and were replaced by "d" and "p" to spell "Adoption." It was a contrast from other places. The United States is truly composed of several regions.

By late afternoon, we neared the exit to the New River Gorge. *Should we stop or keep going?* Oscar was sleeping in the back, so he had no opinion. In the end, I defaulted to yes. If I skipped a terrific site, I would be incredibly disappointed. As the car slowed from sixty-five to twenty-five mph on the off-ramp, Oscar woke up. He leaped into his "Washington Crossing the Delaware" position, staring out the front window, under the rearview mirror. "Well, look who checked in," I said to him. "One more stop: Seeing a bridge."

We walked to the entrance, and I quickly read the sign and noticed the actual scenic view was .8 miles away! *Ugh.* It was too far to run there myself, and I wouldn't leave Oscar in the parking lot for twenty minutes. So, Oscar and I began the trek. Then, stairs appeared in the distance. *Ugh.*

At the stairs, I considered guiding Oscar up and down. But, there were too many; it would take forever. A few months ago, Oscar managed to walk through parts of Rock Mountain in Tennessee. But, he's a bit older, and this was much more difficult. It was going to require carrying Oscar up and down wooden stairs to get a view of the bridge and gorge. Nevertheless, we'd driven too far not to check it out, and I wasn't going to leave him in the car.

I picked him up and started walking, and walking, and walking up and down wooden stairs and platforms. Fifteen minutes later, sweat pouring through my shirt, we reached the view! A few people pet Oscar and commented, "You must love your dog, carrying him this far!!"

"Yeah, he's my pal," I replied while catching my breath. "Always good company. Although, I'm not looking forward to carrying him back to the car."

The overlook provided a spectacular view. Below, I could see the New River at the bottom of the gorge. A coal train was travelling through the green hills. Then, across, there was a clear view of the massive bridge, supposedly the largest wide span arch bridge when it was built in the 1970s. I noticed a large walkway under the bridge away from the cars, and I read that there are BASE jumpers who leap off the bridge. Cool, but no thanks.

The wooden rails were high and narrow. Oscar couldn't slip through or accidentally jump over the top, so I let him loose while taking pictures. Meanwhile, the people in the area either ignored Oscar walking around, or they went over to pet him.

"You mind taking a picture of us?"

"Absolutely!"

I handed the guy my camera and showed him where to press. Then, I lifted Oscar high up to get a shot of him, me, and the bridge in the background. It was amazing.

Scenic view of New River Gorge Bridge, West Virginia

After enjoying the moment, and resting my arms for twenty minutes, we went back. I carried Oscar up the first batch of wooden stairs. Then, I set him down as we walked through a flat section. Then, I had to lift him again. Meanwhile, a few people passed by us, giving me a supportive, understanding nod. Eventually, we returned to the parking lot. I took the bowl of water off the top of the car and gave it to Oscar. While he lapped it up, I joked, "Save some for me!"

Since there were multiple routes into Beckley, I took precautions and phoned the hotel to confirm directions. After driving twenty minutes, I called back, got directions again, and turned around. It didn't make sense, so I stopped at a custard stand for help. Then, at a gas station. Finally, I found the hotel after forty-five minutes. A lot of miscommunication, but that's life without a GPS. But, I looked at the upside: I did get to see all of Beckley and meet a few people along the way.

When we finally got into the room, I turned on the TV to watch the last Jack Bauer 24 episode. Oscar wandered around the room, and smartly put himself right next to the air conditioner.

BECKLEY, WEST VIRGINIA to ABINGDON, VIRGINIA

I OPENED MY eyes. Oscar was sitting and watching me. I turned to look at the clock. 2:35 a.m. "Oy, man." I climbed out of the warm bed into the cold, air-conditioned room, kept chilled for Oscar. Half awake, I grabbed my shoes and threw on a shirt to look presentable. We headed down the hallway, out the back door, and onto the grass area. There was a smell of cigarettes outside the building entrance. I waited as Oscar sniffed. At least, it was a balmy seventy degrees outside, with few mosquitoes.

Oscar lifted one leg and relieved himself. "Nice." This wasn't a total loss. I hated getting up, going outside, and after ten minutes he does nothing.

Oscar looked at me. "No, we're not going for a walk. Are you done?" After a few sniffs, he started to walk toward the hotel entrance. "Beautiful," I remarked, pleased that it was short and sweet. "That was worthwhile." Sometimes we'd go through this routine, but it would turn out that Oscar just wanted a midnight stroll.

Back home, this effort wasn't necessary. The house had a fenced in yard and doggie door. Oscar could go outside by himself. No way was I going to stand outside in a Chicago winter, freezing my ass off, waiting for Oscar to do his business. Also, I didn't want him to burst while desperately waiting for someone to get home.

The easy passageway wasn't just about going to the bathroom. Once, Oscar showed me a present: a little dead rabbit he had found, killed, or played with. It was sitting in the porch. Another time, I noticed an odor. When I went into the living room, I got a whiff of skunk and watched Oscar desperately rubbing his face in the rug, trying to get rid of the stench!! And there were times I came home and found my shoes in the backyard. Sometimes there was too much free access.

On the upside, one time when I got locked out of my house, I simply reached through the doggie door and let myself in. "Aren't you worried about a thief?" my friend asked. "Not really," I replied. "What are they going to steal? My old dinosaur TV? My ancient desktop computer? Besides, if they really wanted to break into the house, they could smash a window."

I had a doggie door—and a brilliant dog. On day one, I showed Oscar the door with the flap. I took a piece of chicken and stood outside the doggie door. Oscar peeked through the flap then pushed his nose through to grab the chicken. Next, I went inside and held another piece of chicken. Oscar immediately walked through the flap and grabbed the prize! And that was that. He was housebroken and knew how to go in and out when he pleased!

We took extra time today to check out of the hotel. While he rested by the air conditioner, I ran to the other building and had breakfast. When he woke up, I turned off the TV and left a tip and thank you note for housekeeping.

After departing the Econo Lodge, we went to the Beckley Exhibition Coal Mine a few miles away. It was a cool little spot. I asked if Oscar could join me on one of the mine tours. The older lady at the ticket office was irritable and said "there should be no dogs anywhere on the homestead." I knew that. I didn't need to hear it from an angry lady. Oscar wasn't bothering anyone. Moreover, there was a designated pet area fifty feet away, so obviously, pets were around somewhere. Anyway, it was no big deal; the tickets were twenty bucks a pop and would've been twenty dollars more to add Oscar's seat. We decided to spend our time and money somewhere else.

On the way out of town, despite stretches of pouring rain, we made good time. It was a straight shot down the I-77 tollway; 70 mph and no back roads. We entered Virginia and sped through George Washington and Jefferson National Forests, passed Wytheville, and connected directly to I-81. After a quick rest stop in Marion to give Oscar a breather, we discovered that we were less than thirty minutes from Abingdon, Virginia!

The hotels in Abingdon were the cheapest of the entire trip. I wondered if this area was poorer or if I had finally left the East where everything was pricier? We stayed at the Americas Best Value Inn. It seemed as good as any. The lady at the front desk was very nice. "There is free breakfast tomorrow."

"Sounds good," I said as I took the room key. "Is that pita place next door any good?"

"I'm not sure. I've never eaten there," she answered. "It's been open for less than a year. It used to be a tavern." I didn't bother to ask about the ice cream place down the road. Any ice cream looks good to me.

Our room smelled of disinfectant, but that's better than cigarette smoke. Once the air conditioner got going, it dissipated. Then, later, the aroma from Pita's dinner freshened the room. As long as the place was safe and clean, I didn't mind.

ABINGDON, VIRGINIA to KNOXVILLE, TENNESSEE

BEFORE LEAVING TOWN, we drove down Main Street, Highway 11, passing a county building and classic colonial-style courthouse. There was a memorial garden and a Civil War statue erected in 1906, a tribute to Confederate soldiers from Washington County, Virginia. It was interesting to see different perspectives over time periods and observe the gradual change in states' histories as we proceeded from the Northeast toward the South.

We continued down Main Street, and just before reaching the I-81 entrance, there was a turn-off for the "Creeper Trail." It sounded like a Halloween movie and was gripping enough to make a stop. Near the parking lot, there was an old train engine, The Virginia Creeper. It turned out that "Creeper" referred to the old trains that creeped around the winding tracks in the mountains. Beyond the exhibit was the start of the Virginia Creeper National Recreation Trail. People were biking and walking along the tree-lined shaded path.

Oscar and I took advantage of the area to get in a morning walk. Along the way, there were odd bits of history and nature spots, including a one-hundred-and-fifty-year-old oak tree. And, farther down, the trail extended more than thirty miles, over wood bridges, bike trails, and Virginia scenery. We covered one mile, before turning around and returning to the car.

Following a brief stop at the Tennessee Welcome Center, we continued southwest on I-81, which merged into I-40. The Smoky Mountains! We were in familiar territory, having traveled on I-40 through Western Tennessee a few months ago. Instead of Chattanooga, we were going to check out Knoxville. We started at World's Fair Park, which contained the Sunsphere. It is easy to find: just look for the gold disco ball on top of a tower.

We passed a big plaza with kids playing in water gushing out of the cement ground. To the right of them, I noticed parents watching their children splashing, and people were sitting on blankets in the grass area. Then, off to the other side, I saw a mother chasing her two kids; they were laughing while she was yelling at them. I looked at Oscar as he let out a yawn. Dog versus kid; it was definitely easier to hang on to the old dog.

We continued through the park, encountering an extensive memorial to soldiers from Eastern Tennessee. There were numerous cement pillars with engraved tributes, recognizing Freedom of Speech, the Holocaust Remembrance, and Medal of Honor recipients, and especially honoring countless Eastern Tennesseans who died in military service. It was a very cool monument area.

We walked along the path to the nearby Holiday Inn. I had read there was a giant Rubik's Cube inside the building. At the entrance, I asked an employee about it. He was very nice, escorting both of us directly to the cube. (Yep, dogs were allowed in the Holiday Inn.) Then, the helpful man took photos of us. I looked down and read a plaque indicating it was one of the most popular icons at the 1982 World's Fair. Makes sense.

A square and cube posing with Oscar

After touring the World's Fair Park grounds, we got in the car and went looking for a Rowing Man Statue, a bronze sculpture of a man sitting in a boat in the middle of the sidewalk. I wanted to see it firsthand. While looking for parking, we passed the Market Square. "That was convenient." I had found our lunch location without even trying! Also, I caught a glimpse of the orange basketball sitting on top of the Women's Basketball Hall of Fame. Everything in Knoxville seemed to be in close proximity.

We parked a couple of blocks from Market Square and went looking for the Rowing Man. Following my hand-sketched map with street names, we found "The Oarsman," the 1988 piece by David Phelps, a well-known sculptor. The intriguing part was that this oarsman appeared to be sitting below the surface of the sidewalk. From a distance, the boat looks half submerged in the ground. It's a piece of art that is definitely part of the cityscape. Two things that struck me: What is the rower looking up at? And, why is he rowing five blocks away from the Tennessee River?!

Bring Oscar

Tiptoeing through Knoxville, Tennessee

Oscar and I followed Market Street straight to Market Square. We passed the Tennessee Woman Suffrage Monument and on to a large walkway between restaurants and shops. Although it was a nice, sunny weekday, this pedestrian mall wasn't very crowded. A few kids were wading in the water fountains spurting from the ground. Everyone else was scattered around, browsing or sitting at random tables. It was a good, wide area for lunch.

I picked a place called Blue Coast Grill. The menu looked good, and I liked the *Superbad* McLovin sketch on their chalkboard. Plus, a few people were drinking and dining on the patio with their dogs. Oscar and I were seated in a quiet corner in the shade. For lunch, I had a tasty veggie burger and sweet potato fries. Oscar had his water, plus leftover chicken from last night. And, I shared some of my fries. It was a pleasant break. A few dogs and people walked by, which kept Oscar's interest. Then a young couple sat at the next table with their chocolate Lab. Oscar gave him a look, but after a few moments, each dog lay on the cool concrete under the tables, just relaxing.

We finished our Knoxville tour by driving toward the big orange basketball above the Women's Basketball Hall of Fame. While the car ran—and Oscar soaked in the air conditioning—I ran inside to see the place. Although I didn't read the details, I got a gist of the exhibits. Very cool. I wouldn't mind returning someday. Outside, I went across the street to look at James White's Fort, the birthplace of Knoxville. After a few photos, of the restored eighteenth century cabin, I returned to the car, where Oscar was comfortably waiting.

At the Red Roof Inn, we were placed on the second floor in the back, which was a pain in the ass, but it was removed from everyone. Being out of the way—perhaps it's safer? But, more likely, it's one of the rooms set aside for pets. Nevertheless, it was spacious. Great for the price.

In the middle of the night, I heard Oscar's tags rattling as he woke up and started walking around. *Oh, no.* I was nice and comfortable under the covers. "Please, sit back down and go back to sleep," I silently pleaded. I didn't want to get up, put on shoes, go downstairs, and walk him at 11:00 p.m. Hopefully, it was a false alarm. Oscar stopped, circled around, and then repositioned himself on the blanket. "There we go," I silently encouraged him. Then I heard him let out a hefty exhale as he went back to sleep. *Yes!* I thought as I went back to sleep.

KNOXVILLE, TENNESSEE to BRENTWOOD, TENNESSEE

A MONTH AGO, my mom and sister scheduled a two-week summer road trip through Tennessee. My plan had been to intercept them at some point. Right now, they were flying to meet each other in Nashville. Oscar and I were headed there today. I looked forward to seeing my sister, who was on school break from Bogotá, Colombia. And, after checking in daily, we would actually see my mom firsthand.

Things were going our way. We were leaving Western Knoxville, so any possible traffic would be behind us. Interestingly, I learned a time change occurs in mid-Tennessee. I didn't realize a time zone could cut apart a state. I wondered how the dividing line worked for neighboring towns on the border. Scheduling events must be an adjustment. For us, we gained an hour traveling from Knoxville to Nashville. Plus, gas was $3.29, far cheaper than the Northeast, and the roads were free, no tolls. There was a 70 mph speed limit, so we cruised one hundred and thirty-five miles through middle Tennessee.

I checked my phone as we neared the Nashville airport to see if my sister had arrived. There was no call. Then, five minutes later at the Nashville exit, I looked again and saw two missed calls. My phone sucks. Or, the user sucks.

Kelly had just arrived—perfect timing. The early departure from Knoxville and the one-hour time change helped.

Oscar and I pulled into the terminal and saw her standing in front of the arrivals. "Aw, hi, Oscar!" she greeted him. He seemed excited.

"Gotta slide, Oscar," I told him. "Hop in the back." Then, I said to my sister, "Just gradually sit in the seat. He'll move." So, she gave him a nudge, and he stepped into the backseat.

We pulled out of the airport, and Oscar put his paws on the armrest and tried to sit on my sister's lap. She gave him a friendly hug. "So, what's the plan?"

"Mom's flight is coming in at 4:00. Then, she'll pick up the rental car. We can meet her back here or at the hotel."

"OK. You wanna grab lunch or look around?" My sister, Oscar in the backseat, and I went around Nashville, part exploring, part catching up, and part killing time.

"So, how's the trip been going? I like the pictures you've been sending."

"It's been great. We've seen a ton of places."

"And, he's OK?" Kelly had seen Oscar many times over the years. This was the first time she'd seen the set-up with the car.

"Yeah, he's enjoying the ride."

We started hunting for a dog park I remembered seeing in the area. After ten minutes of driving past the Two Rivers Mansion and Golf Course, turning around, and asking a local, we found it. "That's the place!" I told my sister. "I knew it. I just didn't realize it was so close to the other parks."

She took a look. "This place is huge."

"And, it's free," I added. The familiar park had water, grass, trees, and plenty of running space. The enormous facility was still maintained and clean.

After Oscar walked and frolicked with a few dogs, he plopped down, rested, and got some water. "Is he OK?" my sister asked.

"It's a little hot," I said. "But, he'll be fine."

While sitting with him, we found a tick. I recalled the tick incident in Dillon, Montana, last year. Back at the car, I pulled out a pocket screwdriver and plastic fork from the trunk. Then, my sister parted Oscar's fur, and I plucked out the tick. "Hopefully, that did the job."

We got back into the car, cranked up the air conditioner, and headed to Vittles to have a good Southern lunch. We were grateful for nice service from the waitress and the owner. We had seats in the shade and enjoyed the comfort dishes. Through the window, I could see the inside with traditional tables and décor, plus some Christian items on the wall—crosses, prayers, and morality stuff. Funny, there was a TV on playing the Fox News Channel instead of CNN, which places in the Northeast consistently showed. There seemed to be a lot of old native Southerners. Most of them greeted Oscar on their way in and out. All in all, a good place.

After our meal, we arrived at the Super 8 hotel where my mom was waiting. "How's the trip going? Oscar looks good."

"Great." We'd been on the road for about one month. "Oscar is enjoying himself, meeting a lot of people."

"He's not too tired?" my mom checked.

"Actually, I notice he perks up when we hit the road. He's excited to see the new hotels and new places. Plus, he loves meeting the people. To be honest, he's doing better now than when we're at home and he's just sitting on the couch."

"They've certainly gone far," my sister remarked, knowing we'd been zigzagging through the East. "But, Oscar looks good. You should've seen him at the dog park today."

"We just take it easy." I explained, "A few hours at a time, stopping for breaks every so often."

"Sounds like road trips with Mom!" my sister joked. "A few hours at a time, stopping for breaks…" We were laughing at the comparison.

"What's that?" Mom asked.

"Nothing," we told her, then switched topics. "So, how's the room?"

"It's good, especially for the price," she added. "I think you could've stayed here, too."

"I don't think so. I checked online, and it wasn't a hotel option for big dogs."

"I know, but I asked the manager. He said you could've stayed there. They allowed mellow pets over twenty pounds." It's too bad, because the location was fine. And, we could've stayed down the hallway from each other. Unfortunately, they were now sold out for the weekend.

After dropping my sister off, Oscar and I drove to revisit my friend, Erich, at his house in Brentwood. At 6:00 p.m., we cruised through Nashville. *Hmm, where is the Thursday rush hour traffic?* The only delay was at the exit to Brentwood, where the trail of cars spilled well out to the freeway. Eventually, we passed through the intersection and drove through the Brentwood neighborhood, viewing the school and more spacious and clean parks. At last, we got to his house.

We caught up on events since our Spring visit. We picked up dinner from Tin Roof, the nearby bar and grill, and added a shake from Sonic. Then, we relaxed in his living room, eating and watching some TV. The end of another travel day.

BRENTWOOD, TENNESSEE to NASHVILLE, TENNESSEE

AS HE LEFT for work, Erich offered breakfast and the use of the house. After a quick shower and breakfast snack, Oscar and I made our exit an hour later. We drove straight to Downtown Nashville. Bypassing twenty-dollar parking, then ten-dollar parking, I found a meter that charged a quarter per ten minutes. Fortunately, I kept a pile of spare change in the car, so we got by for about five bucks.

Oscar and I strolled several blocks and joined my mom and sister near the Honky Tonk and entertainment areas. We weaved through the crowd of visitors, as well as watched weekend partiers go by. Especially notable was the mobile tavern with drinkers peddling to move the bar along. I wondered, after several rounds of beer, who does the steering?

The four of us continued up and down the streets of downtown, looking for a lunch option. There were plenty of choices, but we wanted an easy place with outdoor seating in the shade. Eventually, we reached the Nashville Arcade, a place with galleries, stores, and restaurants. After enjoying lunch together, we parted ways. Mom and Kelly had plans to go to the Grand Ole Opry. So, Oscar and I went to check into our hotel.

We got a studio at The Red Roof Inn, but it was a "renovated" room. Actually, most of this hotel was being fixed. The furnishings and floor appeared new. I discounted any inconveniences. It was a bit small, but the appearance and price made up for that. There was a slight view of the freeway, but I couldn't hear the sound. There were wood floors, but I had Oscar's blanket so he could sleep comfortably. There was no breakfast offered, but again, the price made up for that. With the cost savings, I could easily get a substantial breakfast nearby. Passersby could see into the room, but I just kept the curtain closed. This will work.

NASHVILLE, TENNESSEE – Day 2

MY SISTER AND mom had plans to see Andrew Jackson's Hermitage. No pets allowed. So, Oscar and I went a different direction, driving into Hillsboro Village. We walked up and down the streets, passing restaurants, cafés, and shops. Nearby were Belmont University and Vanderbilt University, so I wasn't surprised to see lots of young people meeting and having brunch. I had brief conversations with a few who wanted to meet Oscar. In the distance, there was a playground next to an open park. We walked along the park, hoping clouds would slide under the sun and cool the temperatures. People nodded and said hi.

Two young girls ran over to meet Oscar. Their mother was in the distance watching. "Can we pet your dog?!?"

"Yes," I answered. "I think he'd like that. He's friendly."

They each kneeled down and began petting Oscar. He was enjoying the attention. "What's his name?"

"Oscar."

"Hi, Oscar," each of them said. Oscar leaned against one of the girls. She giggled.

"I think he likes you," I told her.

The mother came over. "I hope they're not bothering you."

"Not at all," I reassured her.

"This is Oscar," one of the girls informed her mom.

"They love dogs," the mother told me.

"I can tell. Do you have a dog?"

"No," the mother said to me. "They want one. They keep asking. But, my husband and I work a lot. We know a dog is a big responsibility. But, maybe."

"Yes, they're a lot of work. But, totally worth it."

The girls overheard part of our conversation. But, mostly they were playing with Oscar.

"We're considering getting a little dog for her next birthday. But, my husband thinks he'll end up doing all the work."

"Maybe," I said. "You can always try the 'Jim Conley Test.'"

"The what test?"

"The Jim Conley Test. Named after my cousin," I told her. "My cousin, Jim, had two kids around ten and twelve years old. They were dying to get a dog and kept asking their parents."

"Sounds familiar," she said.

"Jim never had a dog growing up. He liked animals, but he was OK living without pets. However, his kids kept asking, so he thought about it. In the end, he was worried they'd lose interest, and he would end up taking care of the dog! But, his kids continued to bring it up, so one day, Jim came home from work with a leash. The kids saw the leash, and got excited. 'A dog?! We're getting a dog?' Jim sat them down, and said, 'Here's the deal: A dog is a lot of responsibility. It needs to be fed, taken care of, trained, and taken outside for exercise. (They lived in a two-story apartment loft in New York City.) But, if you can prove that you're willing to take on the responsibility, we can get a dog.' The two kids listened intently."

I went on. "Here's a leash. Each morning at 6:00 a.m. and each evening at 6:00 p.m., you have to take this leash out for a thirty-minute walk. One of you can go in the morning, and one of you can go in the evening, or both of you at the same time. And,

I'll even go with you! My cousin's thinking was, 'Hey, I get to spend time with my kids. Plus, if they keep up the bargain, they'll show commitment.' He promised, 'If you can walk this leash twice a day, every day for one month, we will go right over to the shelter and adopt any dog you want to put on the end of this leash! You can pick.' The kids agreed to the terms."

"So, what happened?" the lady asked me.

"The next morning my cousin got up for work. He went into the girl's room at 6:00 a.m. 'Hey, it's time to walk the dog.' His daughter rolled over and looked at her dad. She briefly weighed her options. Then, she got back under the covers and went back to sleep…and that was the end of the discussion! The kids never bothered to ask for a dog after that."

"Wow," the lady said to me. "That's a great test!"

"I know. It's clever," I agreed. "For me, I would've done anything to get a dog. We grew up with dogs, anyway. But, if my parents made me prove I wanted a dog, I would've done it. I would've taken that leash and easily walked it twice a day. In fact, I walk Oscar twice a day, every day. It's part of the deal."

"I'm going to remember that bargain." The lady turned to her girls. "You ready to go?"

"Yes, we're ready," they said. "Bye-bye, Oscar," they said as they walked away. Oscar stood next to me and watched them.

"Wanna grab some lunch, buddy?" We walked down Belcourt toward 21st Avenue. While Oscar sniffed around, I scanned the cafés and outdoor spaces, looking for a lunch spot. On the way, a young couple suggested "… a place called Fido." That fits! Oscar waited by the seats out front, while I checked the menu inside. The food looked good, but there was a huge line. I went back outside and asked two female students if they'd watch Oscar while I ordered. A guy overheard me and suggested that I call the restaurant and order take-out. "As long as you use a credit card, you can bypass the register," he told me. "I do it all the time." Perfect!

After ordering, I chatted with the people outside and a few tourists who walked past. The lunch was very good, especially the sweet potato fries. During the meal, the conversations continued. While talking with the two female students, they mentioned some of the cities all of us had visited. Then, a guy called out Lake Placid. "We were there last week!" I told him.

"I have a house out there," he said. We listed off the familiar places. It's a small world.

Also, I met two women visiting from New York. "Girls weekend," they told me.

In between conversations, I read the Nashville local magazine and watched people go by. Meanwhile, Oscar sat and slept by the table. Following the meal, we explored a few more streets. Then, Oscar and I returned to our hotel for an afternoon siesta until hearing from my sister.

For the last night, we drove to the eastern part of Nashville to meet with my mom and sister. We walked around their hotel in the Hermitage area and discussed dinner ideas. We spotted Café Bosna, a European restaurant. While I waited outside with Oscar, my mom and sister went inside to look at the menu. A few moments later, they returned. "It's fine. There are some vegetarian options. It looks good. Come inside."

"What about Oscar?"

"She said to bring him, too," my mom told me. "The owner has a table for us." Wow, I thought. Leave it to my mom to get an "in" with the owner.

I tentatively led Oscar into the restaurant. We walked past a table with ten young people and sat at a table in the corner. This was best. I was able to seat Oscar between me and a wall, somewhat out of sight.

A moment later, an older, Eastern European lady came out. "Can I get you something to drink?" Then, she noticed Oscar. "Oh, there he is!"

"You're sure it's OK to eat here? He's quiet, but I don't want to disturb the other diners."

"My restaurant. I can let you eat here," she proudly said with an accent. I suppose a service dog would be welcome, so why not Oscar? A busboy came over with a bowl of water for Oscar. I set it next to his dinner bowl.

We sat inside the restaurant and had a delicious meal. Afterward, we thanked the owner and left a generous tip. Then, we walked

Bring Oscar

back to their hotel and said our goodbyes. Tomorrow, Oscar and I would head north, finishing our trip. Meanwhile, my mom and sister would go east toward the Smoky Mountains, starting their driving adventure.

NASHVILLE, TENNESSEE to HOME

I MENTALLY PREPARED for the last day of driving. It would be the same route as the Spring trip four months ago: Nashville to Louisville to Indianapolis to Chicago. It was about five hundred miles due north. A map with directions was unnecessary. The downside: The same route may be repetitive, and five hundred miles is a long haul for one day of driving. The upside: The same route makes it easier to skip places and save time or try different attractions. It's more efficient going over the same ground, and there was no hurry to get to the next hotel. The destination was home.

As early as possible, we started our drive north on I-65 into Kentucky. We passed by the National Corvette Museum in Bowling Green. Soon after, I became intrigued by Mammoth Cave National Park advertised on the interstate billboards. Instead of the Corvette stop, we could spend the time investigating the American Cave Museum.

After a hundred miles, we took our first break, exiting the interstate at Horse Cave, Kentucky. We went along a quiet road to the middle of the small town, and parked in front of the museum. There was a big banner: "Hidden River Caves." My plan was to quickly look it over and see if it seemed worth the time and money. As I was setting Oscar beside a pole, a girl came outside. "Come on in," she said.

"We came to check out some caves?"

"Yep, it's this way," she said. "Right through the museum." Oscar was welcomed in the museum and down into the cave! This was shaping up to be a worthwhile dog stop.

Inside the museum were lots of exhibits and history related to cave exploration, the environment, and formation of the cave. After a glimpse at the displays, we followed the crowd down a winding walkway and into the caverns!

It was an interesting tour, although I had to carry Oscar up and down the steps into the cave down to the river. The tour guide and the other visitors were amused by my dedication to Oscar! Also, I had to hold on tight to him, for fear he would lose his footing and fall off the wooden planks. Nevertheless, in the end, I'm glad we did it.

Is that the light at the end of the tunnel?
The last day of our summer road trip!

Back on the road, we passed potential stops in Louisville, but since I had been there multiple times, we circumvented the city and immediately crossed into Indiana. Driving-wise, the trip from the Indiana border to Indianapolis was a nightmare, filled with delays and construction lane closures. Although, there were no construction workers on site. I wondered if I should've driven at night or early morning.

After delays in Indiana, we made up time between Northern Indiana and the Illinois border—70 mph speed limit and the cars were cruising. There were no cops, and it appeared the Indy 500 had spilled on to the I-65. At last, we crossed into Illinois. Moments later, we hit tons of traffic on a Sunday afternoon on the I-94. Ridiculous. The drivers were insane and rude with their cellphones and reckless lane-switching. In the distance, I saw the downtown Chicago silhouette. We passed Comiskey Park where the White Sox played. Then, we ran into the bottleneck of traffic. *Now, I remember why I don't miss this city—poorly designed and maintained roadways, and awful drivers.*

Eventually, we made it back home. Another successful road trip over five weeks. The car needed a cleaning, but we were safe and sound. I looked at the odometer: 5477 miles of driving.

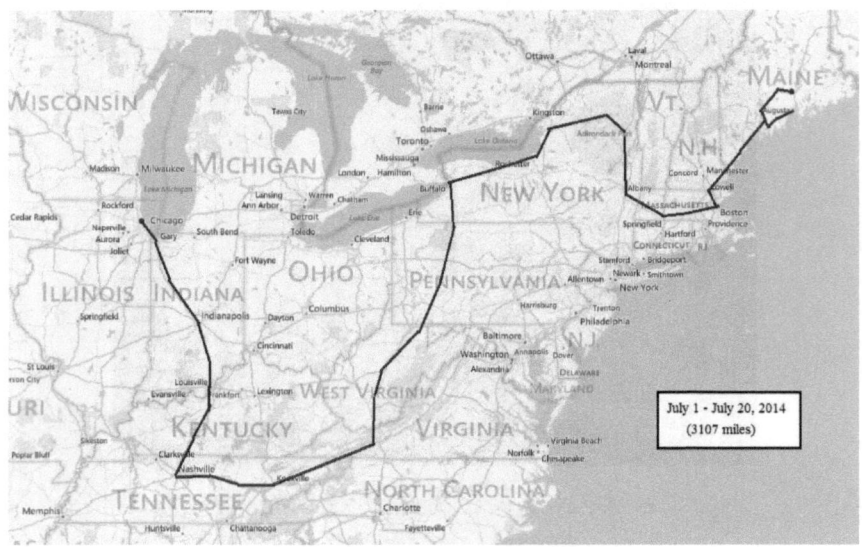

Bring Oscar

As I unpacked the Nissan, Oscar sat outside by the driver's side of the car. He watched me go inside and outside the house. "You don't want to go in yet?!" *I don't think he's ready to come home!* Oscar sat in the driveway and watched me unload the car.

Suddenly, Miguel showed up. "Hey, the house looks good," I told him. I paid him the balance of my housesitting tab. He handed me the key. This time it was on a string that was wrapped around his neck.

"I made a necklace so that I wouldn't lose it again!" I appreciated his enthusiasm.

When most of the car was unpacked, I announced, "End of road trip!" and led Oscar inside the house. I looked in the backyard and saw the garden overflowing with vegetables that grew fine without my help. And, I skimmed over the pile of mail on the table. Both were evidence of the time that had passed.

Trips like these are odd. They start out slow, the first few miles. Then, we pass fifty miles. Then five hundred miles. Then twenty-five hundred miles. Then five thousand miles. And suddenly, it's over and we're home!

While uploading photos from the trip, I was reminded of how much we saw and did. It might have seemed like a blur, but when I looked at the photos, all the details and events spilled out. I realized how quickly the five weeks went by.

Travel can be a paradox: a long adventure that goes by quickly.

But, vivid memories remain...

PART IV

ALASKA

ONE MORE, Alaska.

When friends, family, or my students asked about the next adventure, I replied, "We're going to Alaska, assuming the car and the dog make it—"

"Drive to Alaska?!?" they would ask. "And, what do you mean, if they make it?"

"Well, the car has about eighty-five thousand miles on it. And, the dog has at least fifteen years on him."

Oscar's hearing was impaired and his hind legs had atrophied, but he still had a lot of spirit left.

I estimated that he and I walked roughly four to five miles per day, every day, except when it rained. Like Art, my mailman, we were out there, regardless of snow, rain, and heat. Since four miles per day is roughly fifteen hundred miles per year, we'd gone well over twenty thousand miles on foot. Plus, we had driven about thirty thousand miles in the car. That's a lot of mileage together.

"I can't wait to hear about it," one of my students said. "That sounds like an awesome trip!"

Summer soon arrived, and two old guys in an old Nissan were going to try for Alaska. This was uncharted territory, so I did more preparation than the previous trips. I didn't want to drive three thousand miles and discover a roadblock to the Alaska border; that would be a massive disappointment.

The original plan was to go west to Idaho and Oregon and visit family. We could stay with them for a few days to reset and recharge before heading north through Vancouver to Alaska. Unfortunately, on the map, I didn't see a road through the waterways.

After some research, I called the ferry service. They definitely accepted pets. "But pets are required to stay in the car."

"Can I stay in the car with my dog?" I didn't mind sitting in the cargo section for a few hours.

"Unfortunately, that's not allowed. Passengers have to sit above."

I couldn't risk leaving Oscar in cargo. It would be a three to four-hour trip. What if something happened?

"Most people just give a sedative to their pet," the ferry-service gentleman suggested. "It's not a problem."

Unless it's a warm day. What if it were abnormally hot in the vehicle section? I would never forgive myself if something happened to Oscar.

Travel through the area seemed to require a plane or ferry. I didn't have twenty grand for a plane, and Oscar wasn't going in cargo. So, I needed a plan B. I looked at every possible spot on the map until I noticed a pathway that wound up through British Columbia and entered Alaska through Skagway. Looking closer, I learned the border town of Skagway was along the Alaska Highway! A road!

Instead of going due west and up, we'd go up and across Canada into the Yukon Territory and down. That was our mission. It was a farther distance, but on the upside, it would be land we'd never covered. There were so many variables, particularly the Alaska Highway, but it sounded like a cool trip. Now, I needed to do some more preparation.

Ordinarily, I like to do things on my own, learn firsthand, and find out for myself. But, in this case, I needed some expertise. I started asking around and surfing the Internet. Online, I found an invaluable blog that listed the mile markers along the Alaska Highway. Although it was four years old, it provided several landmarks for our drive.

I looked at maps to figure out suitable overnight rest spots. Then, I checked hotels online. In one town, I found only one dog-friendly hotel listed. I booked that hotel two weeks in advance. Then, I looked to Skagway and booked one of the few available hotels that permitted pets two and half weeks in advance. Again, I didn't want to travel all that way and then have to sleep in the car. I had spoken to someone from the area, and he mentioned that Alaska and the Yukon do get busy during the summer months.

Meanwhile, I loosely outlined the beginning of the trip: passing through Milwaukee and stopping in Eau Claire, Wisconsin (Day 1), then proceeding past Minnesota and reaching Fargo, North Dakota (Day 2). Then, at some point in North Dakota, we'd turn up into Canada.

EVANSTON, ILLINOIS to EAU CLAIRE, WISCONSIN

I PREPARED THE car with the usual items, including an old spare tire, can of flat tire fluid repair, auto tools, duct tape (always have duct tape!), batteries and a flashlight. Then, I added a two-gallon gas container, which was strongly recommended for the sparse Alaska Highway.

I packed a map of Canada, my passport, and Oscar's rabies certificate and meds. In the backseat, I stuffed a large duffel bag, a small overnight bag to carry into the hotels, and a round dog pillow bed.

Oscar wandered outside, sat, and watched me loading up the car. Every so often, I would pet him on the head and say, "Going Alaska!" I'm not sure if he could hear me, but his eyes did light up.

At last, I opened the car door and lifted Oscar inside, placing him beside his friends, Froggie and Sylvester. I locked up the house, got in the Nissan, reset the trip meter to 0, and drove out.

We began our marathon journey cruising up the I-94, past the Six Flags Great America amusement park in Gurnee, across the Wisconsin border, and past the factory outlet stores in Kenosha to Milwaukee. It was routine. As we drove into the heart of Milwaukee, it was a clear, pleasant day—good for walking. Oscar and I went along the Milwaukee River through the middle of town to look around. Eventually, we found the "Bronze Fonz," which is a statue honoring Arthur Fonzarelli (Fonzie, The Fonz), a character in *Happy Days* played by Henry Winkler. The Fonz was legendary for any kid growing up in the seventies. We read—well, I read—the donor's plaque. Then, I placed Oscar next to the life-size statue and captured a few picturesque photos of the statue, Oscar, and the Milwaukee River background.

I admired the scene and the summer day while hoping someone could arrive to take a photo of the two of us. Seeing a site without crowds is wonderful, until you need a photographer. Suddenly, a mother and daughter showed up. "Can I trouble you for a few photos?" They agreed and took my camera. I hoisted Oscar up in the air. After they snapped a few shots, I set down my handsome friend, took the camera back, and looked at the digital photos. *That's a keeper!* I thought. Oscar never takes a bad photo!

Oscar getting thumbs up from The Fonz

"Thanks," I said. "That's a great shot." They gave Oscar a gentle greeting and went on. Oscar and I remained for a few moments. A few boats went by and people passed, as we enjoyed the pleasant driving break.

We continued our stroll along the Riverwalk and returned to the car.

"Son of a bitch!" There was a dent in my bumper. Some idiot couldn't parallel park, or they were careless. No note—just a noticeable dent on the rear right side of the car. At least, the car was drivable, but this was a bad omen.

We retraced our route from downtown Milwaukee back to I-94 and continued driving up through Wisconsin. We made our next extended stop at Black River Crossing Oasis where visitors were welcomed by a huge fiberglass mouse in blue overalls pushing along a block of cheese. Very Wisconsin-ish.

An hour later, we arrived at Eau Claire, Wisconsin. We took the familiar I-94 exit and reached the Econo Lodge. I remembered the hotel from two years earlier. I think there was a mild fountain of youth effect from the car. Oscar seemed more alert and happier when we hit the road. The first day of our two-plus week trek to Alaska had gone smoothly, minus the dent in the car…

EAU CLAIRE, WISCONSIN – Day 1

AFTER AN EASY night, we loaded up the car and checked out. "Ready to hit it?" Oscar was comfortably sitting in the passenger seat.

We began to drive out of the parking lot. Suddenly, I heard a scraping sound. *What the hell?* I gave the car a little gas, and we started to move again along with an erratic scraping sound.

I got out and checked if a branch or something was stuck underneath the car. It was all clear. "That's not good." My old manual car would make that sound when the clutch needed to be repaired. But, does that happen in this car? I drove around the parking lot and back to where we started. There was more scraping. Something was wrong. I pressed the gas pedal while the car was in neutral. OK. Then, I started to ease the car forward. Scraping.

This was not good. We're stuck at an Econo Lodge, over two hundred and fifty miles from home. This car issue seemed beyond my expertise, but I certainly didn't want to drive back to Chicago. Could the car even make it back to Chicago? I needed to find a knowledgeable, recommended mechanic. I went back inside and asked if there was a nearby auto shop. The hotel lady suggested driving about half a mile, making a few left and right turns.

I followed her directions, hoping the car didn't fall apart, and found the local garage and repair shop. I stepped out of the car and saw a mechanic working on a customer's car. "Hi, sorry to interrupt," I called out. He looked up and walked toward me. "I'm on the road with my dog." I pointed to Oscar who was sitting in the front seat looking out the window. "There's a scraping sound coming from the car. Any chance you can quickly look and tell me what's wrong?"

The good-natured mechanic stepped away from his work to look under the hood of my car. While he scanned over the Nissan, I briefly explained what had happened. "It could be the transmission," he started.

"I just had it replaced a month ago! It's brand new." Was the new transmission defective? Or, replaced incorrectly? Then, how could I have been driving for a month without a problem?

"Well, it sounds like the transmission," the mechanic repeated. "I recommend going to Nissan to look at it. It's probably under warranty."

"Oh, my God." I'm screwed. The car wouldn't make it back home. "What a mess. I just came from Chicago, and—"

"No," he said, "there's a Nissan dealer right there." He pointed behind me.

I turned, and just over the tree line, I could see the Nissan sign in the distance! "Alright, what a break." This was a step in the right direction. "And, I just follow that road to the entrance?"

"Yep."

I thanked him, incredibly grateful for the fast assistance.

I drove the car slowly to the Nissan sign in the distance. During the short ride, I heard the occasional scraping, and I agonized over the possible damage I may be doing to get to the next mechanic. We pulled into the lot and parked at the entrance to customer service.

Inside, I repeated my story: I'm travelling across the country, I have a dog with me, and the mechanic thinks it is the transmission. "Ordinarily, I'd have plenty of time," I explained. "But, due to the Alaska part of the trip, I had to reserve limited rooms in advance for certain nights. So, time is an issue." Not to mention, I didn't want to be stranded for days. They seemed very sympathetic. Almost immediately, a mechanic took my car.

So, we found ourselves sitting in a Nissan waiting room in Eau Claire. Oscar napped by my side, unconcerned with the situation. Meanwhile, I half watched TV and half checked email, using the dealership Wi-Fi. Every so often, I peeked at the clock and made mental calculations. *If we can get out of here by lunchtime, we're good. We could race to Fargo.*

As time passed, I ran through other possibilities. Best-case scenario: The transmission is fine, but the technician had made a mistake hooking it up. Worst-case scenario: The transmission is defective, and I need another, taking two-plus days. Worst worst-case scenario: It will take a week and be expensive. Or, it's something entirely different and unrelated to the transmission.

An hour later, the service manager returned with the news: They have to replace the transmission fluid due to a leak. "So, the transmission itself wasn't the problem?"

"No." He explained, "Whoever replaced the transmission last month, they didn't replace the gaskets between. They used the original seals. So, there was a leak."

"So, I've been leaking fluid for the past month. And, it just happened to go dry yesterday?"

"Most likely," he nodded.

The mechanic working on the car had entered the room, so he began answering my questions. "But, the transmission is fine?" An engine running without oil will eventually seize up and be destroyed. I hoped that didn't happen.

"I think so," he answered. "You said the scraping started this morning?"

"Yes, I just heard it. Nothing before that."

"Then, it's possible that there wasn't any damage. But, you'll know in about fifty miles."

"So, I could drive on?" I asked. "Or, should I go back to Chicago and have them replace the transmission again?" I mentioned the planned road trip.

"I don't know. I'd continue driving. If the car is fine after fifty miles, then everything is OK. If you run into problems, then you'll have to replace it."

"But, you can't do it?" I asked.

"We'd have to charge you, whereas your warranty is covered for them to redo the job. We'd charge for labor, but they'd have to replace it all for free," the service manager explained. "Plus, we couldn't get it done today, anyway."

"Was this easy to see? Was it preventable?"

"Doubtful," the mechanic answered. "It's hard to notice, unless you're specifically looking underneath for the leak, especially since you said it was just replaced." Then, he added, "It could take a month of slowly leaking before it ran out of fluid."

"What a mess," I sighed.

"I hear ya," the mechanic sympathized. "But, at least you didn't get stranded. This could've happened any time." They looked down at Oscar and recognized the situation. "We'll try to get you going as soon as possible." I appreciated their sense of urgency and agreed to have them fix the seals and refill the fluid. It would cost two hundred dollars—a bargain, especially if they got us out quickly. Plus, I would be reimbursed later.

In the Nissan waiting area, taking our travel delay in stride

While they repaired the leak and replenished the transmission fluid, Oscar mellowed out and slept in the middle of the Nissan waiting room. The people around were quite friendly, checking on him from time to time. Meanwhile, I watched the clock and ran through more possibilities. Is the transmission ruined or not? Is there extra wear and tear, so it runs, but I should replace it? We were about to drive thousands of miles.

The service manager regularly appeared to update the status. Four hours later, he came with my key. "You're all set."

"Great!" I gladly paid the bill and thanked them for the rush job.

We drove out of the Nissan lot. "No scraping. I hope that's a good sign."

During the ride back, I reassessed our situation. Only one day delay. Fluid leak was fixed. But, did the dry transmission cause permanent damage? Do we go back and check? It would be three hundred miles home. Then, we'd have to turn around and drive three hundred miles again to get back to this point. Ugh, a terrible delay.

Oscar and I returned to the Econo Lodge and walked into the lobby. "Did you get the car fixed?" the desk lady asked.

"I think so," I answered. "Thanks for your suggestion. The mechanic was incredibly helpful."

"So, you need another night?"

"Yep, back for another night."

We got the same room 101, same spot by the exit, same price. Oscar led us down the hallway; he knew the way. Inside our room, I used the same Wi-Fi password to get online and cancel today's arrival to North Dakota. Then, I rescheduled the two hotels in North Dakota. It was a pain in the ass, but everything was easily refunded. Fortunately, it was only a one-day delay, so I kept the other reservations. I had allowed two-to-three days of flexibility. If the driving were slow, we'd still make it in time. Or, if the driving went fast, then we could extend time at favorite spots.

After finishing the online work and updates, I sat on the bed with Oscar and escaped with a TV rerun. Then, I had an idea. Oscar and I returned to the car. The mechanic had mentioned I'd find out if there was significant damage to the transmission within fifty miles. "Let's give it a test drive now." It's better to be stranded near town than thirty miles away. We got in the car and drove down the side streets for a few minutes. "No scraping," I said. "It rides fine."

Then, we entered the I-94 and drove five miles north of Eau Claire. Then, exited, turned around, and raced ten miles on I-94 the other way. Then, we exited, turned around, and drove the other direction. "I think we're good, Oscar."

We drove for twenty-five minutes at various speeds. There was no scraping. Acceleration seemed fine. Did we just get lucky? The Econo Lodge lady, to the right mechanic, to the Nissan dealership, which led to a quick fix. It was a fortuitous chain of events.

We drove around town, stopping for late lunch at Taverna Grill. There was pleasant weather, and the food was quite good. Midway through the meal, the lone couple on the other side of the outdoor patio got up to leave. Oscar perked up his ears as they approached us. The elderly lady smiled. "You have a nice dog. We were watching you share your meal."

"Yeah, he's helping finish it up," I responded.

The elderly man added, "Well, we are grateful and thankful that you are taking such good care of the old dog." They waved as they walked away. Nice people. And, they had those Wisconsin-Canadian accents!

After relaxing for a moment, I paid the check. We drove back to our room at the Econo Lodge. Exhausting day. And, we hadn't gotten anywhere. We were still in Wisconsin. But, we'd reset and try again tomorrow. The trip is still on!

EAU CLAIRE, WISCONSIN to FARGO, NORTH DAKOTA

"WHO LEFT THESE two Lincoln Logs?" I asked out loud. No reaction from Oscar. He just lay on the ground, with his head on his paws, watching me. He had discretely left them at the entrance next to the door. Did he try to wake me last night? At least, they were easy to pick up and flush down the toilet followed by a quick spray of Simple Solution pet cleaner and a swift wipe with spare napkins. No stain, no odor. Just like new.

After cleaning up and packing up, we checked out of the Econo Lodge a second time. With Oscar sitting in the passenger seat, I turned on the ignition. The car sounded fine. I gave the dashboard a gentle, appreciative tap. Despite a bumper dent and almost losing our transmission, the adventure continued!

We left Eau Claire and cruised to Minneapolis. I dreaded this part, expecting the worst in Minneapolis. However, unlike two years ago, going through Minneapolis-Saint Paul wasn't too bad. The tailgating drivers were still there, which sucked, but the roads were slightly better with less delays and fewer potholes than our previous visits.

We stopped at a Minnesota rest stop. I gave Oscar a little walk along the grassy area, walking around the greenery and trees. The Land of 10,000 Lakes still had ten billion mosquitoes. But, this time, I sprayed repellant for our fifteen-minute break. *Experience and Preparation.* Yes, there is a learning curve to traveling.

I did a quick inspection and noticed some liquid pooled underneath the car. I dipped my finger in and smelled it. Nothing. Must be water? Hopefully, it's just condensation from the air conditioner. After the episode yesterday, I was paranoid. When one thing goes wrong on an older car, other problems may follow. I tried an experiment: Driving thirty minutes without air conditioning. Then, I pulled over to look under the car. Result: No liquid dripping from the car. I turned on the air conditioner, and we continued along I-94.

In the afternoon, we arrived in Fargo. Our hotel was located conveniently off I-29, near a ton of restaurants, a mall, and sites. It's an easy town to navigate through. And, while Fargo isn't a massive city, it offers everything one could need.

We checked into the AmericInn. The receptionist sounded like the helpful lady I had spoken to yesterday when switching my hotel reservation. The young man next to her reached down to greet Oscar. We received the key and went to our room at the end of the hallway; another place close to the entrance, good for packing and unpacking or walking Oscar.

We entered the clean, carpeted room with two beds, a microwave, and fridge. I quickly checked messages. Then, to refresh my memory, I scanned over online maps of Fargo. With a few hours of daylight, we had time to check off three items on my list: Nissan, Celebrity Walk of Fame, and dinner. Fifteen minutes later, Oscar and I drove up the street to a Nissan dealership. Yes, incredible luck. There was a full-service Nissan dealer just one mile from our hotel! We pulled into the lot and stopped next to the repair area. After I explained to a technician what had happened, he checked the fluid level in the transmission.

"It's full. Looks good to me." And, after driving three hundred and thirty-five miles today, the car seemed fine to me. We were in and out of the service center within twenty minutes.

We revisited the Convention Center and Celebrity Walk of Fame. While we had stopped there last year, it was still fun to go back. Oscar and I strolled past handprints of Kiss, Alice Cooper, and others, the outdoor Fargo woodchipper, and the notable tourist attractions. It was a nice spot to walk Oscar.

I went inside and noticed the shop had added a section related to *Fargo*, the FX television show. And, by the entrance was the bench with the sign "Is this the end of your quest to visit all 50 states? Welcome to the Club." The tour guide explained that they took a photo and gave a T-shirt that said "North Dakota, the 50th state" to anyone who finished there! The guide added, "Quite a few finish the fifty states in North Dakota." Alaska would be my fiftieth.

The hotel guy suggested Sickies Garage Burgers & Brew, a casual themed restaurant. The outdoor seating was wide open at four o'clock. I picked a table off to the side and ordered a burger for Oscar and a veggie burger for me. While waiting, we relaxed and listened to the classic and hard rock music. My kind of place.

Oscar was comfortable in the sixty-five degree weather. I heard there was a heat wave around the country, but it was quite cool here in North Dakota. While he devoured his dinner, I ate mine. The food was terrific. After eating, Oscar took a nap, while I thought about the day and listened to music. When we left at six o'clock, the parking lot was filled with motorcycles. Tonight was 107.9 The Fox Rock Night. Under a large banner, a DJ was blasting music while a crowd streamed in for dinner. Cool place, but we headed back to the room. I was looking forward to getting a good night's sleep.

"I hope this doesn't become a habit," I said to Oscar at 3:30 a.m.

I got up, put on shoes, and took him outside. Although it was summertime, it was brisk outside. The clouds in the night sky were moving rapidly southbound, so the wind from the north was putting a chill in the air. But, it was worth it. Oscar marked some territory and relieved himself on the grass. When we came back in, I watched a little television, checked email, and looked over potential North Dakota attractions for tomorrow. Afterward, I tried to get back to sleep. Meanwhile, Oscar was out.

FARGO, NORTH DAKOTA to MINOT, NORTH DAKOTA

ON THE THIRD leg of the trip, we continued driving west on I-94/US-52 through North Dakota. It was good driving through this state: open roads and 75 mph speed limit. Someone we met mentioned it was up to 80 mph in parts of South Dakota.

After one hundred miles, we approached Jamestown. It claimed to have the world's largest buffalo and a rare white one. On the map, it appeared to be a good halfway point for today's stretch of driving. When we got to town, I didn't see much. *Where are the buffalo?* The highway billboards advertised them. *I know they're around here.*

I went inside a gas station to ask for specific directions to the giant buffalo. The attendee was unsure, so I tried the motel next door. The older gentleman told me, "There's a spot with a big buffalo and live ones, too." He gave me rough directions. Since he seemed knowledgeable, I asked for a lunch recommendation too. He pointed at the trucker stop/diner across the street. Through the window, I could see S & R Truck Plaza & Cafe with a gas station and mini mart.

Then, he assured me, "That food is good; different than Applebee's and the others. It's inside."

The journey can be influenced by people you meet.

I followed the old guy's directions, which led us to a tourist area containing a museum, old town, amphitheater, and walking trail. And, there was a huge open range where buffalo were roaming around. "We're getting warmer, Oscar," I said as we pulled into a parking space near the museum.

Oscar and I explored the area, seeking the giant buffalo. I noticed several parking spaces were occupied by numbered racing cars of different shapes and sizes, many having overseas license plates. Subsequently, we met some of the owners and drivers and learned they were traveling in a "Trans-America Nova Scotia to San Francisco Rally." We encountered visitors from Arizona, New Zealand, London, and other places. The group recalled participating in road rallies through South America, across the US, and in Europe. It was adventurous and fascinating.

Walking through the Frontier Village parking lot, I admired the cool cars with painted sketches that illustrated maps and roads these international cars had taken. Some of the cars were caked with mud. I imagined a rugged cross-country road race, the sort you'd see in a movie. One of the British drivers mentioned that he was glad to get out of Nova Scotia. He preferred driving in the States. I hoped that didn't mean the next fifteen hundred miles through Canada was going to be hard driving for us. We'd find out tomorrow.

Oscar and I passed a big, red Suburban with the emblem "The Endurance Rally Association." Beside it, two men were standing behind a big utility vehicle. One of the back doors was partly open where I could see large tool boxes, auto parts, and equipment inside. It was a mini-garage. I asked the guys a few questions. They explained the organization, and the fact they were part of the crew that escorted the drivers and offered repairs along the way. I learned that many of the cars had been shipped overseas by the owners.

As we walked away, I looked at Oscar. "Yes, we're on a road rally, too!"

Bring Oscar

We passed an old US Mail stagecoach, an antique Standard Oil cart on wagon wheels, and other Western antiques. Then, we proceeded on Louis L'Amour Lane through the tourist center—and I saw the massive buffalo statue in the distance! Oscar and I followed the paved trail toward the statue, along with several tourists and the road rally racers. As we neared, I pulled out the camera to capture a few photos. This thing was enormous—twenty-six feet tall and sixty tons. I took a picture of an adult couple looking underneath the buffalo. Then, I tried to put Oscar in the frame to gain perspective of the size.

Oscar posing in Jamestown, North Dakota
World's Largest Buffalo, 1959 – "Dakota Thunder"

After reading the plaque on a rock and posted information about the area, Oscar and I returned to the Frontier Village. Walking among the families, couples, and road rally people, we went through a huge library of Louis L'Amour Western books. I discovered that the famous writer was indeed born in Jamestown, North Dakota. Then, we passed by the fire department, decorated with colorful lettering and images on the building, a bank, and a few cafés. It was a neat old western town.

Oscar and I wandered along the boundary of the open field, where the buffalo were grazing in the distance. We paused at the National Buffalo Museum then resumed walking until I spotted a few picnic tables with a view of the open field. Perfect! We sat at a picnic table to eat our lunch and enjoy the beautiful scene. During the past hour, the herd of buffalo had moved closer. Now, I could see them better, including one of the rare white buffalo.

Switching routes, we continued west on I-94 instead of US 52 to the northwest. We traveled almost two hours, reaching the middle of the state, the capital Bismarck. I recalled our picnic lunch at their Walmart two years earlier! We turned onto US 83, heading north toward Canada. There were several ways to enter Canada. I just picked a route that likely had a solid, developed highway.

Forty miles north of Bismarck, we paused at the Lewis and Clark Interpretive Center in Washburn, North Dakota. I had no idea what we'd see, but it seemed like a good place to get some exercise for Oscar. I assumed I'd be able to read a little bit about Lewis and Clark. Maybe learn something about the Missouri River and Northern Plains travelers. Perhaps, more buffalos, too.

In the end, there was a lot of space. Wide open space with a walking trail and some windfarms in the background. One thing there wasn't a lot of: people. Including the Nissan, there were two cars in the entire parking lot. After looking at the outdoor sculptures and storyboards, and stretching in the cool air for thirty minutes, we resumed the last part of today's drive.

Eighty miles later, we finished the day's driving in Minot, North Dakota. Unsure of what Canada would bring, I chose this location, a hundred miles from the border—pretty much the last big town before crossing into Canada. "Minot? Why not!"

Minot seemed set up in grids, similar to the numbered avenues and streets in Fargo. The town was small enough to get around easily but large enough with an adequate selection of restaurants, snacks, and stores. Nice place.

We arrived at the La Quinta Inn and parked in a large lot beside a Sonic and Fuddruckers. *A Sonic milkshake later sounds pretty good,*

I thought. Carrying my laptop bag, I walked with Oscar into the lobby. The nice lady at the front desk recognized my credit card. "I'm a USAA member, too." We had a brief conversation about the Minot Air Force Base and her family's military service. She handed me the key and recounted the hotel offerings: Wi-Fi, breakfast in the morning, cookies and refreshments at the front desk. I learned that on Monday through Thursday, this La Quinta offered a free dinner in their restaurant. As we walked to the hallway, I glanced inside the dining area. The buffet looked and smelled good.

Our room was very nice! It was new and spacious, including a microwave and fridge. So, I could put together a plate from the dining hall and save it for later. On the bed, there was a puppy goodie bag, containing doggie clean-up bags, dog treats, and a welcome card with info.

I popped on the television and noticed this hotel offered HBO, so maybe there was a movie on later?

While Oscar rested, I checked email, uploaded photos, and looked into hotel options for tomorrow. Then, I trotted to the dining area to make a dinner plate and carried the meal, a drink, and a few complimentary cookies back to the room. When I reentered, Oscar was up by the door waiting. "I got us some vittles." He followed me to the desk area where I shoveled some food off the plate into his bowl. The hotel's buffet was good.

After dinner, we had a few hours of daylight left. Last night it didn't get dark until after 10:00 p.m. We went farther north today, and the summer solstice was two days away, so our day would extend even longer. Although tired from a day on the road, I didn't want to skip a chance to see a new place. Rather than watch TV and lie around, Oscar and I rallied to explore Minot.

We visited the Scandinavian Heritage Park with statues, pretty grounds, and a bit of history. Hans Christian Andersen, Vikings, and Winter Olympic legends were recognized, as well as Minot's Swedish immigrants. Plus, some giant, red wooden Dala horses and a huge Japanese-looking building and garden stood out in the park. Honestly, I'm not sure what these were or how they tied into Scandinavian heritage. As the sun was setting, we finished our brief, pleasant Minot tour. We were ready for bed. Tomorrow, we'd make our crossing into Canada!

I thought the evening walk around the Heritage Park would tire him out. But, at 1:30 a.m., he was up and wandering. *Damn.* "You really need to go out?" I couldn't take a chance. I put on my shoes, threw on a sweatshirt, and wobbled half asleep outside with Oscar. He sniffed around the grass, taking his sweet time. The chilly air woke me up. *Ugh.* It's nearly 2:00 a.m., and I was wide awake.

After another five minutes, nothing happened; it appeared Oscar had no interest in relieving himself. He just wanted to walk around. It was a wasted trip in the middle of the night. False alarm. "I give up, Oscar." I took off his leash. He stared at me. So, I lifted him on the bed. Then, I took off my shoes and sweatshirt, climbed under the covers and went back to sleep.

At 5:00 a.m., I felt Oscar moving around. He sat up. "Really?" I looked at him. "You're killing me!" I got out of the warm bed, put on my shoes and sweatshirt, and took him out again. We passed the young guy finishing his shift. He nodded as we walked by.

Outside, Oscar started sniffing and enjoying the cool air. "Oscar, this is not part of the plan. Please do something." He lifted his leg and left his mark on a bush by the entrance. "Thank you."

MINOT, NORTH DAKOTA to REGINA, SASKATCHEWAN, CANADA

DESPITE THE COMFORTABLE bed, I got up. I didn't want to miss the breakfast. Plus, the sooner we left, the sooner we would cross into Canada. "You're good, right?" Oscar was lying on the carpet. His eyes looked at me, but he didn't bother to lift his head. "Getting breakfast," I told him. "Stay here."

I exited the room, making sure I had the key. It would be tough to explain locking myself out, while locking my dog in! I ran down the hallway to the breakfast area, quickly collected anything I could carry—apple, orange juice, eggs for Oscar, fresh fruit and banana, muffin—and raced back to the room.

When I opened the door, Oscar was sitting at the entrance, just waiting. He looked up at me, sniffed the aroma of the food, and his ears perked up. "Yep, got some vittles for you." I ate the fruit and muffins and handed him the scrambled eggs. Breakfast of champions.

We started packing up. After a few trips back and forth to the car, with Oscar following along, we were done. Down the road, the Tesoro gas station offered free air. "Use it when you can; not when you have to." I checked the air in the tires and gassed up the car. All's well. I felt the crisp chill in the air. Cooler weather will be good for driving and for Oscar. I climbed into the car, dropped the gas receipt on the pile of papers under the armrest, and started the engine. We left Minot and drove northwest on US 52 toward the border.

After one hundred miles, I saw the official border inspection signs. Welcome to Canada—Oscar's first trip to another country. The crossing was rather uneventful. There were no other cars when we arrived. The Canadian Border Agent didn't ask me much. When I offered Oscar's rabies certificate and my passport, the agent took a quick glance and handed them back.

That's it?

I was ready to explain my story about our planned trip, why we were going, and where we were going—but he never asked. I guess not many people are trying to sneak into Canada through this Saskatchewan crossing. Besides, there was no true "fence." It seemed to me that anyone could simply go two miles down the road and just walk across. It was all oil and wheat fields and rail.

The agent waved us through, and we entered North Portal. I walked Oscar around the quiet open area, took a ceremonial photo in front of the border sign "Welcome to Saskatchewan! Land of Living Skies," and got five mosquito bites.

Highway 39 was only two lanes, and the posted speed limit was 100 (kilometers/hour). Welcome to the metric system. It was mostly open roads with fast drivers, so we cruised along.

The scenery appeared to be an extension of North Dakota. We passed wheat farms and silos and a ton of energy places: oil drills and miners. Also, trains transporting cargo went by us. The landscape contained lots of lush green due to the recent rains. We saw a deer run across the road. And, there were plenty of cows along the way.

In new areas, I observe the billboards and their advertisements. We passed several with the motto RID—Report Impaired Drivers—a Canadian crackdown on texting while driving. Amen.

In the afternoon, we arrived in Regina, the capital of Saskatchewan. There was tons of traffic in this area. We passed by many recognizable franchises, including plenty of American spots: Chili's, PetSmart, Perkins, and Walmart, to name a few. I even saw a Menchie's Frozen Yogurt next to a Fatburger. *Was that the California Fatburger? Damn, we don't even have Fatburger in Chicago.* While I collected visual information of the city, Oscar watched the colorful stores and cars passing by.

Since this was a half-improvised road trip, I still didn't have Canadian cash. We made two stops at banks along the way. Because I was not an account holder, each one of them refused to exchange my US dollars for Canadian currency. I was reluctant to use an ATM, since I had no idea what the exchange rate would be. And, I preferred to exchange the cash I was carrying in the car rather than add more. I could've planned this better. After twenty-five minutes, I postponed the bank search.

I followed my handwritten directions to the Comfort Inn, just off Highway 1/East Victoria Avenue, a main road through Regina. Check-in was easy. And, the people at the front reception desk were quite nice. I noticed the clock: We had hit a time change along the way, gaining an hour.

The room space was tight, but it worked. There was a patio door to exit directly to the parking lot. This made packing and unpacking the car very easy. Also, walking Oscar in the middle of the night was a short trip.

While taking a break, I turned on the TV and followed my routine of checking email, uploading photos, and making notes about the day's trip. Suddenly, clouds moved in overhead and it darkened outside. Then, rain. Then, pouring rain. Then, hail! *What happened to the seventy-seven-degree, warm day?* After thirty minutes, it stopped, cooled down, and the sky cleared. Small piles of ice were around the outside entrance of the room. *What the hell is with the weather?!* I learned that hail can occur in the summer. Basically, the water and moisture are trapped in the clouds, where it solidifies into ice before actually falling out of the sky. Odd phenomenon.

For dinner, we tried a Chinese restaurant next to the hotel. China Liang's Buffet wasn't too bad. The inside was dated, decorative, and dark. The food at the buffet was a mix of fresh and appealing, as well as items that had been soaking for a while. Instead, I ordered off the menu.

I paid with a credit card. The restaurants and vending machines wouldn't take US currency. I had over three grand in cash, but couldn't buy a candy bar, let alone dinner, with the wrong currency.

I received our food and went back outside where Oscar was waiting. When we returned to the hotel room, I unloaded the white cartons with dinner. Then, on the bathroom sink, I started preparing the *Chef Lance Special*. I placed the bowl with dry dog food on the counter. Then, I added some chicken and beef, making sure to include the sauces. Then, added a dash of Oscar's pain medication under the sauces (to disguise the smell). I mixed the concoction and lowered the bowl in front of my eager dinner companion.

Oscar gobbled his Chinese chicken mixed with dry dog food. "Easy, easy," I said as I watched him eating superfast. Then, he was choking a bit. Obviously, he was pleased with the dinner choice. "Chew, Oscar. You gotta chew."

Meanwhile, I dumped some Chinese food on top of rice and sat on the bed with my dinner plate. I skimmed over the channels on the remote control, eventually settling for a rerun of some sitcom. A few minutes later, Oscar wandered over to me, licking his lips several times, getting the last bit of chicken flavor.

REGINA, SASKATCHEWAN, CANADA to LLOYDMINSTER, SASKATCHEWAN, CANADA

I HAD NO idea what to visit in Saskatchewan, so I relied on RoadsideAmerica.com. I wrote down a few odd attractions, offering places to stop for a quick break: a huge, colorful coffee pot in Davidson; a giant Mountie statue in North Battleford (that seemed very "Canada"); World's largest Tomahawk. Each provided a photo opportunity, maybe some history, and a chance for Oscar to stretch, smell around, and do his business. In addition, I anticipated places to see in between. *It's the journey, not the destination.* The written list of places provided the framework—sort of a scavenger hunt—for the day's drive. Then, who knows what we'd find in between?!?

We started at the Petro-Canada gas station. Measurements in liters, price in Canadian dollars; I had no idea if gas was expensive or cheap. There were lots of oil wells around here; I hoped it was cheaper. While filling up the tank, I did a quick mental math exercise. A liter is little more than quarter of a gallon, and a Canadian dollar is about four-to-three with the US dollar. And—

I stopped trying to calculate. Did it matter? I was buying it regardless of the price.

I finished pumping the gas, grabbed the receipt, and got back into the car. After placing the receipt in the pile of travel notes, I pulled out of the bay and returned to the road. We went to the bank I had seen yesterday, next to the Fatburger, and exchanged five hundred US dollars at an acceptable rate and without a problem. "Now, we're set. Air con or windows, Oskie?"

He meandered into the passenger seat. I cracked open the windows. As we drove down the road, Oscar poked his head out and enjoyed the breeze. When we reached the highway, and the wind was whipping, he pulled his head back inside. I rolled up the windows and cracked the sunroof. Oscar pushed his nose up to the roof, feeling the breeze.

After sixty miles, or in Canada about one hundred kilometers, we picked Chamberlain for a quick stop. I was drawn in by a statue and monument, a sign promoting the "world's most interesting rock," and a cool ice cream/snack bar. Across the road, there was a huge grain silo beside railroad tracks. At the moment, a long line of railroad cars were resting at this stop. One of them had *Saskatchewan* painted across it. That's where we are!

Oscar and I got out and stretched a bit. I grabbed a terrific cherry shake at the Twisted Sisters snack bar then looked for anything interesting. We found the most interesting rock, which looked like a gimmick to get people into a barbeque place. There was metal artwork surrounding a Canadian Maple Leaf flag, as well as a statue, which offered a bit of local history. Mostly, the rest area offered open views of the silos, railroad, and the landscape in the distance.

Thirty minutes later, we stopped at Davidson to view the "World's Largest Coffee Pot"—a pure photo op in the middle of nowhere. It's about twenty-four feet high, touted as the world's largest, and supposedly it could hold one hundred and fifty thousand cups of coffee. Next to the giant pot was a giant coffee cup. I approached the items to get a closer look at the painted images and material. Then, I walked about forty feet in the distance with my camera. Oscar slowly followed me. "Wait a sec, buddy," I told him. "I want to get you in this." I shot a few photos as he continued to hobble toward me. "Oy, you're falling apart," I said as he approached. "Head tilted, arms sticking out, twisted body, but, you're a warrior!" He reached me, and I gave him a nice hug. Then he fell into me.

Taking a giant coffee break? Halfway between Regina and Saskatoon

We passed Saskatoon, the largest city in Saskatchewan, and switched to Yellowhead Highway 16. Thirty kilometers northwest, we randomly stopped in Langham. I was getting hungry, and I knew Oscar could always eat! Beyond a Subway, I spotted a place called Gk's Restaurant next to a cheap motel with a gravel lot.

I cracked the windows open and left Oscar in the car while I checked it out. It was run by an Indian family, judging by the young woman who took my order, the chef, the old guy sitting in front, and kids running around. I scanned over the people eating inside: Their plates looked good. I ordered a wrap and fries. *Hey, if it didn't work out, I could go back to Subway.*

The meal was tasty, confirming you can't always judge a place by its appearance. This restaurant looked like an oversized tin shed with light blue and white paint. But, inside was modest décor, and they made a terrific lunch!

We continued on TransCanada 16, until stopping in North Battleford to view the Giant Mountie Statue. On the roadside, we stretched our legs and got a closer look. The plaque mentioned a dedication to the pioneers and citizens of North Battleford. As cars drove by, we took in the fresh air while I took pictures of Oscar sitting in front of the towering horse and Mountie.

It was comical. I thought, *Who on earth plans to stop on the side of a road to look at a random statue in the middle of Saskatchewan?* I wondered what it looked like to the Canadians driving by. *I am such a tourist.* I laughed at myself as I took photos.

Suddenly, a white compact car pulled over next to ours. Two young women got out and walked over to the statue. I guess I'm not the only tourist. They looked up at the twenty-foot structure, smiled for a few photos, and joked around. Then, they noticed Oscar and me.

"Are you from around here?" I asked.

"We are driving through," one answered. "From Winnipeg; we're on holiday."

They noticed my car. "Are you from the United States?"

"Yes, Illinois," I added, "Chicago. Are you familiar?"

"We've heard of it."

"Never been?"

"No. New York and California," one answered. "Nice puppy."

"Yes, he's a good one," I said. "But, he's not a puppy. He's fifteen."

"Wow. He doesn't look that old." Then, noticing my camera, "Do you want a picture?"

"Sure, why not," I answered. I picked up Oscar and we posed for a few shots. They returned my camera, said goodbye, got back in their car, and left. I guess we weren't so out of the ordinary. Taking photos, on holiday, just like the Canadians.

In the afternoon, we reached Lloydminster, on the western border of Saskatchewan and the eastern border of Alberta. Yes, the city straddles two provinces. We pulled into the Super 8 in

Lloydminster, Saskatchewan, just off the main road next to a gas station and Tim Hortons.

After scouting the room, Oscar and I did some recon. We parked next to the Royal Canadian Mounted Police Station in Lloydminster, Alberta, and walked toward City Hall to visit the Hope Monument, a tribute to the service and kindness of the RCMP. *Why do I think of Dudley Do-Right whenever I see or hear anything related to the Mounties?*

We continued down the road to the giant orange dividers. My online map was completely off, but I found the border markers. It's tough to miss towering orange structures lined along a major street. They were notable symbols of an interesting geographical fact: a major town straddling two Canadian provinces. We walked onto 50th avenue, and I placed Oscar at the border line. His hind legs were sitting across Saskatchewan and Alberta at the same time! This made me think of when we visited the Four Corners at the intersection of Arizona, Colorado, New Mexico, and Utah.

I took a photo of Oscar straddling the border. Behind him was a border marker with the two colorful provincial emblems embedded in the concrete. "Look at you, Oscar. The world traveler, covering two Canadian provinces at once."

After touring and dinner, we returned to the room with a candy bar for me and a big chew stick for Oscar. While he sat in the corner enjoying his snack, I did a quick skim online through maps and RoadsideAmerica. I looked over tomorrow's route and found Vegreville, home of the "World's Largest Easter Egg." Then, I noticed a recommended Asian restaurant in Whitecourt, Alberta. I wrote down these options for tomorrow. After watching TV, I followed Oscar to sleep. I was tired. It was 10:00 p.m. and still light outside.

LLOYDMINSTER, SASKATCHEWAN, CANADA to FOX CREEK, ALBERTA, CANADA

"DAY SEVEN, OSCAR." I opened the map, took out the yellow highlighter, and traced our route over the past three days to our current position in the middle of Canada. Looking at the map, I could see the fifteen hundred miles we'd covered. We were halfway there. We had a long way to go, but I could start to anticipate Alaska.

I assessed the road trip concerns. Oscar's legs were weak, but his spirit seemed good. The car seemed to be going fine. Our lodging so far had been fine. We have rooms going there. *What about the return part?* I'd figure that out later.

"You must be lovin' this," I said to Oscar. "Temperature's gotta be in the low fifties."

Aside from the daily walks, twenty minutes on a stationary bike in the La Quinta Minot gym, and occasional sit-ups and push-ups in hotel rooms, I hadn't done any exercising. That needed to change.

We packed up the car and were back on the open road. Our first stop was in Vegreville to check out the "big egg." In the distance, an ornate, giant aluminum egg was displayed in the middle of a huge community park. Very cool. We stopped beside a group of information boards. Oscar waited beside me as I read about the "World's Largest Easter Egg." The project began in 1974 to commemorate the Alberta cultural centennial. It seemed to have some history recognizing the Ukrainian population. Mostly, the mathematics and science that went into building this ellipsoid structure was interesting. The thing was huge, and the construction was awesome. "If this is the egg, wait 'til you see the Easter bunny!" Oscar just yawned.

Reading further, I saw it was referred to as the Pyzanka—a decorated Ukrainian Easter egg, where the design and color scheme contained all sorts of symbolism. Plus, the large egg swiveled like a weather vane. Impressive.

Oscar's head tilting like the giant egg

We continued driving through Alberta, taking a few breaks at basic rest stops or road pull-offs. The highway went through Edmonton, passing Wayne Gretzky Drive. *Was there a statue of the hockey legend?* West of Edmonton, we made the change from 16 Trans-Canada Highway to the Alberta Provincial Highway 43. This would lead us to the Alaska Highway! At one Alberta pullover, there was a large display describing the construction of the Alaska Highway and its military need during World War II. It recognized the significance of Highway 43, which would lead to Dawson Creek, British Columbia, and the "Alcan Military Highway."

When we reached Whitecourt, Alberta, we made a planned lunch stop at Kujira off 50th Avenue and 50th Street. It checked all the boxes: Japanese take-out, small town, easy to find, and convenient parking. Plus, they were open at 3:30 on Sunday, Father's Day. I trotted inside and ordered a feast: egg rolls, rice, veggies, soup, tempura, and more. Plus, I added a dinner Bento box with teriyaki chicken for Oscar. Kujira was decorative, and I felt good about this choice.

Outside, I prepared our "concrete picnic" out of the rain. I poured some of the chicken and sauce on top of the dog food. Meanwhile, Oscar was sniffing each carton, and he began licking the beef and broccoli carton with brown sauce seeping out of it. "Hang on," I told him. "There's plenty of food for all of us!" That did not deter him. He kept at it.

Finally, I dropped his bowl in front of him. He started gobbling the chicken on top of it. At the same time, I started making my lunch. By the time I set up my plate, Oscar had polished off the chicken. He was sniffing the other cartons. "Damn, that was fast." I poured more chicken and beef into his bowl. Weight was no longer a problem for Oscar. He was down to roughly forty pounds.

I started drinking some of the miso soup and eating the rice and veggies, then I took a bite of the tempura and the salad. It was all tasty. While it poured outside, we remained dry, enjoying our picnic under the overhang. As we finished eating lunch, the downpour turned into a sprinkle. "Perfect," I told him. "Ready to get rolling?" Oscar was still licking his face, enjoying the aftertaste of lunch.

Bring Oscar

Adapting to rain: eating Japanese take-out in the dry corner of a building

In the distance was a small grassy area with a few statues. After placing Oscar's bowls in the trunk, we walked down the street. Suddenly, Oscar did an abrupt, big somersault fall. *Oh, no.* "Are you alright?" He slowly collected himself, and I helped prop him up. We continued walking. A few minutes later, he tripped and somersaulted again over his face. "Oh, are you OK?" I noticed a scrape on his nose. The poor guy looked a bit out of it. "Let's stop for a moment."

I swept the excess rainwater off a bench, and we sat. Then, Oscar fell asleep on the sidewalk beside the bench. I listened to music while Oscar napped. The skies completely cleared, and it was sunny out. If only lunch had been an hour later.

The last part of today's drive offered a clear view of pine trees. It's amazing how the scenery evolved. It reminded me of Arizona, where elevation and scenery can change multiple times. We had a saying: There are six types of climate, and Arizona has seven of them.

We arrived at Fox Creek and found Timber Ridge Inn & Suites, located off Highway 43. In the parking lot were trucks and equipment vehicles. In the next area, there were big rigs, which looked like oil transports. I grabbed Oscar and his leash, and we went to see what kind of place I had picked. As we walked, it seemed as if Oscar had rallied nicely. An hour ago, he seemed exhausted. But, as we entered another hotel, he was alert and raring to go!

The young woman at the desk checked us in. "Do you have a room preference?" she asked.

"First floor is best for him." I pointed to Oscar.

"I can put you by an entrance."

"Great." I thanked her. First floor room close to a doorway was convenient for packing and unpacking and an easy distance for Oscar.

Inside our room, it was spacious and smelled fresh. There was a window view of the trucks and adjacent industrial park. But, it was bright and seemed new. I noted the few cars in the parking lot were heavy pick-up trucks. I wondered if a Nissan Altima was an acceptable car to get to Alaska. *We'll find out soon.*

FOX CREEK, ALBERTA, CANADA to DAWSON CREEK, BRITISH COLUMBIA, CANADA – ALASKA HIGHWAY MILE O

I WAS AWAKE before Oscar. Timber Ridge had a nice laundry room, and as the saying goes, wash the clothes when you can...not when you have to. The next several days may not provide an easy opportunity. I made a trip to the car and grabbed a pile of change—"Loonies" (Canadian one-dollar coins) and "Toonies" (Canadian two-dollar coins). Then, I collected my clothes and Oscar's blanket and went to the open laundry room. It was two Canadian dollars for soap, two Loonies for the washer, and two loonies for the dryer. My first Canadian load of laundry.

After breakfast, we departed Fox Creek. Having crossed through Saskatchewan and most of Alberta, I was excited to be nearing British Columbia, which would lead to the Yukon Territory, and eventually into Alaska. Instead of a smartphone, I referred to the screenshots of online maps saved on my laptop. Also, I used hand-drawn sketches of major streets and landmarks as my guide. Or, sometimes, I'd just wing it. Most towns were small enough that if you simply drive to the downtown plaza, then you'll find it!

The sun broke out when we arrived at our next rest stop, Beaverlodge. There was a gigantic beaver perched on a log! We stopped at the welcome area for a mandatory photo. "Just a quick stop," I promised him. "Then we'll get you some lunch." Oscar went along as I guided him in front of the "World's Biggest Beaver."

"Stay, Oscar." He waited and watched me walk backward. "Stay." Then, as I got the camera ready, Oscar started to wander. "Wait!! Let me get the photo first." He stopped. "Look over here." As soon as he glanced in my direction, I shot the photo. "That's a keeper." Oscar and the Beaver. "Good job." I ran thirty feet to the side of the beaver to get a different angle. (This thing was enormous.) Then, I stepped twenty feet in another direction. Oscar just sat in the grass and waited. He seemed content watching me run around taking photos.

Afterward, we walked over to monuments and etchings in front of the Cultural Centre, which presented a history of Beaverlodge and its early settlers. Then, content with the photos and introduction to this town, we drove one mile down the road, turned a couple of blocks over, and saw Soups, our lunch spot. (Who needs Google Maps when you have a map drawn on paper?!)

The quaint restaurant was filled with locals, and the menu was solid, with baked items as well. *Yeah, this will work!* I ordered a veggie sandwich, pastry, chips, and side of chicken.

"For here or to go?"

"To go," I answered, "I'm going to eat out front with my dog."

"Wait, do you want to sit in the patio?"

"It's closed up," I told them. "We'll just eat in the grass area, if that's OK."

"Not necessary. We'll open up a table for you," the lady said. "We closed it because of the rain the past two days." A guy came outside and opened the patio for Oscar and me and brought water to fill Oscar's bowl. Then, the lady unlocked the chairs and swiftly wiped the table top.

"Wow, thanks," I said to her. I certainly appreciated the red-carpet treatment.

"No trouble." She walked back inside.

A few minutes later, the guy brought out my sandwich, chips, and chopped chicken for Oscar. The food looked tasty. The lady who took my order came out to meet Oscar. "He is so sweet!"

"Yeah, he's a good one," I agreed. "Fifteen years old."

"Oh my God!"

"But, he's a warrior. We've driven a long way."

"Where are you from?" the guy asked.

"We started in Illinois." Then, I added, "Chicago area. Have you been?"

"Yes," the guy said. "I go to school in the US." He nodded toward Oscar. "Does he want more water?"

"He's good. Thanks," I said. "So, what do you do out here? Besides, work at the restaurant." The guy explained that he was from San Francisco. He had met a girl from Calgary and moved to Beaverlodge. At the moment, he was working part-time at the restaurant and part-time as a copywriter. They went back inside to check on the lunch crowd. I handed Oscar some chicken and enjoyed my sandwich.

An older couple exited the café and smiled as they saw us eating. "Nice dog," they said as they leaned over to view Oscar sitting under the table in the shade. Another group, who had been dining next to the window, came out and pet him as they left.

After finishing the meal, I phoned a bed-and-breakfast in Whitehorse. I was thinking a day or two ahead. "We do have a few rooms available on Thursday and Friday," the lady told me.

"Fantastic." Then, I confirmed, "And, with a dog."

"Yes, of course. We have dogs here."

I gave the lady my name, email address, and credit card information. "I'm glad I called. The website said there were no rooms available. I hoped there might be a change or cancellation."

"No, we have rooms." She explained that several of the online outfits will claim a bed-and-breakfast room is unavailable if you're checking less than three days before the stay. "We're trying to correct that error in the system." (It never hurts to ask, even if the property is listed as unavailable.)

"Well, I look forward to meeting you and seeing your place. Thanks." We were set for what seemed like a beautiful spot outside of the Whitehorse town.

After enjoying the break, I asked to wrap up the other half of the sandwich. A moment later, the lady returned the boxed sandwich, and she brought another container with cooked chicken. "Here is a bit more for your dog." There was a small pack of chicken strips for Oscar.

"Wow, thanks. That's very nice of you!" I pointed at Oscar. "He certainly appreciates it."

Soups was a terrific lunch stop. The sandwich with fresh vegetables was delicious, and the dessert—a cinnamon roll—was the best I'd ever had. Tons of cinnamon and sugar. I bought an extra for tomorrow. I wish I could've stuck around to try other items on the menu. *Maybe on the way back?*

Within an hour, we crossed into British Columbia. Then, twenty-five minutes later, we reached Dawson Creek with the big mile marker sign: "You are now entering the World Famous Alaska Highway – Dawson Creek, BC." Above this gateway were three flags: Canada, British Columbia, and the United States. Two thousand miles of driving, and we were here!

We joined several visitors parked in a lot, then each of us walked over to stand under the sign for a photo. Oscar and I took our turn, and a helpful person shot a few souvenir photos.

Alaska is that way!

When the crowd cleared, I read some of the plaques and markers, which explained the history of the Alaska Highway. In March of 1942, troops arrived in Dawson Creek to begin construction of a fifteen hundred-plus mile road to Delta Junction, near Fairbanks. The small agricultural town was immediately converted into a huge industrial area, transporting materials and people to quickly build this road for the war. Incredibly, they accomplished this feat in under one year!

After reading about the highway, we continued to nearby Walter Wright Pioneer Village. The heritage site showed a history of the early pioneers, including buildings that replicated an old settlement, sort of walking through time.

Afterward, we went into the town, filled with shops, restaurants, and tourist items. Also, there were colorful murals depicting the historic area. In the center, we located the circular road where the highway actually begins. The Alaska Highway doesn't start in

Alaska. Mile 0 is in Dawson Creek, British Columbia. (And, no, the TV show *Dawson's Creek* isn't there.)

There was a signpost with the heading "Mile 0 Alaska Highway." Above it, there was a board listing notable towns along the way, including their mileage distances, and at the top, three flags were waving: Canada, British Columbia, and Dawson Creek district.

I took a few photos from a distance. Then, Oscar and I crossed the streets to get a few more pictures from different angles of the signpost in the middle of the circle. Suddenly, a scruffy, old guy approached us. "Gimme your camera." *Huh? Is this guy trying to steal my camera?!* I hesitated for a moment. *Wait, I'm in Dawson Creek. These are just a bunch of nice people.*

"Go over there. I'll shoot a photo of you two."

We waited for the cars to pass, and then I led Oscar to the middle of the street. I picked him up, and we stood in the island next to the signpost. The old guy took several photos for us followed by the thumbs up sign. After the cars passed, Oscar and I crossed back over the street.

"Thanks," I told him.

"I took a bunch of them for ya." He handed me the camera. I viewed the digital pictures. He had taken more than enough to make sure we got a good one.

Oscar and I wandered up and down the streets of Dawson Creek. There were historical markers, info, and old black-and-white photos of the town. Inside the Alaska Highway House, the museum displayed panels about World War II and the need to build the highway. Also, there were exhibits about the engineers, labor, and challenges of building this road in the terrain of British Columbia and Alaska. It further amazed me how it took about nine months to build the highway from BC toward Fairbanks. Just nine months! In Chicago, I watched a patch of highway under construction for years. *What has happened to our government?*

After touring the main streets, we went to the Comfort Inn. The location was good and check-in was easy. The front desk guy was an Asian gentleman who reminded me of my childhood orthodontist, Dr. Tadano.

Bring Oscar

Although it was completely light outside, it was dinnertime. I stayed with a local theme and picked a place called Mile 0 Pizza. Oscar waited beside the lamppost while I went inside. There were nice customers waiting for their orders and pleasant people working and preparing the pizzas. I ordered a veggie pizza, salad, and soda to go. During the fifteen-minute wait, Oscar and I looked at more murals and shops around the area.

After picking up the pizza, we drove back to the hotel. Oscar's nose was on the box the entire drive back. Inside the room, I flipped on the TV and began with the salad. Meanwhile, Oscar started snacking on his food. After the salad, I started on the pizza. At the same time, Oscar meandered over to the desk next to me. "Nice timing," I told him. He assumed the position: sitting on his hindquarters, waiting with anticipation. I tore off a piece of my cheese slice and handed it to him. While he chewed, I took a bite of the rest. It was quite good. As I took another bite, I looked down at Oscar. He was licking his lips and waiting for more. "That was quick." I tore another piece and handed it to him.

DAWSON CREEK, BRITISH COLUMBIA, CANADA – ALASKA HIGHWAY MILE 0 to FORT NELSON, BRITISH COLUMBIA, CANADA – ALASKA HIGHWAY MILE 300

I WOKE UP at 7:00 a.m. Since Oscar was sleeping, I decided to check out the fitness room down the hallway. I picked up a "20" dumbbell. *Is that pounds or kilograms?* It had to be pounds, unless I had gotten massively stronger all of a sudden. I did a set of curls and one-arm push presses. Then, I did six minutes on the elliptical jogger and took a drink of water.

I trotted down the hallway to the room to check on Oscar. He was still asleep, so I went back to the fitness room for another set.

Bring Oscar

The second set was better, and I finally broke a sweat—first in over a week. Dumbbell curls, push presses, elliptical, water. I headed back to the room. Oscar was in the same position. I watched him raise his head once. Then, it went back down. His eyes were closed. So, I went back to the exercise room for a third set: arm curls, push presses, elliptical, water.

In the room, I tossed out last night's leftover pizza and soda. Then, I jumped into the shower. Suddenly, Oscar pushed his head through the curtain. "Somebody is finally up!" I said to him. "Ready to go to Alaska?!"

On a sunny Tuesday morning, Oscar and I entered Alcan Highway 97. We were still in British Columbia, Canada, but it was exciting to start on the road to Alaska. A few weeks earlier, I printed a website's three-page list of km/mile markers, mentioning places between Dawson Creek to Whitehorse to the Alaska border. This outline provided landmarks and options to space out the drive.

The first stop we aimed for was Kiskatinaw River Bridge, located along a five-to-ten mile road off the main Alaska Highway. I looked out for a turn-off around Mile 16 and was half-past the exit when I realized it had been time to turn! I slowed, u-turned, and went back. I found that some signs show up precisely at the turn-off.

We drove down the winding auxiliary road, eventually reaching a sign that read "Old Alaska Highway Historic Site: Kiskatinaw Curved Bridge – 1 KM ahead." Good, we weren't lost already. We continued along the paved road through the green, high trees until we met the bridge, and it was curved. For the most part, it was wooden, spanning high over a river. Very cool!!

Oscar and I pulled over and got out of the car. There was nobody in sight. We walked onto the bridge, and over the edge was a scenic view and river. While Oscar sniffed around, I took pictures and read the placard explaining about the timber bridge's history. The fact that it curved nine degrees, as well as the ingenuity and work it took to build it in the 1940s, was interesting. After photos and doses of fresh mountain air, we continued driving on the side road until it rejoined the main Alaska Highway.

An hour later, we reached Fort St. John at Mile 47. Fort St. John was an established town, with a population of about twenty thousand. By informal measure of businesses, it had the main trio: Subway, A&W, and Tim Hortons. I went inside Tim Hortons to use the bathroom. The menu items looked good, but there was a line inside. Since Oscar was waiting, and I'm not a fan of lines, I skipped it. I liked the Tim Hortons menu, drinks, and prices, and I recognized the long line at the drive-through. I wondered if it were a publicly traded company.

As we were leaving Fort St. John, in the distance, I noticed a big memorial area with flags. So, I turned around, and we made our next stop: Charlie Lake. After parking in a gravel lot, Oscar and I wandered past two kids fishing, toward the waving flags and monument overlooking the beautiful lake. The memorial provided a brief history and tribute to nine workers who drowned during the construction of the Alaska Highway in 1942. Their pontoon boat was moving equipment across the lake when it turned over in the middle of winter, and most of the crew drowned. It was a compelling and tragic story.

The drive was easy, with occasional remnants of civilization. At Mile 101, we passed Wonowon log cabins and motel. "Wonowon at 101. That's original." We stopped at the general store for gas and a snack. Inside, several road workers and truck drivers were eating fast food from Chester's Chicken. *That'll tide us over.*

At 4:30, we arrived in Fort Nelson, Mile 300 of the Alaska Highway. It was a decent-sized town; perhaps around six thousand people. It was originally a fur trading post. Now, my guess is oil and gas and forestry were supporting the area. These places made me think of frontier towns in the 1800s, when people were settling in the West. Today, I was delighted to see this development.

The Super 8 had plenty of parking. After Oscar finished our lunch of Chester's chicken strips and I ate the remaining potato skins, we walked inside. Check-in went smoothly.

"It's just the two of you?"

"Yep, just me and the dog." Then, she gave me two key cards. I carried Oscar's.

We were assigned room 303. I had some hesitations about the third floor; but at least, there were elevators. As we approached them, I noticed an indoor pool and water slide. Plus, there were beach chairs and a hot tub. All of it was unoccupied; however, no dogs allowed. So, there would be no spa day for Oscar. (And, to be honest, I've never been much for public hot tubs, imagining weird people and gross things.)

Oscar and I stepped into the elevator. I pressed 3, and the elevator slowly climbed. We got out, and room 303 was right in front of us. Many people don't want a room next to the elevator, for fear of noise. But, I preferred the shorter walk for Oscar.

As I reached to unlock the door, I dropped the key card to the carpet. "Here's your chance, Oscar," I joked. "That's your key. You wanna open the door?" Oscar just looked at the key. I used the other key card to unlock the door. As we entered, I picked up his.

The TV offered the usual Canadian cable, which I didn't understand. I read the guide the hotel provided, but none of it matched the stations on TV. At the same time, the Wi-Fi was fantastic. This is the middle of nowhere in the Northern Rockies. So, I was impressed with the Internet connectivity. Through the window, I could see the parking lot and Boston Pizza next to the hotel. We got some take-out from there for dinner.

FORT NELSON, BRITISH COLUMBIA, CANADA – ALASKA HIGHWAY MILE 300 to WATSON LAKE, YUKON TERRITORY, CANADA – ALASKA HIGHWAY MILE 635

A NOTABLE STOP along the Alaska Highway is the Fort Nelson Heritage Museum. We parked just past the big "MILE 300" sign. At the entrance, a young woman invited both of us to explore. After I paid the five bucks, she and another lady gladly welcomed Oscar as we entered. We browsed the countless artifacts and random items in the glass cases or lying on shelves and on the ground. It was a nice way to pass the time. There were antique cars, license plates, old farming equipment, photos, and more. An eBay user's heaven.

Twenty minutes later, the curator, Marl, pulled up in an old Model T car. Classic! This fella, thin, about a thousand years old, with long flowing white hair, came out and greeted us with a genuine smile. Marl was eighty-three, a super nice guy, with a sharp, dry sense of humor.

He chatted about the museum, inviting Oscar and me to tour his cars and follow him to another building of antiques. It was an unbelievable number of old items, including his personal car, which was sixty-five years old.

I spoke with the other nice people who worked there. Jen used to make great money with an energy company, but with the drop in oil prices, the operation closed temporarily. Now she was working at the museum. What a difference a year makes. I remembered driving through North Dakota and seeing abundant oil wells. A year later, the energy boom had crashed.

We spent an hour browsing. To some it may appear to be a museum, filled with nostalgia. To others, it might look like a junkyard or flea market. We liked it.

Ten minutes after leaving Fort Nelson, the paved road turned into an asphalt/gravel mix. Then, later in the drive, we hit loose gravel and construction. Sheesh. In the back of my mind, I kept thinking about the condition and durability of the Nissan. I stayed away from other cars to avoid a gravel windshield incident. I wondered if we were nuts, watching trucks and rugged vehicles cruise past our regular sedan. Mostly, I was concerned about the tires. My spare tire was pretty much worthless. Over especially rough patches, I pleaded, *please don't get a flat*. I did have a can of tire sealant, but one sharp rock or a blown tire, and we'd be screwed.

Occasionally, I'd see a little wood cabin with a car in front of it. I'd make a mental note. *If we get stuck, we could walk back to this spot and knock on their door.* Then, miles and miles later, I'd see a camp pull-off with an RV. And, I would mentally reset how far from help we were. We rarely encountered a police car. This is good if you're speeding, but not so good if you need help.

I put worst-case scenarios in the back of my mind. Besides, if Oscar and I got stranded, we could wait it out with energy bars, dog food, and water. In the end, the open road and solitude were wonderful.

The clear morning turned cloudy as we hit Tetsa River Outfitters at Mile 375. I figured we could check it out—and try the advertised fresh-baked cinnamon rolls. We pulled into the dirt and gravel road up to a gas pump in front of a large log cabin lodge. When Oscar and I got out of the car, we were greeted by the local dog. I scanned the surroundings, particularly looking at the decorated porch area. In front was an eye-catching wooden bench: two hand-carved black bears holding the wood seat. *Someone around here is a very talented woodworker.*

I finished filling the tank from the old-school gas pump. Expensive! But I wasn't surprised: It was the middle of nowhere. Nevertheless, I had vowed to top off the tank whenever it was available. Plus, it's good to support the few businesses along this remote road.

Inside, I smelled the tasty baked goods and bought a few items to try now and eat later. I took a brief look at the gift shop, which featured books about Alaska, the Klondike, and the wilderness. Also, there were sweatshirts, videos, and more. I thanked the lady and returned to the car. It was a worthwhile stop.

Much of this driving stretch was pristine scenery and wilderness. Occasionally, I'd see a hollowed out building that used to be a gas stop or diner—a constant reminder of the pleasant mix of beauty and isolation. There was not enough traffic to support business. Plus, where would the owners and workers live between work hours? However, there were outposts along the way: an occasional general store, food stop, or camping area. And, amongst these random spots of civilization, I anticipated a larger town every few hundred miles.

While cruising down the road, I noticed a car pulled over. The passengers were standing outside, setting up a huge camera. Across the street was an enormous buffalo. I would've turned around, but I didn't want to disrupt their shot.

The route continued through endless open road and green trees. Beautiful British Columbia. Occasionally, it was interrupted by some traffic or roadwork. But, again, there was no hurry. We leisurely went thirty-five miles in the next hour. At one construction stop, near Summit Lake, we stopped to watch a moose meander across the street. "That's a frickin' moose, just walking across the street!"

While watching, I turned on my slow camera and waited for the digital lens to set. Fortunately, the moose was taking its sweet time. Oscar watched through the windshield as the creature wandered by, just thirty feet ahead of the car. When the camera was ready, I snapped a few photos. Then, the moose went back into the woods. "Can you believe what we just saw, Oscar?" I looked around and didn't see anyone. Incredible.

A few miles later, we encountered rams. I pulled over for more photos and watched them go up the mountain. We continued driving the open road again. When a truck raced toward us, I pulled over and let it pass. They had business to attend to, and I didn't want a stray pebble cracking my windshield. When a regular car was behind us, I pulled aside and let them go by. If I saw an animal or scenic view, I wanted to be able to suddenly pull over or stop without inconveniencing anyone behind our car.

We stopped for lunch at Toad River Lodge. On the side of a wood building was the welcoming image of a toad with the words "Welcome to my pad" and "Mile 422, Alaska Hwy." The lodge interior had a cool display: thousands of hats that had been collected from visitors since 1979. Fascinating. I looked at the variety and origins of the countless baseball caps while I peeked out the window to check on Oscar. He was napping. It started to rain slightly, but it didn't seem to bother him.

Oscar relaxing at the Toad River Post, British Columbia

After getting a sandwich and chips, I returned to the picnic area. The sprinkle of rain had stopped. Oscar and I ate outside with a water view in one direction and the distant mountains in the other direction. After finishing, I looked down and Oscar was napping again.

Following the break, we drove around the jade green Muncho Lake. The road weaved between mountains that shot straight up from the road and the picturesque lake. Several sheep were just grazing along the road; not a care in the world. And, some could be seen climbing along the steep mountain side. Apparently, the passing cars were just part of the landscape to them.

Suddenly, I saw an enormous bison walking beside the road. Oh, my God! I was about to turn around when I saw another bison ahead. And, another. And, others. I stopped the car and just sat there and watched. I looked behind us, and the road was clear. It was just Oscar and me and the group of bison. I took out my camera and snapped some photos and then just watched. Oscar leaned his head out the window, wondering if he was getting out of the car.

I pat him on the head. "Pretty cool, huh?" He stuck his head under my hand. We just watched the giant creatures walk along the road.

When the bison were out of sight, we resumed the drive until reaching Liard River Hot Springs Provincial Park. It had been recommended by a traveler we met in Dawson Creek. After parking near the campground, I put on some bug spray. Then, Oscar and I walked along a wooden pathway for about ten minutes. A family came toward us, carrying towels.

"How much farther to the springs?"

"About five more minutes or so," they told us.

"Just checking," I said. "Is it worth it?"

"Yes. It's a little bit smaller than we expected. But, it was nice."

"Thanks."

Finally, we reached the actual spring. There was a changing area. And, we saw several people in swimsuits sitting in the hot pools of water. I dipped my hand into the water. Yeah, it was hot. Oscar leaned over. I'm not sure if he wanted a sip or was pondering a dip. "Hang on." I pulled him back. "I don't think this is for you. It's too hot."

It didn't seem to bother the people in the water. I realized some parts were hotter than others. In one section, you could see the steam rising. Then, as the water flowed downward, it cooled off, making it more bearable to swim around. After a look, we turned around and walked back through the wooded area to the car.

I kept an eye out for animals and photo ops. We passed a few bison, a black bear that roamed along the woods, and curious goats on the side of the road. Within two hours, I saw the big sign up ahead: "Yukon – Larger Than Life," with *Plus Grande Que Nature* in French. I pulled the car to the side of the road. Oh, yeah, we had to get a photo of this spot.

Water break at the Yukon border

While Oscar had a drink and a snack, I broke open the Tetsa River cinnamon roll. Damn, it was tasty. I looked at the surroundings for several minutes. There wasn't one car that passed by. Over twenty-five hundred miles from our home in Illinois, and it was just Oscar and I standing near the sixtieth parallel at the border of the Yukon Territory!

When Oscar finished his treat, he wandered over to me. "Pretty nice, huh?" He looked up and smiled. Then, he followed me around the Nissan. I looked at the tires, pleased that there were no car issues after miles and miles on the gravel. "Good to go?" I lifted him into the car, and we continued on the Alaska Highway. When we entered Watson Lake, it changed from Highway 97 into Highway 1, and the gravelly road turned to pristine pavement!

The small town had few hotels. Only one of them had a dog room available—at a whopping price. I briefly considered turning the backseat of the car into a hotel room. I had imagined an instance

Bring Oscar

when Oscar and I would have to sleep in the car. Maybe we couldn't find a hotel, or worse, we got stranded. But cost wasn't an excuse.

I've heard of people who will sneak their pets into a hotel, despite a hotel's "no pets allowed" policy just because they want to stay there. Others just want to avoid the pet fee. That's just wrong. It ruins it for all the good pet owners. I have the same issue with service animals. There are people who apply for the service animal permit so they can take Pebbles on the plane with them. It's just uncool.

The hotel entrance area was acceptable, although it was a little bit dated and musty. The lady at the front desk in the tiny lobby was very nice. She looked up our reservation on a handwritten list of names. Then, handed me a key. Oscar and I walked around back and looked up at the second floor of the next building. We climbed the slatted steps. Oscar did OK as I slowly guided him up. The balcony appeared sort of slanted. *Is that safe?* I imagined the odd shapes of the rooms in Willy Wonka and decided to go with the flow. When we reached the top, I noticed the walkway was significantly sloped toward the edge. I cut the slack out of Oscar's leash and guided him close to me for fear he might tip over or that the rails weren't solid. In fact, I even walked close to the wall, away from the edge.

We entered room 405. Even inside the hotel room, there was a slant. If I set a marble on the ground, it definitely would roll toward the doorway! The room had a 1970s linoleum look. It wasn't vintage; it was just old. "This ain't the Hilton," I said as I put down my laptop and overnight bag on top of the old quilted blanket on the second bed. The one potential upside was the cable TV had a terrific selection of channels. All things considered, it would work. Certainly, for one night. The lady said the hotel was filled. So, I might have to also reserve next week's return.

I ran down to the car to fetch Oscar's blanket and bowls. Then, I sprinted back up the stairs to the room. Oscar was sitting at the entrance when I returned. "No problem, buddy. Just grabbing your stuff."

After setting up Oscar's area, I pulled out my laptop and considered three options for dinner, choosing the hotel restaurant for convenience. We stepped out of the room and down the stairs. I guided Oscar to the entrance of the Golden Dragon Restaurant. "Wait one sec," I told him. I slipped in, grabbed a menu, and returned outside with Oscar. The dining area was full. Either the food was good or there just weren't many dining choices in this one-street town. We'd find out soon. Hopefully, this golden dragon wouldn't blow fire into my stomach.

I skimmed over the large menu selection and picked a few dishes. While waiting to go back inside, I nodded to a young couple we had seen earlier today. In this neck of the woods, it wasn't uncommon to run into someone familiar.

"Hello," the female host said.

"Can I get something to go?"

I placed my order, and she offered to charge it to our room. "It'll be ready in about twenty minutes."

We walked up and down the main street while we waited for our food. The town was sparse; regardless, I always like exploring new places. Plus, we were surrounded by fresh mountain air. Overall, Watson Lake seemed like an easygoing, friendly town.

We returned to the restaurant, and the lady had our bag of food waiting. After peeking through the contents, we took it upstairs to our room. It was quite tasty. Oscar enjoyed it. I liked it. And, neither one of us got an upset stomach. Winner!

After dinner, I uploaded photos from the camera and got some Internet tasks done. I was running the fan in the room, but it was not much help. In fact, it was actually cooler outside than in the room. For Yukon hotels, the winter cold is probably a bigger concern than the few weeks of warm weather in the summer. Oh well, I just adjusted and accepted it. *Always adapt.*

Oscar was sleeping on the floor. Maybe the linoleum would keep him cool. I tried to watch TV, but realized that a lot of the cable channels didn't work. Five hundred channels, but most of them were unsubscribed. Oh well. I looked at the beds with the dated comforters and the not so fresh-as-a-daisy linens and went to sleep in my clothes, on top of the bed.

At 10:45 p.m., I looked down. Oscar was huffing and puffing with his tongue hanging out. The area was stifling. I searched the room to see if I had overlooked the air conditioner. I saw a thermostat but didn't see an air conditioner. I did see a heating vent. So, that must be for the thermostat in winter. I tried a fan by the window. But, it didn't seem to help. I turned the fan to the highest speed, and to get some relief, I took Oscar for a thirty-minute walk.

It was still light outside. The birds were chirping. At 11:25 p.m., we returned to the stuffy room. Unfortunately, the fan couldn't get the air circulating. While I could sweat it out, I didn't want Oscar gasping. I opened the door completely, hoping to mix the cool outside air with the warm space. For most of the night, I kept the door wide open, figuring nobody would pass by our second-floor room at two in the morning.

WATSON LAKE, YUKON TERRITORY, CANADA – ALASKA HIGHWAY MILE 635 to WHITEHORSE, YUKON TERRITORY, CANADA

AT 6:00 A.M., Oscar was sprawled across the linoleum floor, hopefully staying somewhat comfortable. I walked over him, shut the front door, and jumped in the shower to rinse and cool off.

Before leaving, I sent a quick email with a few photos to my mom. I reminded her that if she didn't hear from us in a couple of days, she should call around. I didn't want to worry her, but I wanted someone to be proactive if we disappeared. Oscar and I were continuing on more gravel roads along the Alaska Highway—remote parts of the Alaska Highway. I was warned to bring extra gas and a spare tire. I wasn't sure if the spare tire in the Nissan would cut it, not to mention if I even had a jack in the car. I accepted that if a wheel were shredded, then we were screwed. But, we had plenty of gas, water (of course), snacks, and time.

I turned off the computer, gave Oscar more water, and then we went for a walk. At first, Oscar stumbled and looked terrible, but eventually, he relieved himself. So, his systems were working.

I noticed the cars in the parking lot with Alaska, British Columbia, Yukon, and NW Territories license plates next to our car with Illinois plates. We've come a long way! It had rained a bit yesterday. The vehicles and ground were wet. Still, mud and dirt were caked onto every car and truck.

While we walked in the cool air, Oscar got into a better rhythm. We went by the log cabin chapel next to the hotel. The placard mentioned that it was built in 1942 and later moved to this site. More than seventy years, and it was still used every Sunday.

Suddenly, we were greeted by a couple and their two young dogs. Oscar sniffed the two eager pals. "You have a nice dog."

"Yeah, he's a good one. Old guy."

"How old?"

"He's fifteen," I proudly told them.

"Oh my! He doesn't look it."

"Well, he's got the white whiskers," I pointed. "And, he's a little fragile, but he's doing it." The gentleman acknowledged Oscar's tilted head. It was kind of funny looking.

We returned to the hotel. I carried Oscar up the uneven stairs and lowered him onto the balcony floor. He stumbled and fell back. The crooked balcony and his vestibular issues didn't mix well. Inside the warm room, I took out the leftovers from the mini-fridge and tossed them. Then, we quickly packed and cleared out of the room.

During checkout, I returned the key and asked about reserving a room next week. Although there was no air con, and the place was far from palatial, I needed a place coming back. Beggars can't be choosers. It was slightly more comfortable than sleeping in my car. The one upside: I didn't have to worry about the pet fee or liability for damage. There was no way Oscar could make the room worse than it was.

I led Oscar out to the car. Across the way was the Sign Post Forest. This Watson Lake attraction was over twenty years old and contained thousands of signs and license plates nailed to posts in a huge outdoor area. It's a very cool site! There were submissions by families and individuals from all around the world. I easily found a few from Arizona and Illinois. And, I even noticed a plate from Indianola, Iowa, a small town where my friend's daughter attended Simpson College.

Oscar and I wandered through endless rows of license plates and signs, most of them dated, from as far as Europe. We encountered three travelers, who appeared to be retirees, touring the forest. I asked one of them to take a photo of Oscar and me standing in front of a colorful row of license plates. Afterward, I learned that they were from Missouri. Someone else had driven a long way to get here, too!

While taking more pictures, I watched a caretaker hang the latest submissions to a half-filled post. Next to it, there were several empty posts. "They'll be filled by the end of summer," he told me. I wish I had known; I would have brought an extra license plate from the old Acura sitting at home.

When we departed Watson Lake, the smooth road abruptly went to graveled pavement, but we moved relatively fast. And, I deliberately pulled aside of the passing trucks that sprayed gravel. An hour later, we stopped at Rancheria Falls, located near a KM 1113 marker. Anticipating a photo op, I grabbed the camera along with my headphones. And, noticing the wooded area, I put some insect repellant on my arms and legs. After giving Oscar some water, we went to the walking path that led to a view of the waterfalls.

Listening to music and walking through the boreal forest proved to be a good break from the car. Oscar seemed to enjoy sniffing and exploring the end of the path. Eventually, we reached the water and encountered our three friends from Missouri! They remembered us from ninety minutes earlier, and the old guy offered to take another photo of Oscar and me with a pretty view of the river falls and forest behind us.

We turned around and headed back on the wooden boardwalk. I carried Oscar part of the way. It was a good stop. As I gave Oscar water, I could see the insects coming. Oscar began shaking his head and twitching his ears to shoo away the swarming pests. Luckily, I had brought the OFF! Insect repellent, and it did the trick. Time to go.

We continued winding through the endless, beautiful scenery of trees and lakes. In the distance were mountains embellished with patches of snow. Breathtaking.

We stopped at a rest area with a wonderful overview of Teslin Lake, the Nisutlin Bay Bridge, distant mountains, and green trees. While Oscar sniffed around, I read about the salmon that travel over eighteen hundred miles from the Bering Sea, upstream through Alaska, all the way to Teslin. Amazing.

Suddenly, the white sedan with Missouri plates pull into the lot! Again, the three travelers got out of their car and began sightseeing. The old guy walked over and asked for my camera to take another shot of Oscar and me. Then, we had another round of friendly greetings. I continued to look at the surroundings; a terrific place to enjoy a break from driving. Meanwhile, Oscar found a comfortable dirt area to relax. He was less interested in the view.

Oscar napping at the rest stop in Teslin, Yukon Territory, Canada

Following Oscar's nap, we drove down the hill, toward the bridge, and found a place for lunch: the Yukon Motel & Restaurant. In the front, there was an enormous life-size stuffed grizzly bear. "Yep, this is the Yukon." Also, there were colorful summer flowers adorning the wooden front, giving it a welcoming accent.

We parked in the gravel lot among the row of cars and trucks. This spot was bustling with people going in and out, eating, socializing, and preparing for the drive ahead. Fortunately, there was a row of chairs and tables under the eave out of the way, so I set Oscar beside the wooden railing and went inside to get us lunch. I ordered a veggie wrap and fries, trying to keep at least half of what I was eating healthy. While waiting to pay and get my food, I could see visitors acknowledging Oscar peacefully sleeping as they walked by him.

As I set up lunch, Oscar woke up from his brief nap. When I set down his food, he gobbled it up. As long as Oscar was eating, I felt he was OK. I ate my lunch while watching everyone packing and refueling. Also, I met a few people who took a liking to Oscar.

After a relaxing lunch, we continued the drive. Most of the road was clear. If a car caught up to us, I let it pass. There was no hurry. I enjoyed the space and being off the grid—except for listening to XM Satellite Radio and news. The satellite reception in the middle of nowhere was incredible.

I noticed several lodges and rest stops had closed. Some were up for sale; others had closed part of their business down, leaving the gas station open. It'll be years or decades, if ever, before this area is developed enough to comfortably support these establishments again.

Following a hundred miles of wide-open driving, we got to Whitehorse! We passed the airport with a big Canadian Pacific Air Lines plane mounted on a swivel display. It supposedly is the world's largest weather vane, with the nose of the plane always facing into the wind.

While passing the Whitehorse main road toward the inn, I made a note of street signs and landmarks. I had the address and detailed directions to the Hidden Valley Bed & Breakfast, but I didn't want to get lost in the middle of nowhere. After some left and right turns, highways, and gravel roads, I found the wooden sign and entrance to the inn.

We were greeted by a caretaker for the bed-and-breakfast property. As he showed us around, Oscar was greeted by two dogs who roam freely around the property. I liked the vibe. We were led to the "Blue Room," a small room with two single beds. It might be a bit tight for Oscar, but he would find his sleeping spot. And, it was comfortable. The fan seemed to circulate a nice, cool breeze from outside. I didn't see a television, and I didn't bother to ask. Overall, this worked.

After the introduction and tour, the caretaker left us to wander around the inn. Oscar and I picked a spot on the patio outside. Perfect! Terra, the woman who took my phone reservation, arrived. She and I chatted for a bit. She had a dog that was nineteen years old! A Shepherd Lab mix. And, she said the dog's canine sister died the previous year at eighteen. I'd like to think Oscar could go that long.

The Hidden Valley Bed & Breakfast was peaceful and remote. It was a terrific two-day retreat. However, it was about twenty minutes from town, and there were few nearby dinner options. I was informed that there was a relatively close market to pick up food to cook. But, after a day of driving, I wasn't hungry enough to make the effort. Instead, I decided to call it a night.

We went to the car, where I collected my small suitcase, treats for Oscar and a protein bar for me. Then, Oscar and I wandered back through the patio and along the brick path past flowers and brush to the doorway.

Oscar settled into a spot by the door. I gave him a few strokes on the back, and then I rolled him over. He had an erection. It had emerged in Watson Lake over ten hours ago. Then, it got a bit bigger. And, he still had it. Moreover, I was becoming concerned. There were red patches in his crotch area. Was it a rash? Or, was it something internal? Otherwise, he'd been behaving the same. Although he was having a tough time with his rear legs.

When I called the vet, the answering service forwarded me to an emergency number. They suggested I bring him in for examination, or try K-Y Jelly to lubricate so the penis could recede. I tried my third option: Rest and hope it goes away. I pulled the dark window shades down and slept.

After a pleasant nap, I got up at 10:45 p.m. It was still light outside. It wasn't dusk. It was light outside. The bed-and-breakfast was quiet. While Oscar slept, I did computer work for an hour. At midnight, it looked like it was 5:00 p.m. Through the window, I could see the glow from the sun. Oscar woke up, so I carried him down the stairs and outside. I led him around, hoping he would take a leak and that his erection would subside. He took some treats and drank a bunch of water, but no leak. And, the erection was still there. I didn't look under his crotch partially because I didn't want to bother him, partially because I didn't want to know, and partially because I couldn't do much about it. Irrationally, I hoped drinking water would flush out the red splotches.

At 2:50 a.m., I peeked under the dark shade. Outside, there were no lights on, but I could still see everything! It looked like dusk. I could see a bright glow over the mountains in the northeast. Or, was it the southeast? It looked the same as it did at midnight, except the glow was over a different section in the horizon.

I checked Oscar's status. He was limping badly, favoring his front left arm. Was his front right arm sprained? His erection seemed to be subsiding. Maybe it'll be gone tomorrow? During this walk, he didn't drink any water. It was cool outside, so maybe he wasn't thirsty? He did a little squirt at the end of our time. After a twenty-five-minute walk/limp/stumble, we came back inside.

I moved his blanket to the corner by the door. After some shuffling, Oscar found a comfortable position and he went back to sleep immediately. I lifted a leg to take another look: "Still got a red splotch on the crotch."

WHITEHORSE, YUKON TERRITORY, CANADA – Day 2

I'M GLAD I skipped dinner last night. The bed-and-breakfast had a phenomenal breakfast! It was prepared by Terra's boyfriend, Scott, a meat and fish distributor who helped at the inn "both for the money and because I enjoy it."

In the classic dining hall, the guests were served a fresh fruit cup, eggs, banana bread, toast, juice, tea, and coffee. While the inn discouraged pets from nearing the kitchen, they were OK with Oscar joining us in the main dining area.

At the breakfast table, I met a nice, retired couple from Saskatchewan. They had traveled for ten days around the area, using this inn as their base. While I enjoyed the broad conversation with them, Oscar slept underneath the table. He was quite tired.

When Oscar perked up around noon, we took a ride to explore Whitehorse. Overall, it's a very cool town: a good mix of history, scenery, and nice people. Surprisingly, there was traffic. Perhaps, the capital city was outgrowing its roads and infrastructure?

Our first stop was the S.S. Klondike National Historic Site, a restored sternwheeler that had been used to transport freight and passengers around the Yukon in the 1930s. At the waterfront, I learned that "Whitehorse" describes how the river waves and white caps appear as they rumble along.

While standing outside the boat, a woman, her son, and mother were drawn to Oscar. I had a fifteen-minute conversation with the woman, who was born and raised in the area. She was delighted to offer plenty of suggestions. I realized there were a ton of extended possibilities. Dawson City was three hundred miles north and the gateway to the Arctic Circle, or travel west led to Anchorage and Fairbanks.

We continued to the Yukon Transportation Museum, where out front was the DC-3 airplane on a swivel. At the entrance, Oscar waited while I checked inside the museum. I gave myself five minutes to see as much as possible. I skimmed past a tribute to mushing dogs and other canines. Then I saw a display about neighboring places, including Skagway, and another area with images related to the Gold Rush, Alaska Highway, and the region's growth. Overall, it was a beautiful set of exhibits with a lot of cool items.

When I returned outside, I found two young guys who work at the museum keeping Oscar entertained! We had a ten-minute conversation about the area where I learned about the thousand-mile Yukon Quest in Canada. "It's more rugged than the Iditarod," one claimed. "In fact, hard-core German racers are big fans of the Yukon dog race." They cheerfully answered questions and offered tourist suggestions. "Do you want to go back in there?" they asked.

"Nah, I'm good." There was so much to see, I wouldn't know where to start.

"We don't mind watching your dog."

"Thanks. Maybe we'll come back later."

"We'll be here," they replied. Very hospitable people around here.

"Looks like you made two more friends," I said to Oscar.

Our next stop was Miles Canyon. Carved out by the Yukon River, it produced a great hiking area with beautiful scenery. We walked along a dirt path with an unobstructed view of the surroundings. I didn't see any railing or fence to border the fifty-foot drop to the water, so we maintained a safe distance from the edge overlooking the canyon river below. There was a white, wooden bridge that crossed to the other side of the canyon, but we just walked back and forth instead.

We headed into City Centre for lunch. I picked out a pizza place, Bocelli's Pizzeria. I took our medium pizza and salad to nearby Rotary Peace Park, where I spotted a few picnic tables. I quickly ate while sharing some of the pizza with Oscar. It tasted pretty good. After absorbing two vicious mosquito bites, we got out of there.

We walked down the way and looked at the White Pass & Yukon Route Railway station. Near the entrance, I read a wooden sign that provided a brief history timeline, including the Klondike Gold Rush, building a railroad through the mountains in the 1890s, and the route from Skagway through Carcross to Whitehorse. Then, we walked along the railroad station to explore. I saw a totem pole towering in the middle of a plaza next to the railroad tracks. There was a large promotional poster with a Siberian Husky's image set on the left with a background of ten sled dogs pulling a competitor. "Yukon Quest: 1000 mile international sled dog race" and "Whitehorse: official start and finish line." That must've been the race the guys at the museum told me about.

I looked down at Oscar hobbling around I remembered when he was younger. Oscar would have loved powering through the chest-deep snow, dragging me along! He loved the cold, icicles hanging off his face, and the snow powder. Sometimes, that white powder would be all over his face. "Remember when you looked like Pacino in Scarface!?" Oscar paused, looked up at me, and gave me a smile.

All in all, a good day. Oscar managed quite well. We returned to the Hidden Valley Bed & Breakfast. Without TV in the room, I listened to music on my MP3 player until I pulled down the dark shades and went to sleep at 8:00 pm. I was tired. Oscar was sleeping. I knew we'd be up later. Besides, what's the difference between 8:00 p.m., 11:00 p.m., or 2:00 a.m.? It's light outside.

WHITEHORSE, YUKON TERRITORY, CANADA TO SKAGWAY, ALASKA

AFTER GETTING CLEANED up, we went down to the dining room and had another terrific breakfast. This time, we dined with a retired Canadian couple and an Asian couple from Vancouver. The guy from Vancouver had been to forty-one states, eleven Canadian provinces and territories, and eighty-three countries! The conversation was substantive, covering several Canadian issues, such as roads, schools, and medical care.

Following the pleasant meal, we said our goodbyes. It was a sunny day. Boy, the sun was bright. Brightest I had ever seen. Anticipating a wonderful drive, we backtracked on Alaska Highway 1 then turned onto Klondike Highway 2. There were tons of amazing scenery with plenty of places to stop and get great photos. One of the most spectacular was Emerald Lake. This blue lake was stunning. It has a vibrant blue, green—well, emerald—color. It was cool and clear. There was a plaque displaying information about the lake, the chemistry behind the bright colors, and other sites in the area.

For ten minutes, I took photos of the view, then photos of Oscar in front of the view, shots in the distance of the Alaska border, and shots straight ahead at the blue water. Then, a bird perched with the setting behind it—absolutely beautiful. Almost three thousand miles of driving, so I definitely wanted to take advantage of this one-of-a-kind spot, which I'd likely never see again. I'm sure I could see photos on the Internet, but there is something about being in the crisp, clean air, with a 360-degree view of this area. It's tough to duplicate. I just stood with Oscar. It was a moment. Something that was amazing yet temporary. We couldn't stay forever. I just soaked it in.

Oscar and I continued our journey to the Alaska border. As we drove along the Klondike Highway, I kept an eye out for scenic stops and animals while admiring the snowcapped mountains that decorated the background. Suddenly, I saw a bear on the side of the road! Wow.

We also stopped to look at the Carcross Desert. It's a peculiar place, full of dunes, but not really a desert. There were several illustrated boards explaining the science behind the ancient lake and current dunes, as well as the rare plants and insects in the area. Fortunately, the air was cool, and I didn't see any mosquitoes. Oscar and I walked past the large "Carcross Desert" wood sign into the large, white, sandy expanse. This was a good place for a quick stretch.

We continued along the south Klondike Highway, when ten minutes later, the Bove Island Lookout appeared. At a roadside pull-off, we stopped for a scenic photo. Oscar and I went to the wooden deck to view the islet in the middle of the Tagish Lake. Meanwhile, I read interpretive panels, showing the history and explorers of the Klondike.

Highway 2 exited Yukon and entered British Columbia. We made one more stop, out of curiosity, at the Yukon Suspension Bridge. It was impressive, with a long pathway high above the Tutshi River rushing below. We could've walked over the bridge to the other side, but the sway seemed too much for Oscar.

There were two people on the nearby café patio. One of them was Kim, a cute woman who worked there. She was the owner of a two-year-old dog, Alice, who had a run of the place and took a liking to Oscar. We had a great conservation, and I learned that she and the dog both lived on the site and had a place in Skagway. I wondered where the people who run these isolated places lived. She offered some ideas for our trip.

"There's a Thai place I get take-out from all the time," she suggested. And, she gave insight to the town while drawing an accurate map on the back of a receipt. In between, we talked about her experiences working on ships for ten years before settling here. She had plans to travel south during their winter. I liked her vibe.

That's the nature of travel. You meet people along the way, but it's a passing moment. It's unlikely I'll ever see them again. If I lived there, we'd become great friends. And, the dogs would get along. But it'll never happen. A forty-five-minute encounter and then gone forever.

"Welcome to Alaska"

We reached the border! With excitement, I pulled the car to the side of the road near the sign. 'Welcome to Alaska: and, the Gateway to the Klondike'. Oscar and I got out. The freezing wind was whipping off the snowy mountains.

There was a motorcycle group of four bikers with Louisiana plates. I recognized them from earlier stops. Each was taking the classic photo in front of the "Welcome to Alaska" sign, while sitting on their motorcycle.

I walked over to ask, "All the way from Louisiana? How long did that take?"

"It took us nine days to get here," one of them answered.

Nine days? I thought I was traveling at a good pace. "That's gotta be four hundred or five hundred miles per day." I asked questions and learned that they knew each other back home. They had previously done rides together. But this was an epic road trip.

"I just decided I wanted to do it. Ride all the way to Alaska," one told me. "Sort of a bucket-list thing. Then, he wanted to come along," pointing at one of his friends posing in front of the Alaska sign. "We were planning the trip, then the other two decided to join us."

And, that's how it starts. Someone gets a big idea and decides to go for it. Then others join in. Suddenly, you have a memorable adventure.

"Wow, that's a long trip. A lot of time riding." I looked at the motorcycles and there wasn't much space for luggage. And, it seemed like a long time to be sitting in one position. I wondered if they had any music. There's no one to talk to.

"Nah, the miles go quickly," one said. "Look at the scenery. Open road."

As the wind was whipping, it seemed awfully cold on a motorcycle. But, I suspect Southern heat would be much worse.

"How far are you going?" I asked.

"To Skagway. We wanted to do the entire Alaska Highway, but we don't have enough time." I, too, had considered going all the way to Fairbanks. But, that was hundreds of more miles. "We have less than three weeks of time off," he continued. "Gotta go back to work."

The four of them were a diverse group. One mentioned he was a business owner, another said he was involved in oil services in the Gulf, and one was a lawyer. The other one may have been retired, or just a free spirit. Although they all appeared to be in their forties or fifties, one had a long beard and looked like a biker. The black guy had an earring and short hair with gray blended in. And, the other two looked like clean-cut, middle-aged professionals. By appearance, their leather jackets and sleek motorcycle helmets seemed to be the only thing they all had in common. But, these buddies were sharing a bonding experience.

I mentioned my story, traveling with Oscar, just closing up the house and disappearing for several weeks.

"Aside from work, it wasn't much of an issue," they responded. "Hell, I think my wife is having a good time without me there," one of them joked.

After taking pictures of the scenery, the other two bikers walked over. They nodded toward me and Oscar. We stood around, admired the view, and recognized the journey it took to get here.

When the welcome sign was open, I asked, "You mind taking a few pictures of me and the dog?" No doubt, after all this way, it was the photo I wanted. One biker gladly and patiently took several shots of Oscar and me. Oscar wasn't as into it, but he let me hoist him up to pose for the picture. We got the shot that took thirty-two hundred miles to reach!

HALFWAY!!

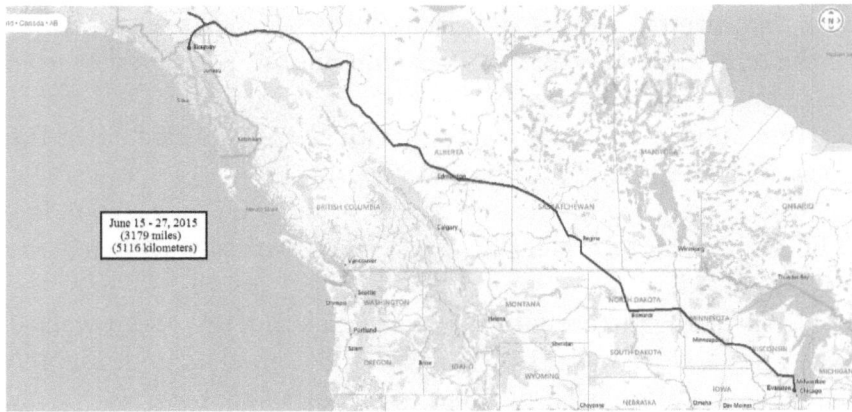

Bring Oscar

We actually made it! On the modest building were the black letters "US Port of Entry, Skagway, Alaska." We passed through US customs, a small location bridging Canada to the United States. We entered my fiftieth state, and by a rough count, Oscar's thirty-sixth state.

I drove down the switchback road through the scenic mountains. Within an hour, we were in the middle of Skagway, Alaska. It seemed to be a nice town with the feel of a Yukon Territory village. There was a mix of scenery, history, tourist shops, restaurants and bars, fishermen, and seasonal workers. I looked forward to a couple of days to relax and enjoy our vacation.

The Westmark Inn was easy to locate. In fact, the commercial area was quite small, so everything seemed easy to find. In the distance, I saw one cruise ship and some tour buses, but at the moment, it wasn't crowded at all. There was a breeze, but it was milder near sea level. The "Welcome to Alaska" sign at White Pass Summit was almost three thousand feet higher. I was excited to walk around and explore as soon as Oscar got motivated.

We settled into our hotel room on the first floor. The room had no air conditioner, but that wasn't a surprise. The Alaska air is anywhere from cool to freezing, so a crack in the window and the fan should suffice. In the end, the room had the essentials.

There were a few inconveniences. We had to park across the street in a gravel lot. If I forgot something, I'd have to go outside down the block to my car. And, there was no complimentary breakfast. Most of all, there was no Wi-Fi signal in the rooms. Instead of Internet while relaxing in the room, we had to go to the lobby or restaurant. And, the Wi-Fi was public, so I needed to avoid use during busy network times. The woman in Whitehorse had warned me that the town included about five hundred residents, but that in a matter of two hours, it could have ten thousand when the cruise liners come in.

Oscar and I did a quick recon, walking down the block to check out Starfire, the Thai place that Kim had mentioned. It looked great! I picked up the pad thai and egg rolls. Thirty-three dollars. American dollars. Sheesh. I had no idea if that was reasonable in Alaska. Or, was it tourist town prices? Judging by the number of young people eating there, it must've been priced fairly. At least the food was good, with a spicy kick, and generous portions.

After dinner in the room, we walked around the quiet town where the occasional passerby gave us a pleasant greeting. A group of four young people came toward us and stopped to meet Oscar. They were friendly and introduced themselves. I learned they were seasonal, part-time workers. We talked for thirty minutes about summer life in Skagway. Oscar enjoyed the attention, face massages, and pats on the head.

Next, we ran into two of the Louisiana motorcycle guys. Afterward, we finished our evening route at an ice cream shop. Just before they closed, I bought two scoops for seven bucks. Maybe I should've stuck with the one-dollar vending machine candy bar?

We returned to the room, I grabbed the laptop, and took Oscar with me to the hotel lobby. The Wi-Fi situation proved to be positive because there was a couch near the lobby entrance. For forty-five minutes, I worked on the computer and watched the people walk by. Meanwhile, Oscar napped on the rug beside my feet. It worked great! We stayed until about 11:30 p.m. Tomorrow, I knew we could sleep in, and I looked forward to a few days with almost no driving and lots of time to explore.

SKAGWAY, ALASKA – Day 2

AT 7:45 A.M., Oscar got up and seemed ready to go. I jumped in the shower and threw on some clothes. I decided to skip the café and save my appetite for some fry bread down the street. We walked around the quiet town for a bit. Sunday morning. Mellow.

We walked past the Red Onion Saloon Brothel Museum, then a brewery and a jewelry shop. In front of a bookstore, I scanned over the books displayed in the window, noticing an old book by Benedict and Nancy Freedman. *I think that's my old math professor!* I remembered Benedict had written episodes for *My Favorite Martian*. Then, he taught math. A true renaissance man.

Oscar was a people magnet. Two of the merchants at Richter's Jewelry & Curio stepped outside and gave Oscar some treats. An Israeli woman named Yuli came over to us. She worked at one of the other jewelers. As she leaned over to Oscar and said hi, she told me about the several dogs she had. As we chatted, I hoped nobody would notice Oscar's red underbelly. If they did, no one said anything.

So far, it was a pleasant morning. When the sun was shining, it was quite comfortable and warm, but when the clouds came and the wind kicked up, the temps dropped about fifteen degrees! So, we returned to the room for a break.

After relaxing in the room, I woke up Oscar from his two-hour nap. We went to the Klondike Gold Rush National Historical Park where there was a plaza, a statue that paid tribute to prospectors and settlers, and a view of the surrounding mountains. Also, there were railroad cars, a giant rotary snow plow that attaches to a steam engine, and the White Pass & Yukon Route Railway station, established in 1898. We had seen the other end of the route in Whitehorse!

We drove to the other side of town to see the Gold Rush Cemetery. Skagway's famous graveyard had burials from 1898 through 1908, a rough period of time in a tough environment. As we walked up the hill along the trails through the trees, we passed many tombstones that had readable etchings on the stones, giving some historical context.

We followed the trail higher and higher, past the signs, until reaching Reid Falls. It was a beautiful spot to watch the water crashing down the hills through the rocks and greenery. As we were ready to leave, two people were coming up the hill. "Can I trouble you for a photo of me and my dog?"

"Of course," they answered. They took a few shots of Oscar and me with the pretty background. As the guy handed my camera back, he asked if I could return the favor.

"Of course," I said as I gladly took his camera. After taking a few photos of the couple, I guided Oscar down the hill, past the cemetery, back to the car.

After dropping off the car and picking up a few items in the room, Oscar and I went for a late lunch. We walked across town to the Skagway Fish Company for king crab legs, melted butter, and salad. I'm not sure if the crab legs were in season, but they tasted great. Plus, we had a scenic outdoor view of mountains and boats in the harbor.

Oscar ate his chicken lunch, and immediately went to sleep. Meanwhile, I just sat and snacked on my dessert, listening to music on my MP3 player, and enjoying the view. Occasionally, there would be a cold breeze coming off the snowcapped mountains. But, the crisp, clean air was refreshing. On the way out, I noticed Bears and Blackhawks items on the walls. I asked the lady if the owners were from Chicago. "Yes, they are," she answered.

"Incredible," I said. "My dog and I drove all the way from Chicago! Are the owners here?"

"Unfortunately, they aren't today. They would've loved to meet you." I would've loved to have heard their story. *How does someone come up with the idea to relocate and start a restaurant out here?*

We returned to the room. I recharged my camera, relaxed, and watched TV. I handed Oscar a treat to work on. After finishing, he went to sleep, so I snuck out to take a quick jog around the town. Running is a great way to take a brief tour of new surroundings. Plus, I hadn't had a full workout in two weeks, except for the exercise room last week at one of the hotels. I ran only about a mile and half, but the distance covered several streets around town and the residential neighborhood. And, I was pleased to take advantage of the beautiful weather and clean air. Great conditions.

When I stopped to walk the last block, a truck dropped off one of its passengers.

"Where's the dog?" he called out. It was one of the young summer workers from last night.

"Napping," was my friendly familiar response. "We'll be back out here later!" He gave me an easygoing nod and walked off. Funny how people remember Oscar.

In the produce section at the supermarket back home, a woman came up to me. "You have a black dog, don't you?"

I didn't recognize her, but I answered, "Yeah, I do."

"I see you walking him past my house all the time." She continued, "Even in the winter."

"Yep, twice a day," I said proudly.

"I should walk my dog more often. He could use the exercise," she said with some regret.

"Yep, I'll bet he'd like that."

"Your dog must be very happy," she said and continued past me. These random meetings happened from time to time. The neighborhood didn't know me, but they knew Oscar.

My plan was to spend several days in Skagway. After a three thousand-mile journey, I wanted to take time to just hang out, with minimal driving, and enjoy the vacation. I figured this was a peaceful place off the grid to relax before the long trip back. However, I was concerned about Oscar's permanent erection.

For years, he'd gotten erections during car rides, getting excited to ride shotgun as we drove to the lake, PetSmart, or any activity. But, this time, it wouldn't go down! It persisted for several hours. Then, overnight. Then, days.

I turned him over to look at the veiny red marks around his nether regions. Because of his age, I was worried. Also, it was more severe than two days ago in Whitehorse. So, I went back to the Internet to find an answer. Of course, it proved useless.

First, I had to figure out, what do you search under? Canine erection, veiny dog scrotum, Viagra dog, eternal puppy pleasure? I found some info, but it varied. One remedy that I tried was Vaseline. Yes, I had to massage the Vaseline onto his thing. But, it didn't work. I couldn't push it back. And, I didn't want to snap anything. From the waist up, Oscar seemed OK. He was a bit tired, but nothing unusual. Still, I worried what was possibly underneath the surface.

In the evening, we walked around Skagway. The cruise ships were gone, and the town was quiet. We saw a few people touring the streets. A group came over to chat, recognizing Oscar from earlier. We continued up and down different blocks, some with touristy shops, others with restaurants, and then a couple of rows of residential areas. A few of the houses had people sitting on the porches, enjoying a pleasant Alaska day.

"Dude, your dog has a boner." I looked to my right and saw a few college-aged guys drinking beers, sitting on a porch.

"Yeah, I know," is all I could reply with. *What would you say?*

I don't think they were concerned or being offensive. Instead, they were just noting the obvious. And, if you take away the possible downsides, it was a funny sight. Part of me thought it was comical, then another part of me felt bad for Oscar. Poor guy. Also, part of me felt a bit embarrassed. I don't know why. It wasn't me with the erection. Mostly, I was worried.

Bring Oscar

We continued our way back to the hotel room. Oscar appeared to walk just fine. Inside the room, I reluctantly looked at his belly area. The discoloration was the same, veiny and red. It hadn't gotten worse, but it hadn't gone away. I wondered if he was uncomfortable walking with this thing stuck between his legs. I hoped it wouldn't break. I decided to cut my Alaska stay short and start heading home. In ten days, we could see his veterinarian.

SKAGWAY, ALASKA to WATSON LAKE, YUKON TERRITORY, CANADA

THERE'S AN OLD mountaineer saying: The toughest part isn't ascending. It's getting back down. We had made it to Alaska. Now, we were turning around and beginning the journey home.

We got ready for the first leg, an extended ride back to Watson Lake. I anticipated losing an hour in the time change, and there would be winding roads—scenic—but that takes extra time. I headed outside to load the car and realized it was raining! Thank goodness we had eluded the rain for two days in Skagway and two days in Whitehorse. The cold is not a big deal, but rain sucks for sightseeing. And, I could imagine the miners one hundred-plus years ago. Crummy weather, climbing up and down the mountains for a chance of striking it rich. That was a rough life.

There was an upside to rain: There's no incentive to stop and take pictures, which saves travel time, especially since much of this drive was retracing the route we already took. And, there was a downside: The visibility and slippery roads would worsen the driving conditions. Hopefully, it will at least clean the car.

I trotted back to the room and dumped Oscar's water bowl out in the sink. Then, he and I walked across the street in the rain to the lobby. After using the Wi-Fi to read through email and review our route, I checked out of the hotel.

We left town and encountered fog in the mountain pass just outside of Skagway. Nobody was on the road, and I drove slowly. The dashboard oil light went on, so I stopped on the road shoulder. The car seemed to have a burning smell. Or, was it my imagination? I added a quart of oil. Hopefully, this wouldn't become an issue. We were at the farthest point from home.

While descending the mountains, we were surrounded by beautiful scenery among the clouds. On the roadside, water was running down the mountains, and there were trees growing out of the rocks, proving nature can work anywhere. I was attentive to the winding and wet road. It was a bit intimidating in some of the narrow turns with poor visibility.

As we dropped to a lower elevation, the range of vision improved. With anticipation, I was on the lookout for any wandering animals. At one point, we stopped abruptly when I spotted a bear in the road. Then, Oscar and I watched through the windshield, our heads slowly swiveling from left to right, as the bear crossed the street and hopped the highway rail.

It felt like sitting on my couch watching the Discovery Channel, as if my car windshield was a big screen TV!

We crossed the border back into Canada. Miles changed to kilometers, and the Alaska Time Zone changed into the Pacific Time Zone. We stopped at the Yukon Suspension Bridge. Unfortunately, Kim and Alice the dog were not in yet. Instead, a few other workers and another dog greeted us. After a breakfast cup of hot chocolate, we continued the trek.

An hour later, Oscar and I reached the Carcross Desert. We pulled to the side of the road to have another look at the "smallest desert in the world." We detoured to the town of Carcross. A big sign advertising the fry bread/sour bread bakery caught my eye. I went in and bought a white chocolate, raspberry scone. They're usually too dry for my taste, but these looked flavorful. Plus, I liked to support the local business.

As I snacked on the scone, Oscar and I walked around the small historic district. There were some cool sites, including the "Golden Spike" site where the railroad from Skagway stopped. History came full circle. The train goes from Skagway to Carcross! Also, I realized the name Carcross is short for CARibou CROSSing. I'm glad we stopped, especially learning how this location fit with the other towns.

After buying another tasty scone for tomorrow, we returned to Klondike Highway 2 and cruised north. Two miles later, we— Damn, we flew by the turnoff to Highway 8. These signs were abrupt. By the time you read them, you've passed the turn.

I slowed down five hundred feet later to turn the car around then got onto Highway 8, which would feed into the Alaska Highway. It appeared to be a shorter route than going up to Whitehorse and over. However, the slight change meant we would not pass Emerald Lake again. It was acceptable, since the visibility wasn't clear.

We reached the Alaska Highway and retraced our route to Watson Lake. The second visit to Watson Lake would be fine. I knew I wanted to go back to the Signpost Forest. Then, I knew we had to return to the same hotel and restaurant. Mostly, we didn't need to explore the town again, leaving extra time to rest.

A friend asked, "You stayed at that hotel again?" I did. It was still my only choice. Perhaps there were nicer, no-pets hotels, but I wouldn't sneak Oscar in a side door. It makes all dog owners look bad. And, I'm not going to claim Oscar is a service dog to get him in. Besides, after one look at Oscar and his wobbling legs, tilted head, and glazed eyes, who would believe he's a service dog, especially if I'm carrying him!?!?

In the afternoon, we arrived at Watson Lake, passing by the Northern Lights Space and Science Centre. It looked like a cool place to visit, but no dogs allowed. Highway 1 was the main street through town. One block further, there was a bank. While Oscar waited in the car, I ran inside to exchange currencies. A minute later, I returned to the car. "Well, that was convenient," I told Oscar.

Bring Oscar

We drove across the road to the hotel. Same deal: plain furniture, stuffy, linoleum floor, and the old television set. Thankfully, it was on the first floor this time. No separated steps and tilted balcony to navigate. Also, the good Chinese restaurant was only fifty feet away. I ordered the same #4 Combo: rice, beef broccoli, egg roll. Oscar would be pleased with the beef. Sometimes it's better to stick with what works.

After dinner, we watched a movie and fell asleep. Since we were on the first floor, leaving the door open wasn't an option. Fortunately, the circulation in this room was a little bit better than the last. Oscar woke me at 11:00 p.m. when he was wandering restlessly, bumping into everything. I walked him briefly, hoping the fresh air and exercise would help him. And, it did. When we returned, he went back to sleep.

Around 3:15 a.m., I heard him bumping into things and restlessly walking in circles. I got up to take a closer look at him. He seemed OK, aside from the crotch situation. It was still a bit splotchy. We went back outside. The sky was clear, and I could see the moon on one side and the glow of the sun on the opposite horizon. "Yep, still light out." It looked like dusk.

Back inside, I tried the Wi-Fi again. At 3:30 a.m., I managed to get a decent connection and rechecked the hotels. Still didn't find anything yet. I hoped for better luck tomorrow. Then I went back to sleep on top of the old bed.

WATSON LAKE, YUKON TERRITORY, CANADA to FORT NELSON, BRITISH COLUMBIA, CANADA

I WOKE UP at 8:00 a.m. and gently turned Oscar over. The erection was still there, but the discoloration was fading. Hmm? Nevertheless, the porn star seemed to be mending. After I propped him up on the tile floor, he followed me outside. While I half-packed the car, Oscar strolled around. Then, we returned to the room. I was too full of Chinese food to even consider breakfast. Instead, I made some complimentary tea and added two sugar packets with the "Whitehorse, Yukon" label. We've been there! While sipping sweet tea, I checked the Internet for messages, hotels, and travel routes.

I still needed a room for tomorrow night, so I retried the Aurora Park Inn & Suites. "Last night, I checked your website. There were no available rooms. Any chance someone cancelled?"

The woman on the call mentioned the Aurora doesn't use online booking agents. "So, you have a room tomorrow?" I hoped. It was July 1st, Canada Day.

"We do," she answered.

"That takes a dog, too?" I checked.

"Yes, we take dogs."

"That's fantastic! Yesterday, I saw your place online. It looks great, but the website said there were no available rooms."

"Yeah," she sighed. "That happens." She explained that the online programs had no idea if there were extra rooms available. In order to get a room, you must call.

"Well, I'm glad I called." I gave my name and reserved a room for that night in Dawson Creek. I was pleased, because it looked like a good one. And, I was relieved that we had a place. I suspected the Canadian holiday made it tougher to find a room.

We crossed over the British Columbia border, where I spotted a bison sitting on the side of the road. In North America, buffalo and bison are often used interchangeably. Buffalo are prevalent in Africa and Asia. Bison are found in North America and have thick hair, short horns, and a hump. No doubt, this was a bison.

The large animal was sitting, just lounging in the grass. I slowed down to turn the car around then noticed another one up ahead. So, I eased the car forward, rolled down the window, and stopped to shoot photos. Meanwhile, Oscar stuck his head out the window to have a look. Incredible. We were watching this big creature about twenty yards away. Although it was oblivious to us, I had no interest in getting out of the car for a closer look.

As we watched, I was delighted to note that we were all by ourselves. Even after five minutes, not a single car had driven by in either direction. The bison was grazing, Oscar was watching, and I was enjoying this moment in a place three thousand miles from home.

Oscar watching the "British Columbia Nature Channel" from the passenger seat

We continued along Alcan 97 and saw much of what we'd seen while traveling west last week: bison, bears, rams, and moose. And, there were plenty of beautiful lakes, mountains, and rivers in between. We weaved along the jade-green Muncho Lake and made stops to admire the rivers running through the mountains.

We also encountered some relentless insects. At a scenic spot along the highway, Oscar and I got out for a moment to stretch and enjoy the scenery. A few bugs hovered around us. They weren't bees that would bite. And, they weren't mosquitoes. But, they were annoying. A few moments later, there were tons of them, swirling around my face and body. Meanwhile, Oscar was shaking his head, trying to flick them off. I took off my hat and tried to swat them away.

We made a break for it back to the car. I tried to shoo them away before I opened the car door. The swarm was unstoppable. "Ready." While opening the door, I launched Oscar into the front seat and then quickly followed him and slammed the car door shut. A few persistent pests got inside the car. As we drove away, I opened the window and shooed them out of the car.

We returned to the Toad River Lodge at Mile 422 for lunch. This time, I decided to try my first "buffalo burger," or bison burger. While waiting, I strolled up and down the gift shop and looked at the hat collection on the ceiling. The food was tasty. Oscar snacked on his dog food and some of my scraps. Across the way, I watched a bush pilot land a little plane on a grass airstrip across the street. "Yes, this is remote British Columbia."

Suddenly, four motorcycles pulled up. It was the Louisiana bikers again! After meeting at the "Welcome to Alaska" sign and crossing paths in Skagway, we found ourselves at another common stop off the highway. They greeted us with friendly nods on their way inside.

Including a return stop at Tetsa River for cinnamon rolls, it was a smooth drive back to Fort Nelson. We arrived in the late afternoon and tried the Lakeview Inn & Suites. I wanted the variety and to see if the suites were more comfortable than our hotel last week. The two women at the front desk were terrific: efficient and accommodating. There were DVDs at the front desk along with baked cookies and candy. This place was off to a great start.

We walked down the hallway to room 102. I opened the door and found a huge room with a doggie bag. It was definitely a suite. Sweet! While Oscar wandered around the large room looking for a comfortable place to relax, I popped open the laptop and learned the Wi-Fi had smoking fast internet. Outside, the sun was shining bright. Blindingly bright.

I woke up at 2:00 a.m. to use the bathroom. Oscar was sound asleep on his blanket by the entrance. I stepped over him and noticed paw prints all over the shower area. "Well, I wonder who did that," I said while looking at Oscar. "Or, was someone sleepwalking!?" I was surprised I hadn't heard his tags jingling.

FORT NELSON, BRITISH COLUMBIA, CANADA to DAWSON CREEK, BRITISH COLUMBIA, CANADA

"I GOT YOU some breakfast!" I dumped a cup of eggs into his bowl and mixed it with a tramadol pill. When he finished, I took a peek underneath. The Yukon/Alaska erection was completely gone. That had to be some sort of record. Stamina! Oscar seemed to be back to his old self.

Before leaving town, we drove through the main street and saw residents waiting along one of the roads. A parade! Canada Day! Floats, old cars, and city vehicles lined up in front of the A&W and local store, getting ready for the celebration. If you swapped the flags, it could've been a scene from a small, rural USA town on July 4th.

We made our lunch stop at Alaska Hwy Mile 147, Sasquatch Crossing. There was a bistro, gift shop, some lodging, and a ten-foot-tall wooden carved Sasquatch. I ordered a Sasquatch sub (chicken, cheddar cheese, lettuce, peppers) with fries. It was a pretty good picnic lunch.

Continuing our drive back through British Columbia, I counted down the miles on the Alaska Highway. Bye-bye, Alaska Highway. A moment later, we reached the Aurora Park Inn & Suites. I hoped it would be like Lakeview Inn & Suites last night. During check in, I noticed free DVD movies available along with snacks at the front desk: cake, coffee, tea, candy, and fruit. In our room, there was a fridge, microwave, cable TV, and good air con. This suite was as sweet as last night's suite. That's two for two in British Columbia.

Since we toured Dawson Creek last week, it wasn't necessary to see those attractions again. Instead, we tried the Walter Wright Pioneer Village, which was five minutes away. There were a few interesting exhibits and restored log cabins. But mostly, it was a place to walk around during the sunny, pleasant day.

On the way back to the inn, we picked up dinner and returned to the room. After another three-hundred-mile day of driving, I was delighted to eat, sit on the bed, and find something on the TV. As I set up our dinners, Oscar stood beside me. His head was tilted, and his tongue was hanging out. He looked happy. "Long day, huh?" Oscar continued to watch me. "We got in a lot of miles," I said to him. "Great job, today. Ready for some vittles?" I set down his bowl of food, chicken on top, and tramadol. "Dig in!"

DAWSON CREEK, BRITISH COLUMBIA, CANADA to HINTON, ALBERTA, CANADA

OUR PLAN WAS to turn south onto Route 40 and head toward Jasper, Banff, and Calgary. In the afternoon, we arrived in Hinton, just outside of Jasper National Park. Before the hotel, we visited the Beaver Boardwalk. It was a pretty area to walk around, although we didn't see any beavers. After speaking to a few people, I learned that it was more likely to see them come up around dusk.

As Oscar and I followed the wooden deck path to leave, an older couple walked toward us. "Nice dog. What kind is that?"

"He's a mix: I think Shepherd, Lab, with some terrier and Schipperke," I answered. "He's a rescue, so I don't know for sure."

"He looks like a Shepherd," the lady said.

"Well, he's smart like a Shepherd, and friendly like a Lab. But, he's kinda small, so I think he's got some sort of terrier," I guessed. "But, some guy told me he has Schipperke."

"A mutt," the guy said.

"Yeah, his mama got around!" I joked. They gave a polite smile. Since they were entering the area, I asked, "Is it true the beavers come out later?"

"Yes, at dusk is when you can see them. But, we're here to look at the birds."

"Are you from around here?"

"Yes." They added, "We come here quite often."

"It's a nice spot. I guess we'll come back later." I wasn't interested in the birds, but the beavers piqued my curiosity.

Oscar and I walked back to the car and drove to the hotel de jour, the BCMInns. I dropped off my bag on the bed and looked online for nearby restaurants. We ended up at a Japanese sushi restaurant. While we ate, I watched a group of teenagers playing football in the distance. Then, a lady walked by with her collie. It was a pleasant summer atmosphere. A moment later, I looked down, and Oscar had cleaned out most of his dinner, leaving bits of dry dog food in the bowl. I poured some more of the chicken and sauce, in case he was still hungry.

After an hour of relaxing, we headed back to the Beaver Boardwalk. Oscar and I walked to a platform where a few people were standing. I figured they knew more than I did. An older couple pointed out a few beavers swimming, but it was tough to see any others. Every so often, I could see the water move or a current from a swimming beaver in the distance. But, it was difficult to see any of them up close. Nevertheless, you could see the extensive network of dams they had built. No doubt, they were there.

As the sun was setting, I continued to look for any beaver that might swim up close. Meanwhile, Oscar just slept on the wooden deck. When he was younger, he'd have tried to chase every bird and anything that moved! Today, Oscar made a brief effort at some movement in the water. But, quickly, lost interest and just napped on the platform.

Eventually, I called it a day and woke him up. We carefully walked along the narrow wooden boardwalk. I held the leash tight. The last thing I wanted was Oscar to stumble and fall into the pond. Then, I'd have to jump in and grab him. What a mess that would be.

HINTON, ALBERTA, CANADA to COCHRANE, ALBERTA, CANADA

OSCAR WAS CURLED up on his towel under the air conditioner. I went to get a cup of egg for his tramadol pill. There was a line of people looking over the pancakes, fruit, eggs, and bagels. I watched several kids enjoying their vacation as they walked through the buffet line, looking over the items. It was bustling. The 8:30 a.m. crowd was too much for my taste, and I hoped it wasn't foreshadowing the travels through Banff.

I watched some impolite and hurried people filling their plates. One big person in front of me piled eggs, hash browns, and greasy sausages on her plate, which didn't leave much room for fruit or grains. It was a physician's nightmare. And, I wouldn't give those dripping sausages to Oscar, let alone eat them myself. I slipped in, scooped some scrambled eggs into a Styrofoam cup, and went back to the room. After feeding Oscar his egg and dog biscuit breakfast, I took a quick shower and packed the bags.

We traveled to Jasper National Park, the largest in the Canadian Rockies. I'd always heard of Jasper and Banff, and this was my chance to see what I had been missing. At first, we met a lot of traffic and some construction. However, I did get an opportunity to stop and view two majestic elk minding their own business next to the road. The picturesque animals seemed to be park ambassadors welcoming the stream of cars.

We entered the park and distanced ourselves from the bottleneck of traffic. That was the theme of the day: Try to avoid the tourist crowds. The scenery was tremendous: mountains, lakes, falls, ice fields, and the woods. Plus, there were the little things: seeing a long train going between the lake and mountains, an airstrip with planes for the area, off-road biking paths, and rafting places. Despite all that, there seemed to be plenty of space to go off the trail and be alone.

We stopped at a scenic spot overlooking the mountain pass. There were crowds of people wandering and taking photos. I took in the fresh air and walked with Oscar. While he sniffed around, I took a few photos and read the placards that provided a brief history of the area. As I read one of the stories, a young guy stepped right in front of me to read it. Rude or oblivious? I moved on. A friendly couple asked if I'd take a photo of them. Of course, I did. I'm always happy to return the favor. Suddenly, after five minutes, the several cars were gone, and it was just Oscar and I. It was peaceful, and I noticed the mountain peaks in the distance and the birds. Then, a few minutes later, another batch of cars pulled into the scenic view.

We continued along TransCanada 16 into Jasper then connected onto Highway 93, the Icefields Parkway. Thirty minutes later, we reached Athabasca Falls. Very cool. It's not as vast as Niagara, but the intensity flowing through the rocky area was awesome. Plus, the background view of the mountains was spectacular.

I picked out a traveler who was holding a large-lens, expensive-looking camera. He seemed best for our souvenir shot. The European gentleman was gracious and did have a good sense of photography, angles, and backgrounds.

Posing with a lightweight Oscar at Athabasca Falls, Jasper, Alberta, Canada

There was a large crowd, but we were able to maneuver among the people. Plus, I felt good that we had gotten rock star parking next to the entrance. I didn't have to carry Oscar too much. He was walking along and seemed to enjoy the cool air and the smells. This stop was a pleasant surprise.

While we drove through the next scenic part of Alberta, Oscar looked through the windows. Eventually, it steamed up inside the car, so I cracked open the windows. I could feel the cold breeze pour into the car. Oscar enjoyed it. So, I relented and dropped the windows farther and slowed down the car. Oscar hung his head out the window as I maneuvered a sweatshirt over my head. I was running the heater while allowing cold air from the snowcapped mountains to pour in. Yeah, that made sense.

In the distance, the Columbia Icefield appeared. I stopped the car and took a photo of the sign and the icefield in the background.

Very cool. The largest icefield in the Rocky Mountains covers British Columbia and Alberta, and falls between Jasper and Banff National Parks. Also, the massive expanse lies on a triple continental divide, where the meltwaters flow all the way to the Pacific, Arctic, and Atlantic Oceans.

I jumped back in the car and drove to the parking entrance. The lot was full, so we parked on the road leading to the parking lot and base of the mountain. After a few minutes, I realized we couldn't go. Besides the half-mile walk to the base of the hike, there was a stream of people going up and down the trails. It was too far to walk with Oscar, too much to climb, and again, too many people. I'd been on other glaciers, so I was OK with moving on. And, Oscar didn't mind.

We resumed driving through the mountain area toward Banff and Calgary. I could smell a campfire aroma. Within two hours, we passed Lake Louise and went toward Moraine Lake. I had heard Lake Louise was popular, so I wondered if Moraine Lake could be a nice alternative to avoid the tourists. A young couple pulled up, and I asked if it was worth it. They said, definitely. After forty-five hundred miles, I realized I needed to find out for myself. So, we turned around and went back to Moraine Lake.

We followed the path to the lake. Oscar took a drink of the glacial water. Then, we sat on a bench and admired the setting. The lake's turquoise-blue color from the refraction of light off the rock deposits was awesome. We had a spectacular view of the lake and the towering mountains around it. This is a place worth a visit. I met an elderly couple who had been to both lakes and asked them which one they preferred. Moraine, they said. I learned later that the image was featured on the back of the Canadian twenty-dollar bill during the 1970s. It was certainly worthy.

After the Moraine Lake stop, we returned to the 93 Highway, which had merged with TransCanada 1. We were headed straight for Calgary. We passed through the town of Banff. There were a lot of tourists, but I was glad to see the place I had heard so much about. It was the middle of summer, but as I drove past the shops and lodges, I could sense the appeal this place had as a winter ski destination.

After Banff, we drove and drove until we arrived in Cochrane, Alberta. Last night, I searched for a stop near Calgary and came up with Cochrane. It seemed like a nice town, a bit off the beaten path.

I found the "TRUST" Mural Mosaic. It was an incredible, enormous display filled with a patchwork of scenes from Alberta. The two hundred and sixteen individual paintings combined to create a grand portrait of a cowboy and his horse. Since I had driven through, I recognized the significance of the images. But mostly, it was a beautiful piece placed in the town center hall. Once I was alone in the display area, I took some open photos of the mural mosaic from all angles.

After a long, adventurous day, we were ready for dinner. At Tim's Gourmet Pizza in the "historic downtown," they prepared a terrific pizza with all-natural ingredients. It was tasty. Plus, it had outdoor seating. After dinner, we walked down the street to MacKay's Ice Cream. One of the paintings in the Cochrane mosaic was a MacKay's ice cream cone. The shop touted its "70-year tradition." I like tradition, and we like ice cream.

The town's people were outside enjoying the summer evening. I noticed two women, and one was wearing an orange Illinois sweatshirt. I asked if she went to U of I. And, she had! She was surprised that I had recognized it. It's a small world, even when you're far from home.

We stayed at the Bow River Inn. It was fine. It had a quick stop, motel feel. The floor had no carpeting, so Oscar was constantly slipping and sliding, but he'd sleep fine on his blanket, a makeshift island in the floor. In the end, we got in so late that it didn't make much difference.

COCHRANE, ALBERTA, CANADA to MAPLE CREEK, SASKATCHEWAN, CANADA

IN THE MORNING, I peeked into the bathroom and saw Oscar lying on the cool floor. He opened his eyes and saw me. Then, he struggled to sit up, like a new skier stuck in the snow. He couldn't get his hind legs under himself to stand up. "You got it?" He flailed for a bit and lost the struggle. I walked over and gave him a quick lift up. "Good to go!"

After checking out of the hotel, we headed east on Highway 1A, an auxiliary route along TransCanada 1. Twenty miles east of Cochrane, I could see the skyline of Calgary. We merged into TransCanada 1 and drove through the middle of the city. Calgary seemed rather modern.

We drove the next one hundred miles through open fields. It was a sunny day, and there was a 110 km speed limit on a smooth road, so the drive was routine.

"Doesn't it get boring?" people ask.

I never think of it that way. I have friends who enjoy spending hours sunning by the pool. And, others who can binge watch a season of *Dexter* in a day. Does that get monotonous? I didn't mind driving mile after mile. For me, it was like watching television, where the windshield was the TV screen that provided content. "Today's scheduled programming will be scenes from Alberta, Canada, featuring oil rigs, cows, and crops." And, in between were billboards with promotions and commercials. "Need oil services? We know the Drill. Call us at…" Mostly, I just appreciated the time I was getting with Oscar.

We continued along the Canadian Badlands of southeastern Alberta. An hour later, we reached Cypress County and found the Medicine Hat "Gas City" welcome center. While Oscar roamed and stretched, I noticed a clever exhibit called "David's Weather Stone." *If rock is wet, then it's raining. If rock is white, it is snowing.* Funny.

Next to the small tourism building, there was an open field with a giant tepee. Oscar and I went over to investigate the open-aired structure. Constructed of steel and concrete, I learned the Saamis Tepee was originally built in 1988 for the Calgary Olympics. It was moved to Medicine Hat in 1991. It had to be the largest tepee in the world, towering over two hundred feet high, with a base diameter over one hundred and fifty feet. When you step inside the massive structure and look up, you can view large, round painted portraits of famous natives and spots in the area. Also, there is a visual history of the region. Then, on the ground were placards with descriptions giving context to the portraits. While Oscar sat in a shaded spot, I toured the enormous structure. It was a meaningful, unique attraction.

One of the ways to make a trip more meaningful is to seek out interesting things. It's easy to go to big cities, museums, and famous sites. But, the trick to traveling extensive miles, especially over lower populated areas, is to seek unique sites. When we were kids, one of us would sigh, "We're bored." My mom would tell us to "go outside and play." In other words, make up your own fun. Make up your own games. Or, go out and explore. Sometimes, you'll find a hidden gem. And, many times, nothing out of the ordinary. But, the search utilizes the time.

We stopped in the middle of Medicine Hat and found the spot I was seeking: the giant chess set. Oscar and I walked to the twenty-by-twenty-foot square area. Standing on the board were wooden chess pieces that were two-to-four feet high. Since Oscar didn't play chess, we explored the surroundings. There was a plaque displaying a certificate from Guinness World Records, proclaiming it the "largest chess set board." Above it were colorful flowers in a garden shaped like the queen of a chess set. A few feet away was a sign showing all of the town's sponsors who helped construct and maintain the park since 2005. There were benches and tables with regular-sized chess boards too. Next to them was a guy selling soft drinks and hot dogs.

We skipped the hot dog vendor and drove through Medicine Hat, looking for a potential snack. When we reached the TransCanada entrance, we changed plans, got on the highway and looked toward tonight's destination. As we drove along the flat, open land, it occurred to me: It's July 4th, Independence Day in the United States. There were no celebrations here in Canada, which was OK with me. Over the years, the appeal of fireworks had fizzled out. Although, I wouldn't mind seeing a ten-second fireworks show. Just take all the fireworks from the entire fifteen-minute show and launch them at the same time. Now that would be spectacular!

Fourth of July didn't matter to Oscar. Although, he loved it when I fired up the barbecue. The sound of bursting fireworks never bothered him. On rare occasions a thunderstorm might bring him into the living room onto the couch next to me. And, some fierce, hard rock music got a reaction. The deep base pounding on the surround sound would get Oscar scampering to the backyard. Now, since he's lost most of his hearing, none of it had an effect any more.

We passed over the Alberta-Saskatchewan border. Within an hour, we turned onto Highway 21 and reached the city limits of Maple Creek in search of the Motor Inn. The outside of the building looked suspense-movie scary. A gravel lot with a few weeds and shrubs and faded, painted walls. Whatever, it was inexpensive and pet-friendly. I grabbed Oscar and the laptop, and we headed to the hotel entrance. It smelled of smoke. The inside was dated, but the people were polite.

After a quick pit stop, we were off to dinner. I decided to go with a place called Caroline's Drive-In. I tried a Canadian cuisine offering called poutine (poo-teen), which was fries, curds, and gravy. It reminded me of chili cheese fries. I added a salad (something healthy), and soft serve ice cream for dessert. I carried out the two plates of food. Oscar was waiting in anticipation. He took a sniff of the salad, but immediately he was drawn to the pile of fries and gravy. So, he assumed the position, waiting for me to hand him a gravy-covered French fry in between my bites. All of it was quite good. "I think this poutine thing is going to catch on!" I handed Oscar another gravy French fry. "Although, this may not be the healthiest thing to eat."

I wondered if poutine was French for clogged arteries.

Everyone was so nice. The lady who took my order, the local guy who was eating there, and all the drive-through cars that waved to us as they left. Then, a mother and daughter had biked over. We had an interesting conversation about local life. They talked about wanting and needing rain for the farmers, as well as the flood five years ago, and the local rodeo going on. I actually heard the end of it. I think it was a block or two away. I saw a few families with the fathers and sons wearing cowboy hats.

After I finished my ice cream and Oscar ate most of his dog food, we returned to the hotel. At 10:30 it started to drizzle outside. Plus, the temperature continued to fall. It was actually chilly out there!

When it rains, we usually sleep soundly. But, this was a brutal night. Oscar was pacing most of the night, butting his head against the furniture and walls. I had no idea why. The room wasn't overly hot. He hadn't eaten anything extraordinary. Hopefully, it wasn't a mental health issue. It bothered me, but mostly, I didn't want the knocking sound to wake the others in the motel. I walked him three times. At 12:15 a.m., 3:00 a.m., and 5:30 a.m., we went out the fire exit door, did a loop, and walked back inside. Each time the weather worsened, including a bit of rain, wind whipping in, and cold air. It must've dropped thirty degrees since we had dinner outside.

MAPLE CREEK, SASKATCHEWAN, CANADA to REGINA, SASKATCHEWAN, CANADA

WE BEGAN THE day's two-hundred-and-fifty-mile drive with a quick break at Tim Hortons. I liked that place. It was better than Starbucks (and cheaper), and it beat the selection and taste of Dunkin' Donuts. I ordered a bagel with cheese, tomato, and lettuce and a large hot chocolate and a muffin. While waiting for the food, I kept wondering where their stock trades. Always busy, good food, and clean; seemed like a good investment.

Forty minutes later, we made our next stop at Reed Lake, near Morse. It was a chance to walk around, read a few placards, and take a longer break. There were two people walking along the water, but otherwise, it was wide open lake and birds. I read how this vast, shallow body of water was a terrific refueling place for migrating birds. We went down the path to a two-story wooden tower. It was too much for Oscar to climb, and I didn't want to carry him up the steep steps.

"Wait here for a second." I darted up the steps, and when I reached the top, I could see the lake from above. I looked down and saw Oscar sitting below. I took a few photos and raced back down. There was not much else to see, but it was a quiet, pleasant place to stretch our legs.

We resumed our drive across southern Saskatchewan. A casual observation: Plenty of open fields, dotted with oil rigs, cattle, and farmhouses. Occasionally, I saw cows sitting by the oil rigs! The road was clear and smooth, temps were cool, so no air con was needed, and we were moving at 110 km/h. About seventy-five miles later, we reached Moose Jaw. The welcome sign proudly stated it was "The Friendly City." That's some good marketing.

I spotted the tourist center, with a terrific photo op: a giant moose. There was a small Canadian plane, with "Snowbird" on its nose, mounted on a stand, towering in the air. It seemed random until I learned the Royal Canadian Air Force Snowbirds, an elite squadron, were based in Moose Jaw. Makes sense.

We got out and stretched, walking from "Mac the Moose," to the plane, to the information center. Inside the visitor's gallery, I discovered Moose Jaw had ties to Prohibition and Al Capone. The downtown had a bunch of murals. That seemed like a good place to start with Oscar.

In town, we parked facing a colorful mural with a symbolic history of Capone, Prohibition, and speakeasies in the 1920s. Oscar and I walked past the tourist Tunnels of Moose Jaw, Little Chicago, and several murals along the streets. I wondered how the painted details and colors could last after years of rough Canadian winters. Continuing along the sidewalk, I peeked through the windows of the shops. Eventually, I stopped at one to pick up homemade fudge and take souvenir photos.

On the way back to the car, I saw a place called Smoke's Poutinerie, a Canadian chain. So, we paused for a late snack. I ordered veggie poutine, which had guacamole, sour cream, and other toppings mixed with veggie gravy on fries. While waiting for our order, I looked at the wall displays describing the history

Bring Oscar

of poutine: potatoes/fries, cheese curds, and gravy. Created on the eastern part of Canada, it was spreading throughout the country. I anticipated the tasty creation would reach the US soon. It had glutton written all over it!

The young worker handed me a soda and box containing the poutine. I took it outside to the table, where Oscar was eagerly waiting. I opened the box and dove into the pile of food. I handed a few fries covered in gravy to Oscar. Then, I shoveled some dripping fries into my mouth. Damn, it was good. The gravy reminded me of the Swanson gravy from TV dinners. This place would be a hit in late night cities, especially after the bars close.

During the remainder of the drive, I pulled out the fudge for a snack. It was fantastic! I had bought four bars to get two free. More than I needed, but I convinced myself that I was supporting the local businesses.

An hour later, we reached Regina. We passed the familiar hotel and Chinese restaurant from two weeks ago. I was looking for the RCMP Heritage Centre. On the way, we passed by the stadium where a football game was being played between the Saskatchewan Roughriders and the Calgary Stampeders. I could see local fans outside the arena, dressed in green Roughrider jerseys.

Oscar and I walked to the Heritage Centre entrance. Luckily, the museum was open until 5:30. I looked at my watch. It was 5:10 p.m. We made it on time. I found a shady spot near the doorway for Oscar. He could peek through the entrance window or stare out to the parking lot where people walked by in the distance. I gave myself three minutes to take a quick look inside.

I wasn't concerned about Oscar waiting I was worried that someone might take him! It seemed kind of irrational. Who would take a dog, especially in front of the Royal Mounted Police museum next to the academy? It's like stealing a car in front of a police station! Nevertheless, my mind sometimes wandered to a worst-case scenario. What if I return and Oscar is gone? He didn't have a chip. Then, I'd have to scramble to try to find him, like some movie of the week.

"Oskie, I'll be back in three minutes," I promised. Then, I darted through the doors. The museum was well worth a visit. It was large, and I didn't have nearly enough time to see everything. But, at least, I could get the gist of it by passing through a few exhibit halls. After the three minutes was up, I returned to the entrance. I peeked through the window and Oscar was just sitting in the shade, watching. He seemed to enjoy relaxing outside.

I gave myself three more minutes and raced to another part of the museum. Then, returned. This time, there was a college-aged woman sitting with Oscar. She saw me peek through the window. She pointed at Oscar. I nodded that he was mine. Then, I walked outside.

"Yeah, he's mine."

"He is so sweet," she said. "We were just sitting here."

"He's fine. I gave him some water before. I'm just trying to see a bit of the museum before it closes." I wanted to assure her that I was a responsible dog parent. "We've been traveling a while, and he doesn't mind a shady spot to rest. He's an old guy."

"He is so nice and great with people. If you want, I'll sit with him while you go inside."

"Really?"

"Yes, I'm done with work. I don't mind."

With the extra time, I took a moment to find out more about the museum and what to see with the ten minutes I had. The woman at the front desk was very helpful and welcoming. She even went outside to meet Oscar and later took a photo of me in one of the displays. The exhibits were wonderful. A lot of original Mountie items. Plus, the story of the origins in the NW territory resonated, because I had just returned from the Yukon!

When I returned to the entrance, the young woman was petting and playing with Oscar.

"Thank you so much for keeping him company!"

"He was great," she said. "What kind of dog is he?"

"I believe he's part Lab, Shepherd, and bit of terrier and Schipperke."

"Well, he looks like a Lab."

"Yes, he's got a Lab face and he's gentle; great with kids," I mentioned. "But, I think he has some Shepherd, because he's smart and protective. Plus, when his ears are straight up, he looks like one. But, he's got Schipperke, because he's a bit smaller."

She continued to stroke Oscar's head. "Do you have a dog?" I asked. Usually, when people are comfortable with dogs, they have one or had one.

"My parents do," she said. "I'd love to get one, but my apartment is too small. But, my parents have two Golden Retrievers that they rescued."

"Mine is a rescue, too. Got him at a shelter. Best forty bucks I ever spent!"

"That's great that you did that," she said. "He's a lucky dog."

"And, I'm a lucky owner," I agreed. "He's been a terrific travelling companion."

"Where are you from?"

"Chicago area. Are you familiar?"

"Yes, I went there once to visit. Wow, that's far. You drove all the way here?"

"Actually, we went across British Columbia to Alaska."

"With him?!"

"Uh-huh," I nodded. "Now, we're heading back."

"So, you are just passing through?"

"Yep, just wanted to see the museum." I added, "Cool place."

"Well, if you are here tomorrow, there is a big ceremony for the latest graduating class. It's a big deal."

"Anyone can go?"

"Yes, it's open. You may have to arrive early to get a good seat. But, anyone can go."

"Even him?"

"I think so. It's outside."

"What time?"

"The ceremony is around 11:00 or 12:00, I think."

"Hmm, that might be too late." I'm not sure if we had the time and energy, leaving at 2:00 p.m. then driving three hundred miles to our next destination. It would likely require another overnight stop. "But, you never know."

The museum was closing, and I was ready to finish the day of driving. The woman gave Oscar one more pat on the head. Then she said goodbye. Oscar and I trotted back to the car.

We drove back through Regina, looking for the hotel. On the way, we passed by the stadium. The game was over, and I saw a lot of fans and cars with Roughrider green jerseys and banners. Using a Bing map screenshot for guidance, we arrived at the Hampton Inn.

What a difference a day can make. The accommodations were a big improvement: maintained building, easy parking, and open lobby area. The furnishings and atmosphere seemed more upscale and corporate. The room had a fridge, new furniture, coffee maker, and great decor. There was a comfortable desk for work, a big screen TV, and very good Wi-Fi. Although we were on the third floor, we were next to the elevator, and the ice machine and snacks down the hall.

My number one rule was Oscar comes with me. No leaving him. But, by this point, I had started to bend the rule. Oscar was just about deaf. If I clapped, he could hear the high pitch or sense the vibration, but if I talked ordinarily or was walking carefully, he couldn't hear at all.

When I saw him sleeping, I threw on my workout clothes and running shoes and quietly exited the room. I took the elevator down to the spacious fitness room. It was a basic set-up, containing several machines that were relatively new. Large selection of weights, ice cold water, and two televisions. Since nobody was in there, I could pick the channels.

I warmed up with a quick ten-minute set and returned to the room. When I saw Oscar was still asleep, I went back down the elevator to do another ten-minute set. Returned to the room; he was still asleep. I saw his chest gently going in and out. He was good; I went back for the rest of my workout.

Afterward, I trotted up the stairs and returned to the room. Following a shower, I did a little work and watched TV while outlining the next day's drive. And, then I heard the sound...*oh no*...I checked down and saw that Oscar had relieved himself. It wasn't completely solid, but it was on his towel! Excellent; we were prepared! I gently pulled the towel away and replaced it. Then, I rinsed the soiled towel in the bathroom. Oscar slept the entire time.

At 10:45, I turned off the TV and went to sleep. At 11:15, Oscar woke up.

"Nice timing, pal," I said to him.

After a walk, he eventually did his business. We came inside and the night receptionist greeted us. He was very nice, offering Oscar a treat. He said he used to have a two-year-old Greyhound, but when he moved to Canada, he left it with his family. During a holiday, there were fireworks, and the dog got scared, ran into the street, and was hit by a car. Sad tragedy. Our midnight chat changed to lighter subjects. Meanwhile, Oscar enjoyed the biscuit. He offered him more treats. I said, I'd likely see him later that night.

We did see him later—three more times.

REGINA, SASKATCHEWAN, CANADA to PORTAGE LA PRAIRIE, MANITOBA, CANADA

I GOT UP and showered. It felt like I had just pulled an all-nighter—three walks between 2:00 a.m. and 6:00 a.m. But, it's part of the marathon journey, so we pressed on. Oscar poked his head through the curtain. He looked up at me as the shower spray hit him in the face.

"Tough night, huh?" He just watched me with his head tilted.

We skipped the RCMP ceremony. It wasn't worth a three-hour delay. Plus, I wasn't willing to risk Oscar getting overheated or sick in a crowd during the afternoon event. So, we departed Regina, and rather than retrace our route south into the US, we continued east toward the next province, Manitoba.

I rarely had a driving day where I was tired. I had plenty of time to sleep, it was almost always light outside, and the radio could keep me occupied. But, after last night with Oscar, plus a stretch of unchanging scenery, I was exhausted—and Oscar was unable to

Bring Oscar

take the wheel. During the three hundred miles, I stopped several times at gas stations, rest stops, and even on the side of the road. I'd step outside with Oscar for a few moments and get back into the car.

After college graduation, a buddy and I were planning to drive from Pasadena back to our homes in Phoenix. I was especially bummed because it was the end of college, and now we faced the final long drive without air conditioning.

The 1970 Dodge Challenger was a three-speed and a fun ride. But, it didn't have air con. That would've required getting a larger radiator and an entire air conditioning system, and I didn't have the money. Hell, my car radio was held together by a thread, allowing the dials to move across the spectrum of radio stations. I was a broke college student.

It was mid-June and we were dreading the long desert trip. My friend's brother said to us, "I usually drive back in the middle of the night."

"Really?" I asked.

"Yeah, I leave around 8:30 p.m., after LA traffic. Then, I drive in the middle of the night. Open roads, stars out in the sky, and just me and truckers. I get back to Phoenix the next morning. But, it's clear and cooler outside."

It sounded reasonable to us. Sort of glamourous; a cool way to drive through the desert. So, my buddy and I agreed to try it. We left after traffic hours and drove back on I-10 to Phoenix. Unfortunately, by midnight, I was exhausted. Driving in the dark for long periods of time was tiring. Plus, I didn't have a chance to rest or nap before leaving. I tried opening windows, blasting Van Halen on my cassette player, and playing a copy of a rock mix my friend Rob had given me. He called it "Religious Experience." Anything to stop drifting and remain awake.

Eventually, there was a small rest stop with a Carl's Jr. My friend Roger raced ahead in his Mustang and waved at me to follow him to the stop. We had a snack and loaded up on large sodas for a jolt.

"Lance, I thought you were going to drive off the road!"

"I know. I'm exhausted."

"A few times, I was honking, yelling, and flashing my lights to get your attention. You were riding on the shoulder of the road!"

"I don't remember any of that." I was a zombie driver. I don't know how truckers can do it.

We continued the long overnight journey home to Phoenix. I remember pulling into the driveway, near dawn, exhausted, and relieved that I didn't drive off the road and kill myself!

A week later, I ran into Roger's brother. I explained our long night and how I struggled to stay awake.

"I don't know how you do it," I said to him. "I could barely keep my eyes open." Then he mentioned he usually got tired too, so he'd just pull over and take a nap on the side of the road for an hour or two. Why didn't he tell us that in the first place!?!

Back in Canada, I struggled to maintain focus and tried opening the windows. I turned to a rock station and blasted the music. I tried singing along, but my eyes were fighting to stay open. I pulled out a soda from the cooler and a bag of Fritos. I wasn't hungry, but snacking was a decent remedy. I managed to stay awake.

Little Dog in the Prairie, Manitoba, Canada

Bring Oscar

The journey east along Highway 1 took us past Indian Head, Moosomin, the Manitoba border, a few rodeo signs, and two small-town stadiums. We reached Brandon, Manitoba, for dinner and a visit to the 26th Field Regiment Museum. Then we went to Marino's Pizza for dinner. It was fantastic! The veggie pita was more like a calzone. Huge portions and tasty. I figured it would be good because they said they needed thirty minutes to make it. Oscar got chicken strips, which he devoured out of the carton before I could put them into his bowl.

Feeling refreshed and finishing strong, Oscar and I made it to Portage la Prairie, just west of Winnipeg. The Super 8 in town was easy to find, and we got a room right next to the entrance.

I was glad to finally catch up on sleep.

PORTAGE LA PRAIRIE, MANITOBA, CANADA to FARGO, NORTH DAKOTA

OUR LAST CANADIAN night was an easy one; we slept uninterrupted. I grabbed Oscar's leash, and we wandered outside. One of the housekeepers saw us and was charmed by Oscar. A woman smoking outside asked about Oscar's limping and his paw. When I said he was fifteen, she was surprised. Oscar wandered to her. Holding a cigarette in one hand, she gave him a gentle pet with the other.

After a brief walk around the area, we went inside. Suddenly, while we were in the hallway floor area, Oscar crouched over. Uh-oh. "We were just outside!" I couldn't pull him away without interrupting. I reached into my pocket for a bag. After a few moments, he dropped a load. By now, I had a bag in my hand, and like a catcher, I received the drops into the mitt. It wasn't the most orthodox way, or pretty, but it did work.

I picked up a complimentary newspaper and a few breakfast snacks, and we returned to the room. After eating, packing, and relaxing, I left a tip beside a written note, "Thanks, from Oscar, the old dog!" directed to the housekeeper who greeted us this morning.

After we left the hotel, I took an extra ten minutes to drive through Portage la Prairie. After all, when would I be back to see it? It appeared to be a quiet town with a lot of places to eat and refuel; a solid stopover. We got back on the TransCanada 1 and continued east to Winnipeg. I wanted to see the city behind the hockey team, the Winnipeg Jets, as well as the "Winnie the Bear" statue. It occurred to me that Winnie, short for Winnipeg, is what inspired the Winnie the Pooh stories.

Within an hour, we reached the city, so I followed my map and tried to find Assiniboine Park and the statue. It took forever. My city map was too general. I should've prepared better. After pulling over several times to ask people, while trying to figure out the layout of the city, I found the Assiniboine Park entrance.

The park was huge and beautiful. We began our walk in the English Gardens. It's a wonderful place, filled with ornate sculptures, fountains, and colorful flowers. Plus, it was a sunny day, making it a perfect time and place to walk with Oscar. After touring the sculpture garden, we searched for the bear statue. That took forever too. My diagram of the large park area wasn't detailed, and when I asked, not everyone knew exactly where Winnie the Bear was. I knew for sure that we weren't leaving until we spotted this bit of children's cartoon history.

After forty-five minutes of wandering, we took a break and sat in a grassy space with a view of the pond. Then, I noticed a little dry space in the shade. I walked over to it. "Oscar, come over here." He couldn't hear me, but eventually he turned in my direction. I put out my arms, "Come over here," I invited him. He started to stumble over toward me. Then, he fell into my lap and sat down. "That's my boy!" I told him. He smiled a bit, pleased that he made it, or just happy to be sitting with me.

We rested for fifteen minutes, watching the other visitors. We resumed our search, backtracked, and found the Winnie the Bear statue. There was a plaque dedicated to Winnie the Bear, containing the history of the bear and its ties to A. A. Milne, the author of Winnie the Pooh. Next to it was the statue of a soldier kindly holding the paws of an upright little bear.

This stop in Winnipeg took a lot of time, but it was worth it. We walked through the park and gardens, back to the car. Then, I found the way back to the highway, and we started heading south on Highway 75 through Manitoba to the US border. Along the way, we passed yellow fields. I wondered if it was colored wheat or some sort of flower. Also, there were beautiful purple areas. Up close, they were separate plants. But, from a distance, it was a gorgeous portrait. A lot of scenery reminded me of the US heartland.

In the afternoon, we still had almost two hundred and fifty miles to go. To make up for lost time, we drove straight through with a brief break at Dominion City. I followed the RoadsideAmerica map and directions to a local sculpture: a huge replica of the four-hundred-pound sturgeon, the world's largest, that was caught in the Roseau River a hundred years earlier. "Yeah, that's a big fish," I said to Oscar while he stood under it.

We made one last stop in Canada at a random petrol station. Then, I followed my ritual of getting rid of the foreign currency. I emptied my wallet of all the Canadian dollars, plus most of the Canadian coins in the car. After buying gas, I went inside to purchase candy bars and snacks.

"I'm sorry to do this," I said to the young lady at the register.

"No trouble. I understand." Then, she and I counted the pile of coins.

I often did this in airports. It seemed easier than going to a currency exchange where they take a percentage of the transaction.

"And, I'll grab one of these," I said as I took a beef jerky package. *Oscar would like this*, I thought.

The lady counted and then swept the rest of the coins off the counter. "That will do it."

"Thanks," I said as I walked out with the bag of items.

We went through customs at the US border, Pembina, North Dakota. Karma was cooperating. There was a large line for trucks, but nobody was in the car line. We drove up to the window. The guard came over and asked a bunch of questions: Where did you go? Where are you from? What do you do? Do you have any firearms?

He barely noticed Oscar. And, when he saw him, he didn't ask for papers. After I popped the trunk, the agent looked at all the junk and waved us through.

Over the border, we resumed our trip on US Interstate 29 heading south into North Dakota. The speed limit signs returned to 75 mph. We cruised the last two hours, where the traffic was going 80. By dinnertime, we reached Fargo. It was our third visit in two years, so I was familiar with the city layout. I knew exactly where the AmericInn hotel was located.

Inside the room, I did a quick scan. It was as expected. There was a bunch of staining on the carpet. This wasn't a problem, but I didn't want to be charged for it! Actually, I didn't mind stains because it meant an Oscar accident or tracks wouldn't be the first. Right on cue, I turned and saw Oscar staring innocently up at me. Firmly standing in place. All four paws attached to the ground. *Uh-oh*. I dove toward him, and just as he started to take a whiz, I threw a towel under him. Without any expression, he streamed onto the towel while I waited. After he was done, I grabbed the towel and doused it inside the shower. Catastrophe avoided. Poor guy; sometimes he can't hold it any more.

We skipped the tourist spots that we had seen already and headed to dinner at Sickies Garage again. I ordered two burgers and sides. I gave Oscar the turkey burger's meat. He earned it! And I took the veggie burger, salad, and fries. After Oscar finished his dinner, he slept beside the table. Meanwhile, at the other tables, there were bikers, families, and people who were drinking and listening to the rock music. Another stretch completed. Just two more driving days left!

FARGO, NORTH DAKOTA to EAU CLAIRE, WISCONSIN

I TOOK OSCAR outside and carried him down the steps. "Lance's Elevator, at your service."

I informed the front desk that my room had some stains from previous guests.

"I'm very sorry, sir," the lady apologized.

"Oh, it's not a problem for me," I assured her. "I just don't want to be blamed or charged for it. Or for the dog to be blamed."

"I understand," she said. "You don't have to worry." Oscar and I made a final trip to the room. After leaving a brief note and tip for the maids, we left.

We drove out of Fargo, across to Minnesota. To stop or not to stop? I let the weather decide. The rain ended, so we did a quick detour through Fergus Falls, Minnesota. We saw a few sites and got a feel for the basic Midwest town. We passed by the Otter Tail River, a giant otter at the playground, a tribute to a school that closed after eighty years, and other local landmarks.

Bring Oscar

Within the town, there was a highlighted Otter Walking Trail. We followed part of it along the waterway, past the dam and power company. Along the way were a few plaques, outlining the area's history. One thing about traveling, it's important to be open to new knowledge and weird or different things. Finding little odd sites in between the major destinations makes the trip more fulfilling. At the end of the walk, under a waving flag, kids in the park were climbing on Otto the Big Otter. The Fergus Falls Otter!

After our break, we returned to the I-94 toward Minneapolis, where I prepared for the expected road rally through Minneapolis-Saint Paul. Crazy drivers, roads going in every direction—a mess. I had a plan to visit a list of sites in Minneapolis, but we hit too much traffic and construction. I've never had luck going through that city. So rather than stop, we pushed through and passed by as soon as possible.

At this point in the journey, I had mixed feelings and a changing mindset. While grinding through traffic in Minneapolis, I was looking forward to finishing this trip and getting home. Yet, during the pleasant dinner in Fargo, I wished time would slow down so we could extend the experience.

Oscar and I arrived in Eau Claire, Wisconsin, around 3:15. I passed the Econo Lodge hotel and drove to the Nissan dealer to say thanks to the crew, staff, and managers. I was excited to tell them we actually made it! Curtis from service recognized us and greeted me by name. "Hey, pup," he said to Oscar.

"Almost six thousand miles without a problem," I told him.

We chatted for a few minutes. As we walked through the lobby and auto bays, everyone at Eau Claire Nissan remembered us. Of course, they remembered Oscar! I explained we got to Alaska and thanked them for their help.

As we were driving out of the Nissan entrance, the manager started waving to me. I pulled over and rolled down my window. "Your rear tail light is out," he pointed out. "Do you want us to repair it while you're here?" Why not? They did a good job with the transmission fix. I drove the car into the garage.

They replaced the break light and added an oil change and tune-up. After sixty-five hundred miles, an oil change was needed, and the air filter was toast. Meanwhile, we enjoyed a nice break after driving all day. In the waiting room, I watched TV and used the Wi-Fi. Oscar napped. The young woman receptionist who loved dogs came in a few times to greet us. Two hours later, the car was good to go.

We went down the street to Noodle Wrap for our final takeout dinner. Chicken pad thai, rice, and spring rolls (the chicken and rice for Oscar). As we left, I realized this was the same Chinese restaurant I had ordered from two years ago when we ended our Idaho road trip. In fact, much of the area seemed quite familiar.

After 6:00, we checked into our room at the Econo Lodge. Everything about it was reliable. I put chicken and rice with Oscar's dog food. I placed the bowl on the floor and went down the hall to get a soda for myself. When I came back, he had cleared his bowl. Five minutes later, he was asleep. He was a road warrior. Meanwhile, I had my dinner, listened to the cable TV, and skimmed over the free newspaper from the front desk. From time to time, I like to look at local newspapers to learn about the different towns. When Oscar woke up, I took him outside for a lap. Afterward, we took a ride to the Dairy Queen. We were celebrating our final night.

EAU CLAIRE, WISCONSIN to HOME

IN THE MORNING, I took Oscar for a brief walk around the entire hotel again. After a lap, I stopped in the lobby to grab some breakfast items. This time when we left, there were no car problems!

After several trips through Wisconsin, I decided to finally visit Madison, the capital. After viewing the capitol building, we drove to a few landmarks and the University of Wisconsin campus. I parked along Lake Mendota, and we walked around for a while. It was summertime, and people were enjoying the nice weather by reading, sunbathing, or playing basketball on the outdoor courts. While there was a college town atmosphere, it wasn't too crowded. It struck me as odd (or crazy) how many attended school here during the cold winter. Then, when the weather is good, they return home for summer break.

I had a friend who attended University of Michigan for law school. The winter weather was fierce. Then, during the summer, he would return to Phoenix where it was blazing hot. One exception: He spent a summer clerking at a law firm in humid Dallas. No relief.

Oscar and I drove up and down the streets, looking for a lunch place with outdoor seating. We ended up at Monty's Blue Plate Diner where I would savor the last meal before heading home. It was sunny, and we enjoyed the falafel sandwich and fries, sitting on a bench near the entrance of the café. Families, college students, and others walked by as they entered and exited. They gave a polite smile or nod as they walked by me and Oscar. I kept thinking, *We were in Alaska two weeks ago. And, now we're here. What an incredible journey, and the only one who shared the experience was the dog sitting next to me.*

At 3:00, I took my last few photos, and then we finished the home stretch of our trip. We took the road to I-94 east. I put away the map and drove past Milwaukee, past Kenosha, over the Illinois border, and straight home.

During the drive, I recognized this was likely our last road trip. Our travels had extended to the East coast of Maine, to the western part of Canada and Alaska, to the edge of Alabama and Mississippi. I wish I had thought of these road trips years earlier. There were so many more places and experiences Oscar and I could have had. But, in the past two years, we'd covered a lot.

We pulled into our driveway. I looked at the odometer: 6578 miles. I took out the yellow highlighter and map from the glove compartment. I finished tracing our route on the map, proud of the distance we had covered. Then, I said a quick prayer, thankful that we made it. And, I gratefully looked at Oscar: Road warrior.

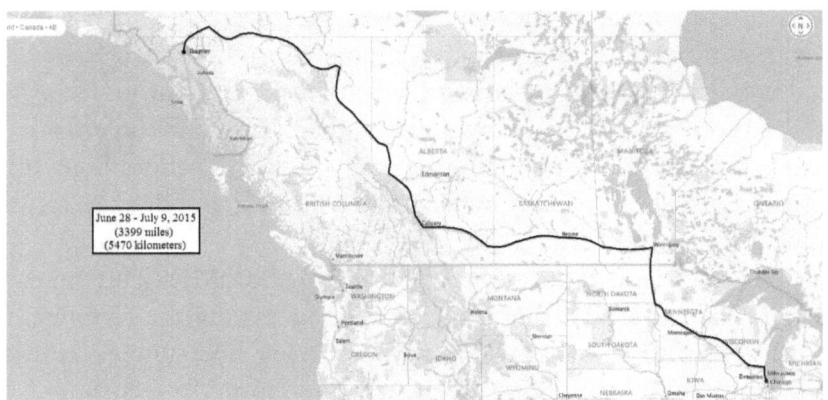

Bring Oscar

I helped Oscar out of the car. He followed me into the house. I checked the basement and walked around the house. It was the same as the day I left. Incredible to think we were in Alaska two weeks earlier. But, that's how time goes. Enjoy the moment, because it passes. Only written notes, memories, and photos can remain.

I watched Oscar climb through the doggie door into his backyard. Through the window I could see him sniff around and wander through the garden filled with vegetables that had grown while we were gone. Then, Oscar picked out a favorite spot in the shade and lay down.

Best dog ever...

Epilogue

Road trips are enriching in so many ways. It's a chance to learn geography and history in a firsthand, engaging way. At times, it's relaxing. Or, fun. Or, challenging. And, while it can be monotonous, there is always the anticipation of what could happen next. But, you'll never know until you get in the car and start with mile one. Give it a try!

Like a road trip, there were turns, detours and rough patches while writing this story. I hope you found it worth reading. If there are incoherent parts, imagine them in the most positive light.

Credits

Thanks to the following people who helped in the process of this book:

Christine Schmidt with True-Blue Editing. In her developmental edit, she guided me through the process of removing peripheral detail from my meticulous travel log and streamlined my storytelling.

My sister, Kelly, who read the first long, unedited version and offered encouragement along the way.

The book design team, Jetlaunch for their fast and efficient services.

This book was a labor of love. One hundred percent of the profits will be donated to Oscar's favorite places.

www.ingramcontent.com/pod-product-compliance
Lightning Source LLC
Chambersburg PA
CBHW031054080526
44587CB00011B/684